(IN)SCRIBING BODY/LANDSCAPE RELATIONS

(In)scribing
body/landscape relations

~

Bronwyn Davies

ALTAMIRA
PRESS

A Division of Rowman & Littlefield Publishers, Inc.
Walnut Creek • Lanham • New York • Oxford

For information contact:
AltaMira Press
A Division of Rowman & Littlefield Publishers, Inc.
1630 North Main Street, Suite 367
Walnut Creek, CA 94596
http://www.altamirapress.com

Rowman & Littlefield Publishers, Inc.
12 Hid's Copse Road
Cumnor Hill
Oxford OX2 9JJ, England

4720 Boston Way
Lanham, MD 20706

Library of Congress Cataloging-in-Publication Data

Davies, Bronwyn, 1945–
    (In)scribing body/landscape relations / Bronwyn Davies
        p. cm.
    Includes bibliographical references and index.
    ISBN 0-7425-0319-4 (alk. paper) — ISBN 0-7425-0320-8 (pbk.: alk. paper)
    1. Self in literature. 2. Australian fiction—20th century—History and criticism. 3. Japan—Civilization—20th century. I. Title: (In)scribing body/landscape relations. II. Title.
PN56.S46 D38 2000
809'.93384—dc21   99-055137

The paper used in this publication meets the minimum requirements of American National Standard for Information Sciences—Permanence of Paper for Printed Library Materials, ANSI/NISO Z39.48—1992.

Editorial Management by Jennifer R. Collier
Interior Design and Production by Rachel Fudge
Cover Design by Joanna Ebenstein

~ Contents

Prologue: or, Where does this book come from?   7

Part 1 ~ (In)scribing body/landscape relations: Australia   **11**

1. Landscapes and bodies   13

2. Writing stories of (be)longing   37

3. Australian men talk about becoming environmentalists
[with Hilary Whitehouse]   63

Part 2 ~ (In)scribing body/landscape relations: Japan   **87**

4. Remembering Japanese childhoods   89

5. Traveling in Japan   111

6. Japanese environmentalists talk about Japanese
body/landscape relations   145

**Part 3 ~ Subjection and the eclipsing of the constitutive power
of discourse through fictional texts**   **167**

7. An exploration of body/landscape relations in
Kawabata's *Yama no Oto*
[with Takeshi Osanai]   173

8. Reading and writing *The Kadaitcha Sung*:
A novel by Sam Watson
[with Sam Watson]   189

9. *The Second Bridegroom*: A narrative of
captivity in Australian landscapes   215

10. (Be)longing in the writing of Janette Turner Hospital:
Eclipsing the constitutive force of discourse   233

Conclusion: The ways and the song of the book   **249**

References   257

Index   263

Permissions   275

About the Author   277

~ Prologue: or, Where does this book come from?

IT IS STRANGE BEING AN AUTHOR IN THIS POSTMODERN AGE. It is an age-old discursive habit to create one author, who supposedly gave birth to the words on the page (as if they lay within, waiting to come out), who is then "known" for her words. This construction of oneself as writer-who-can-be-known attends the writing of books, however poorly known we may actually be, as we struggle to assemble, to scribe, to find the words that make "the way and the song of the book" (Cixous, 1998, pp. 144–45).

Foucault (1977) wrote in his article "What is an author?" that writing emerges out of conversations with others. He suggested we should think about a practice of not signing our names to what we write, but instead signing the names of those in the group who had the conversations in which the ideas for the writing emerged. If I were to do that here, the list of authors would be very long. There are so many wonderful conversations that have shaped this book, and those conversations have been with many different groups—in different countries, and in different spaces and times within those countries.

This is a multivocal text that enables an exploration of body/landscape relations from many moments of being. It comes from the lives of environmentalists, of fiction writers and of their fictional characters, of academic writers, of students, of children (as they are remembered), and of travelers, each of these in at least two countries, and in many different landscapes within those countries. This book comes not just from conversations, but also from written texts of fiction writers, and from texts produced by collective biography participants. All of the people I have interviewed or worked with to produce this text are named throughout the book, though the Australian environmentalists have chosen to use pseudonyms. But there are many conversations and contributions that are not visible here, and so I would like to spend some time, at the beginning, acknowledging those people who have made their mark, invisibly, on this book.

As I wrote each chapter I took it back to the people I was writing with (and about), to see what other points of view/being they wanted to add or change in the writing. Their interactions with the text have added new dimensions, new ways of writing. That process of renegotiating and rewriting is very difficult to make visible in the new text, but the text that you read arises in large part out of those conversations around earlier drafts of chapters and of the book. Each reading, each conversation, has contributed to the unfurling of the multiple points of meaning-making you find here. I am deeply indebted to each of the people you find in this book, either as joint authors of chapters or as people who have worked with me to create some part of the text of this book. It is not possible for me to write adequately about the special feeling of love, of gratitude, and of respect that I feel for each of the people with whom I have worked.

There are times, too, when, alone in my study with my computer and my books, I have had silent conversations with authors whose books I have turned to when the writing hasn't flowed, when I have not been able to see where the words of the participants might take me. The authors whose work is quoted in this book have often provided the conceptual flares that light up the possibilities that are lying there, waiting, in the texts I am working with, or provided me with the conceptual flight paths that have taken me beyond the limitations of the conceptual ground I have been working on.

And there are not only the conversations recorded here, but significant conversations that contributed to the germination of this book. Hilary Whitehouse persuaded me to include male environmentalists amongst those I should study in the work I was then undertaking on masculinity. She set about gathering data at a time when I was so overwhelmed with administrative tasks that I could not imagine how I would ever be able to find any extended time to think or read or write again, let alone collect data. There were also postgraduate students during that time whose work was so fascinating, and with whom I had such inspiring conversations, that I did not allow my writing, questioning self to become extinct, no matter how much my job pressed me in that direction. Individually and collectively, my students, colleagues, and friends have contributed to the creation of the intellectual space out of which this book could be written. Many of them are listed below as readers of various chapters or readers of the whole book. They include Margaret Allan, Yukihiko Asayama, Lise Bird, Paul Davies, Sylvia Ditchburn, Suzie Dormer, Heidi Eng, Sue Gannon, Pam Gilbert, Jill Golden, Rodney Hall, Hanne Helgesen, Eileen Honan, Lekkie Hopkins, Fusayuki Kanda, Hiroyuki Kasama, Professor Katanuma, Anne-Mette Kruse, Cath Laws, Hillevi Lenz-Taguchi, Robyn Longhurst, Helen McCann, Rosie McLaren, Gina Mercer, Tessa Morris-Suzuki, Karen Nairn, Seiji Nakaya, Lorri Neilsen, Elisabeth Nordin-Hultman, Masako Onoda, Michiko Osanai, Takeshi Osanai, Annette Patterson, Sharn Rocco, Paula Smith, Bettie St Pierre, Margaret Somerville, Dorte Marie Søndergaard, Hiroko Tanaka, Kaori Tanaka, Minoru Tanaka, Janette Turner Hospital, Terry Threadgold, Sam Watson, and Hilary Whitehouse.

It is not possible really to pin down the beginning point of this book. It might also be said to have begun in conversations long before I came to Townsville, such as those with Margaret Somerville when she was writing her Ph.D. thesis, now published as *Body/landscape journals* (Somerville, 1999). Or the work I did with Mary Sutherland, a

Feldenkrais practitioner, who taught my body new ways of moving and being aware of itself. Another significant point of beginning may have been moving to the tropics and walking on the beach at dawn, watching the early morning light through the rolling mists, and realizing that my body was running rivers of sweat—or later that year, seeing the leaves of the sea almonds turn red and drop off the trees at the beginning of summer rather than at its end. The carpet of brown discarded leaves in my garden heralded summer, not winter. Each strange moment in this new landscape brought me to an intense awareness of being embodied, of realizing how much my body knew and anticipated old patterns and became deeply troubled in these (at first) unpredictable and unknowable surroundings.

There are also many invisible workers who have contributed to this text. Annette Ryan has provided excellent transcriptions of interviews. Many people have generously helped with translations (spoken and written). These include Eiko Asano, Chie, Kelly Dietz, Joseph (a student from Alaska), Professor Katanuma, Katsumi Kanazawa, Kosaku Kikuta, Yuko Kurosawa, Chika Morioka, Masako Onoda, Yu Sato, Kaori Tanaka, and Victoria. I would also like to give special thanks to my editor Jennifer Collier and my copy editor Rachel Fudge. Clearly, much of this book would not have been possible without their generous and untiring work. There were also people who were both hospitable and helpful, taking me from one place to another, providing me with beautiful food, making it possible for me to see and know Japan. These include especially the Onoda and Suzuki families, including Mr. and Mrs. Onoda, Keiko and Iguchi, Minoru Tanaka, Mamoru and Emiko Gotoh, Takeshi Osanai and Michiko Osanai, Dean Abe, Yachiya Takashima, and Chie. In Townsville, one of the people who looked after me during the period of writing was Jennifer Jefferies, my brilliant masseur. The person to whom I have turned often for illuminating conversations about flora and fauna and zoological discourses is Paul Davies.

I, and this book, are indebted to all of these people. In another place and time they might all be listed as the authors of this work. In this place and in this time I simply extend them my heartfelt thanks.

Part 1 ~ (In)scribing body/landscape relations: Australia

THIS BOOK TROUBLES THE SEPARATION of bodies and landscapes. In Chapter 1 I develop a theory of body/landscape relations in which bodies are understood as taking up their material existence within landscapes, and as landscape. Landscapes are understood as bodies and as coextensive with bodies. The concept of (in)scription is developed as texts written on the deep/surfaces of the body/landscape, not in the sense of scarifying but in the sense of bringing the subject into being. That being is understood in terms of process rather than in terms of essence, and as such is motile, fluid, open to change. The dominant means through which we know body/landscapes is discourse—this does not deny the materiality of bodies, it simply recognizes that unmediated access to the material body is rare. Discourse (with all its fluidity, contradictions, mutiplicity, and explosive power) is a major constitutive force in the (in)scription of bodies. The power of discourse, in its double sense of subjecting and at the same time constituting speaking/writing subjects who can move beyond the terms of their own subjection, is explored throughout this book—through the work of fiction writers, through the experiences of environmentalists, and through the development of strategies of writing throughout the book generally, but in particular in the work of collective biography.

In the second chapter I explore in detail the concept of embodied writing as it is used in collective biography. Here, a group of Australian women explore, through stories of childhood in specific landscapes, the ways in which belonging with/in landscape is achieved in the double sense of becoming appropriate and being appropriated with/in Australian landscapes. The indigenous politics and history that affect that embodiment are also explored.

The third chapter is based on interviews with Australian male environmentalists and explores the ways in which they become embodied as environmentalists, reinscribing their bodies in ways that attempt to evade those aspects of culture they see as alien within "natural" landscapes, and that enable them to become coextensive with "nature." In the take-up of environmental discourses and practices, these men distance themselves from "culture" and immerse themselves in a variety of landscapes in ways that demonstrate the extreme motility of body/landscapes, as they are (in)scribed now one way and now another.

~1~ Landscapes and bodies

THIS BOOK IS ABOUT BODIES in and of landscapes and landscapes in and of the body. It is a set of explorations of body/landscape relations and of the practices of reading and writing through which bodies and landscapes and body/landscape relations are (in)scribed. It is an attempt to make the invisible visible and to find strategies for bringing embodiment to consciousness and into writing. What I want to do here is to free up the language from its "sinister, frequently lazy, almost always predictable" (Morrison, 1992, p. xiii) capacity to determine our modes of being, and in particular our embodiment in relation to landscape. Theoretical writing about the body generally constitutes the body in isolation from the physical spaces in which it exists. Some go so far as to say that writing about the body even ignores the body: the "body may be back but the new body theory is just as . . . disembodied as it ever was. . . . Postmodern theorising about the body has all too often been a cerebral, esoteric and, ultimately, disembodied activity" (Davis, 1997, p. 14). At the same time, it is often the case that environmental discourses are written as if "nature" in its ideal form (i.e., wilderness) is separate from human existence. My position is similar to that of Spinoza, who believed that "identity can never be viewed as a final or finished product as in the case of the Cartesian automaton, since it is a body that is in constant interchange with its environment. The human body is radically open to its surroundings and can be composed, recomposed and decomposed by other bodies" (Gatens, 1996, p. 110).

What we think of as nature is saturated with desire—desire for a particular kind of embodiment or a particular kind of landscape—but the thing we long for and imagine is illusory and elusive and reflects our longing as much as what is actually there. Some environmentalists, for example, imagine an ideal "nature" untouched by humans. They long for a form of embodiment that makes them part of that "nature" that they imagine. Through their take-up of environmental discourses, they reinscribe their bodies. What environmentalists in Australia and Japan say about body/landscape relations is explored in Chapters 3 and 6. I am also interested in the ways some fiction writers are able to anticipate new forms of life in their writing, through close attention to their own embodiment in landscape and their own language practices. The writing of four different authors is explored in Chapters 7 to 10.

I also use the technique of collective biography or memory work developed by Frigga Haug and her associates (1987). Chapters 2 and 4 are the stories of childhood embodiment remembered and written by

groups of Australian and Japanese students using the technique of collective biography, in which listening to others tell their stories helps to
fill in the gaps and silences of knowing oneself as an embodied being.
As one story unfolds, as the words are found with which to reveal the
embodied memory, other memories rapidly unfurl from their hiding
places, threading onto the original memory, bringing it to life in the
same gesture as bringing other buried stories to life. The collective
nature of biography is revealed in this collective unfolding: "the pearls
and corals of the 'language' of the soul . . . (these) jewels, materials of
the earth" (Cixous, in Cixous and Calle-Gruber, 1997, p. 29) are experienced as deeply private and personal, but they are also keys to collective knowledges—not just keys lying randomly to be picked up or
ignored but keys that are in some sense "overdetermined," demanding
to be picked up and used to unfurl the collective wisdom to be had
in storying oneself as an embodied being in landscape.

These diverse ideas are brought together in a series of studies of
body/landscape relations, in which the folding and unfolding of embodied beings is read in the contexts of the folds in the landscapes through
which they move and take up their being. A fascination with the constitutive power of discourse in the opening of new folds in landscapes
and bodies (and body/landscapes) is the thread that holds these studies
together. The Australian collective biography and the study of some Australian environmentalists make up Part 1 of this book. The Japanese collective biography, the story of my travels in Japan, and the study of
Japanese environmentalists make up Part 2 of this book. The third part
is devoted to the fiction writers from both Australia and Japan.

The explorations you find here open pathways between discursive
fields that are usually held separate. In troubling the boundaries
between bodies and landscapes I also trouble the boundaries between
sociology, psychology, environmental studies, literary theory, and history. The particular meaning of *trouble* that I am intending here is the
same as when we say "the seas were troubled," where *trouble* means
to agitate or make rough. I use the word *troubling,* rather than
"deconstructing" or "putting under erasure," since I find that too many
readers of deconstructive texts take deconstruction to mean a disman-
tling that obliterates the binaries and the boundaries between them.
Binaries are not so easily dismantled, and deconstructive work often
can do no more than draw attention to the binaries and to their constitutive force. For some people, in some readings, deconstructive work
may facilitate a different take-up of meaning, beyond the binaries. But
this does not undo the continuing force of relations of power that
operate to hold the binaries in place. I choose the word *troubling* to
represent more closely what it is that deconstructive work can do.

Awareness of being embodied and, in particular, being embodied in
relation to landscape, is something we have little practice in observing
or articulating. "The body" is generally understood as natural, and as

such is taken for granted. It is not made observable, generally, until it ceases functioning in ways that various authoritative discourses, such as health or fitness or religious discourses, say that it should, or until we find ourselves in an entirely different discursive or physical landscape. In an interview on Australian national television, Andy Thomas, an Australian-American astronaut, talked about how, on returning to earth, he became aware of gravity for the first time, and of the way his body functioned as a result of being embodied on this planet. After twenty weeks on the Mir space station, he found coming back into gravity extraordinary and surprising—what had not been noticeable before was now noticeable. He found lifting his leg off the earth to take each step very hard, and when he raised his arm in the air, he was amazed that it did not just stay there, that it took a lot of energy to keep it there. Living in a landscape in which there is gravity we develop the musculature and bone mass, along with the taken-for-granted practices that make our embodiment as gravity dwellers invisible. We learn to do the work and then we forget we are doing it, until we find ourselves on the moon (or returned from it)—or until we find some way to trouble the obviousness, the taken-for-grantedness, and the general invisibility of body/landscape relations.

Elizabeth Grosz talks about the inscription of bodies as a permanent and unnatural feature of human embodiment. I quote her at length here because she makes clear how the overt, violent practices of controlling and shaping bodies are only one aspect of how bodies are inscribed. Equally relevant is the covert shaping that takes place through the establishment of "norms and values" and patterns of desire. But there are important ways in which the thesis I am developing in this book parts company with Grosz's, in particular her claim that such bodily inscription is as permanent as scarification of the body surface, and also in her construction of "the natural" as that which is unscarred and unshaped:

[I]n our own culture as much as in others, there is a form of body writing and various techniques of social inscription that *binds all subjects,* often in quite different ways according to sex, class, race, cultural and age codifications, to social positions and relations. These modes of scarification are *no less permanent or more removable* than tattooing or epidermic or muscular lesions, although they may be less readily observed or directly readable. . . . In our own culture, inscriptions occur both violently and in more subtle forms. In the first case, violence is demonstrable in social institutions of correction and training, prisons, juvenile homes, hospitals, psychiatric institutions, keeping the body confined, constrained, supervised, and regimented, marked by implements such as handcuffs, the traversing of neural pathways by charges of electricity in shock therapy, the straightjacket, the regimen of drug habituation and rehabilitation, chronologically regulated time and labour divisions, cellular and solitary confinement, the deprivation of mobility, the bruising of bodies in police interrogations, etc. Less openly violent, but no less coercive are the inscription of personal and cultural values, norms and commitments, according to the morphology and categorization of the body into socially significant groups—male and female, black and white, and so on. The body is involuntarily marked, but it is also incised through "voluntary" procedures, life styles, habits and behaviours. . . . *There is nothing natural or ahistorical* about these modes of corporeal inscription. Through them, bodies are made amenable to the prevailing exigencies of power. They make the flesh into a particular type of body—pagan, primitive, medieval, capitalist, Italian, American, Australian. (Grosz, 1994, pp. 141–42, *my italics*)

Grosz constructs the body here as fictionalized, with the fictions being written on a natural surface. I also see the body, in all its forms, as a powerful fiction. That fictionality does not make the body any less "natural" than anything else that we might like to (in)scribe as nature. To (in)scribe the body as natural does not fix its nature, nor does it separate it off from the (in)scriptions with which we struggle to make it understandable.[1] To (in)scribe the body's surfaces does not fix the ways it can be read.

In order to highlight my difference from Grosz, I have bracketed (in)scription to draw attention to the acts of reading and writing—the *scription*. In doing so, I also want to draw attention to both the constitutive power and the shifting nature of scription. Bodies and landscapes are not impervious to language and are shaped through our acts of reading and writing them. At the same time, texts are volatile, liable to change and movement, capable of action, capable of rupture and disruption, even of themselves, as Grosz so beautifully elaborates in *Space, time and perversion* (1995). The capacity for change is written into the body—though it is also true that some (in)scriptions make deep and knotty folds that may make the body less fluid, less amenable to change. It is also true that bodies can become exhausted and debilitated through too much change.

Benterrak, Muecke, and Roe ponder on the way our speaking seems so insubstantial, yet (in)scribes (sometimes unintended) traces

---

1. There are two related points here. The first is that many flora and fauna actively inscribe themselves in a wide range of ways. To be uninscribed cannot be the defining feature of that which is "natural." That which is natural is what we call natural. The second point is an epistemological one. A mistake that occurs in some poststructuralist writing is to assume that because poststructuralist theory focuses on the constitutive power of discourse and on the fact that we cannot know bodies and/or landscapes in any way that is unmediated through language, the body does not have materiality, or does not exist except through discourse. But poststructuralist analyses of the constitutive power of discourse are about our ways of knowing, and they do not set out to prove anything about the ontological existence or otherwise of material bodies. For my purposes here, I will assume the materiality of bodies and landscapes, assuming also that I can only know that materiality in ways that are mediated through discourse.

on the landscape that signal who we are, not as individuals, but as speakers of one sort of language or another. They compare language to the marks a lizard makes as it moves across the sand: each signals who the being was who passed through the landscape:

> [S]poken language . . . traces an arc in the medium of sound waves before disappearing in minute echoes. . . . [O]ften we leave these traces unconsciously like a lizard scuttling across the sand. It has left a writing which says very clearly: "I am *barni* going this way". People writing English leave themselves open in the same way. They can be tracked down as individuals cohering to a particular set of Western European beliefs. (Benterrak, Muecke, and Roe, 1984, p. 64)

In their description individuals "cohere," they stick to and are consistent with the beliefs embedded in their language practices. But language practices change, and the trace left on the landscape may change with it. Many speakers have more than one language, and in colonial contexts one language may be repressed or lost and another imposed. And within any one of these languages there are multiple and contradictory beliefs and practices. The relations between the words available to us and what we can say or know are extraordinarily complex. Taking up a language, or a way of speaking, does not necessarily *induct* the speaker into the assumptions and beliefs of that language, let alone *fix* the speaker in them (Davies, 1997). Janette Turner Hospital's portrait of Ethel, an indigenous Australian woman sitting in the desert, longing for the language she has been deprived of, reveals some of this complexity:

> Consider Ethel. She sits there, cross-legged in the red dust at the edge of the bora rings, smiling to herself, rocking gently backwards and forwards as though she hears singing and the rhythmic stamping of feet in the gidgee boughs. She has been putting the scattered rocks back where they belong, filling gaps in the circles and centuries. They have been there, the bora rings, for over twenty thousand years, it is believed; it is only in the past hundred, a hiccup in time, that indifferent graziers and the treads of their four-wheel drives have scattered the stones and have imprinted zippered scars across their sacred clay skin.
>
> From time to time Ethel grins at me, and her teeth flash in her black face like stark white lightning.
>
> 'My mob chuckling up their sleeves,' she tells me. 'My mob been here all along. They been waiting for this.'
>
> 'I wouldn't have thought your mob were wearing sleeves.'
>
> 'Fuck off Jess,' she grins. 'Whitefella Maroo been and gone once, and been and gone twice, and we're still here, my mob and me.'
>
> She is waiting for a lost language to come back to her. She believes it will rise out of the stones. It will drift into her, into the place where

words are made, with the smoke from the gidgee leaves. She pokes at her smouldering branches with a stick. She is waiting for a name other than Ethel to rise out of them, for the name she was never given, but should have been, for the name history took from her. She is waiting to meet her other self. She is waiting for her name to settle into her cupped hands, knowing that it might not come from the smoke because there is no predicting the ways of the Old People. It might fall from a passing bird. The *Wandjinas* might bring it. It might slither over her arm. *She, the rock python* might set it down beside her. She waits. (Turner Hospital, 1996b, p. 40)

In this story, the language does not reside in Ethel but in the landscape in which her ancestors are still present. The landscape can speak to her if she listens carefully enough, and may do so through the smoke of the fire she has lit, or from a bird, or the *Wandjinas,* or a rock python. The white presence with all its destructive power, with its capacity to reinscribe the landscape with zippered scars, and fences, and the scattering of sacred stones, is a minor power compared to that of the Old People. Ethel positions Jess as one with far less powerful knowledge than she has. Even though the language eludes her, she takes it on trust that it is there in the landscape, and that it has given and will go on giving her and her people the capacity to survive. Her (in)scription of the landscape may be less visible to some than the zippered scars, but it is no less powerful in its effects. In Chapter 8 I explore these ideas further with indigenous writer Sam Watson. In Chapter 9 I explore the writing of Rodney Hall as he takes us back into Australia's past, and in Chapter 10 I further explore the writing of Janette Turner Hospital and her fictional inscriptions, her dreamings, of body/landscape relations as they are lived out in the Australian landscape.

Foucault observed that bodies are shaped and disciplined through the systemic pattern of power in our society, which "reaches into the very grain of individuals, touches their bodies and inserts itself into their actions and attitudes, their discourses, learning processes and everyday lives" (Foucault, 1980, p. 39). His emphasis is on the patterns of power and powerlessness. The attention that I bring to language in this book is in part an attempt to wrest language out of its invisibility as a constitutive practice and so gain some greater power or agency in our use of it. In particular I wish to examine the effects of language on the shifting grain of ourselves, a grain that, I argue, is not so separate from the landscapes in which we are enfolded. The separation is an artefact of discourse, an artefact that, in my view, is in need of troubling.

It is extraordinarily difficult to explore what Foucault's words actually mean in terms of lived experience, given the extent to which we are already constituted through humanist discourses that lead us to read ourselves and our bodies in ways quite contrary to what he is saying. In our most familiar discourses, mind is separate from the body and given an ascendant and controlling position in relation to the matter of bodies. It is thus our minds that we are practiced at knowing, rather than our bodies. In those discourses in which the body is constituted as natural (such as medical discourses), we leave the knowing and the reading of the bodies to experts who know how to read and interpret the body's signs. In contrast, by making bodies and embodiment my central focus, I am aligning myself with the Spinozist idea that the mind is no more than an idea of the body—albeit a very powerful idea with material effects.

> For Spinoza the body is not part of passive nature ruled over by an active mind but rather the body is the ground of human action. . . . [R]eason is active and embodied precisely because it is the affirmation of a *particular* bodily existence. . . .
>
> The Spinozist account of the body is of a productive and creative body which cannot be definitively "known" since it is not identical with itself across time. The body does not have a "truth" or a "true" nature since it is a process and its meanings and capacities will vary according to its context. We do not know the limits of this body or the powers that it is capable of attaining. These limits and capacities can only be revealed by the ongoing interactions of the body and its environment. (Gatens, 1996, p. 57)

Because of the lack of practice in reading our bodies in this way, I have sought here to develop a new form of embodied writing. I adopted a number of strategies for disrupting my taken-for-granted and clichéd ways of knowing my own body/landscape relations. One such strategy was to travel out into unfamiliar places to make my own familiar body/landscape relations strange, and to write about what I came to see as a result. Chapter 5, "Traveling in Japan," is the story of one such adventure. I did not need to go as far as the moon to make the invisible visible. In encountering Japanese language, my unexamined practices of reading my own body were immediately interrupted. Many Japanese people point to their hearts when they say "I think." The heart (*kokoro*) and the stomach (*hara*) are central to many of the processes English speakers locate in the brain. *Kokoro ga ugoku* (heart moves) means worry. *Kokoro ni kakeru* (to hang [something] on one's heart) means intend, look forward to, bear in mind. To get something "off one's chest" is *hara o waru*—literally, to slit open one's stomach. Brian McVeigh (1996, p. 39) writes:

> A *hara no suwatta hito* is a person who has accomplished his or her belly, meaning a person who has reached a high level of self-improvement. Someone with an unfinished belly has not morally progressed and remains immature. People should not think with their heads, but rather

with their bellies; that is we should go beyond mere rational, intellectual thought and focus on the deeper, essential aspects of a problem.

My limited perception of my head as the place where thinking took place was made both visible and revisable: in pondering this different linguistic system of reference to the body, my capacity to think of the whole body as engaged in thinking, with thinking legitimately and inevitably tied to emotion, began to unfold.

Moving outside my own language and culture, then, has been one important strategy for making visible the invisible folds of body/landscape relations. Working on the collective biographies was another, along with talking to environmentalists who have developed a particular awareness of their being in relation to landscape. Examining the texts of fiction writers in both cultures has also been a way of finding the detail through which we (in)scribe body/landscape relations. It has, at the same time, been a way of opening my imagination and my writing to other possibilities. The writers open possible landscapes in which bodies might be released from old folds in which they have been caught; folds, for example, in which they could not see or feel their coextension with the landscapes in which they found themselves. The ways in which fiction writers and other creative artists bring a detailed awareness to embodiment come from the creative state that Drusilla Modjeska calls *reverie*:

> Reverie is an interesting word. It captures something of a dream state, and yet it is not sleep. It is a state of absorption, or play, and it is also serious; it conjures a state of not quite being in the world, a little apart, and yet it is in reverie that life is often at its most vivid and alive. It is, if you like, an *in-between* state . . . [that] dissolves the distinction between thinking and feeling, between watching and experiencing. . . . Bachelard, recognising that the creative mind does not function well in the full blaze of attention, talks of "sheltered space" in which we are at once open and attentive, sheltered from the blasts of worldly demands and distractions. It is not quite a meditative state, but akin to a meditative state. The Buddhists talk of "bare attention" as the capacity to be at ease with oneself, to burst through the endless cycle of desires and obsessions and attend to the world simply as it is—the ordinary world most of us overlook, or look at without seeing, regarding and disregarding it in the same glance. It is the capacity to be held in a space in which you are alive to the world, and the world is alive to you. (Modjeska, 1999, pp. 309–10)

Body/landscape relations

I will begin this initial analysis of body/landscape relations with a story of my own embodied being in the landscapes of my childhood. I will move from that story to an analysis of body/landscape relations, tying that discussion to my embodied being here, now, sitting at the computer in my study in the tropical north-east of Australia, with the verandah of my house visible through the windows of the French doors on my left-hand side.

I was born in a rural town in a valley nestled in the Great Dividing Range, a thickly forested range of mountains that hugs the east coast of Australia. It was this range of mountains that for a long time kept the "invading hordes" out of the ancient spaces so different from the landscapes of the northern hemisphere from which the invaders came. It was a valley like mine that the explorers found when they finally made their way through the dense forest to the table-lands and valleys and vast plains. Tamworth was an ugly, lovely town with broken, mysterious, and decaying houses alongside smug-suburbed stretches of square brick houses, each with its neat square apron of green lawn.

Our rambling brick 1930s house in its vast garden nestled up against the hills and looked out over flat dusty plains and distant mountains. A sluggish brown river ran through the centre of the town, providing swimming holes in summer. And then, when the leaden sky rained for days on end, the river flooded the plain, rose as high as the roofs of the houses built alongside it and surged brown and relentless through the streets and shops in the centre of the town. On weekends when the sun was shining (which was almost always) my sister and brothers and I climbed the hills, braving the bull in the paddock along the way, or we explored the cool, dark, dusty catacombs that appeared to stretch forever under our house, or we built tin canoes patched together with the melting tar from the hot roads and sank with them in the sluggish brown river.

The pores of our bodies were open to the air, we felt sweat on our skin and sought out cool breezes to catch the drops of sweat, to caress our body surfaces. We learned to spread the surface of our bodies in front of the fan or in pools of deep shade under the spreading jacaranda or the thick vines of wisteria and clematis and honeysuckle. We knew the rise and fall of body temperature and the interaction between the air and the liquids of our bodies rising to the surface. We loved cold water. Almost every day in the summer we went to the town swimming pool. When our strong, muscular bodies, tanned by the sun, became cold, covered in goose bumps, we sought out the warmth of dry hot cement to lie on, like lizards, drawing the heat into our shivering bodies, readying them to leap again into the water, to experience the shock of coldness and the pleasure of strong movement leaping through the air and into the water.

In summer we wore as few clothes as possible. We wore bare feet and the soles of our feet were brown and tough. The air was laden with dust and pollen—it hung in the curtains and lodged in the grain of the wood and in our skin and hair. I sneezed all the time and my nose bled at night and I developed so much scar tissue in my nose that breathing was almost impossible anyway.

When we played in the water our nasal passages were washed clean, our skin wrinkled like an old person's, our hair bleached from the chlorinated water, and our muscles grew strong.

In winter we got chilblains on our toes. I rode to school with my frozen fingers clamped onto the handlebars with the cold wind whipping my clothes and freezing my face. At night we warmed our kidneys by the open wood fire; we watched the flames glowing on the brass fire dogs; we smelled the singed hearth rug when hot sparks leapt, with a loud cracking sound, out of the fireplace. We curled up in big comfortable armchairs and read books and dreamed—dreams that transported us somewhere else—since the words were never about houses and gardens like ours, about valleys and hills like ours, about families like ours. Dreams were made out of somewhere else—other countries, other times. Our minds drifted free of our bodies and entered other bodies, other ways of being and knowing. Other possibilities lay in words on the page. The sometimes claustrophobic circle of mountains and ready judgments about how one ought to be seemed to exist outside the imaginary possibilities found in books.

The landscapes we lived with/in (and our reading of them) shaped our bodies, our mode of walking and running and jumping and breathing and talking and laughing—and sneezing. They scribed us, they (in)scribed us, as much in our imagining of possibilities as in the actual physical substance of what we were.

When I was about nine we started to go to the beach for our holidays—driving up over the mountains on winding dirt roads, then down to a small fishing village perched high on headlands looking out over the sea. I remember reading comics, eating caramello chocolate, and oysters and prawns, and fish straight out of the sea. I remember learning to go the toilet where there was no flushing; the powerful odour of our accumulated excrement in the pit beneath us taught us to make going to the toilet as quick an act as possible. I remember long walks on the beach and swimming out beyond the powerful breakers and catching huge waves in to shore. I remember coming home from the beach with my long hair so tangled from the hours of swimming in the sea that the only solution was to cut it all off. With regret. With relief. Later, I remember sitting on the flat green grass of the headland watching the waves crash against the rocks, listening to the sound of the waves, and searching, with no success, for the words that might adequately tell the rhythm of the waves, the magnetic, hypnotic, repeated sound, the dream quality, the bright light, the spray of salt water caught in the wind. The sea repeatedly moved me to a search for words, but the absence of words was all that I found. Australia for us, then, was an untold landscape. Our bodies in those landscapes seemed so natural they were not in need of words.

The definition of landscape that I am developing in this writing disturbs the binaries of body/landscape, built environment/natural environment, and human/animal. I use the term "landscape" not just to signal the pastoral scenes of landscape paintings, but also to signal readings of and relationships with the physical environments in which we come to exist as embodied beings. I include not only the land-scapes of houses and other dwelling places, but also others' bodies. While landscapes are often defined in terms of that which is "natural" (as opposed to "manufactured"), I consider all landscapes to be natural insofar as everything is natural, and I consider them, at the same time, to be discursively constituted. All landscapes are transformable, over time, or through the advent of a different presence in them, or through the conceptual/linguistic frame through which they are (in)scribed.

The first landscape we encounter, as animals who are born as sen-tient beings, is the internal landscape of our mother's body folded around us. This experience of first knowing inside a fold of the mother's body is an experience not only of humans and other placen-tal mammals such as whales and rodents, but also of monotremes whose eggs are hatched in a temporary pouch where the baby suckles until it is fully formed, and of marsupials who give birth to fetal young that also suckle in the pouch. It is also the experience of gas-tric brooding frogs who lay eggs that are externally fertilized and then swallowed, growing to fully formed frogs in the mother's stomach. All these give birth to sentient beings, of whom it could be said their first landscape is a fold in their mother's body, whether that fold is a womb, a stomach, or a pouch. The fold creates an interior, a holding place, a deep surface on which the baby lives and from which, or in which, it finds its sustenance.

The body is not separate from landscape, in this example, but is itself, in the case of the mother, a landscape with/in which another being dwells. In the case of the baby, it is connected to or held within the landscape, and it either draws sustenance directly from the substance of the mother's body or from the yolk created from the mother's body or, in some rare cases, from the other unhatched eggs inside the mother's body. This original body/landscape relation is ideal for my purpose here, in troubling the easy assumptions of separation and easy distinctions between where bodies begin and end and where landscapes take up. Bodies and landscapes might be said to live in such complex patterns of interdependence that landscape should be understood as much more than a mere context in which embodied beings live out their lives. I choose this image of mother as landscape as my beginning point to trouble the human/animal binary and with it the assumption that humans are separate from and dominant over landscape in a way that other animals are not. I am at the same time troubling the body/landscape binary, which is a central plank in the construction of humanist subjects whose rational controlling "nature" makes them separate from the contexts in which they find themselves.

To dwell a little longer on that prior-to-birth landscape that some of us experience, it can also be thought of as one in which language, or systems of communication, have already been experienced and made relevant as the vibrations of sound pass through the physical matter of the mother's body. We hear/feel the patterns of sound that our mother makes, and we hear/feel the sounds around her, whether we are in a womb or a pouch or a stomach. When we take up our existence in folds other than the fold of the mother's body, the patterns of sound take on a new importance. Discourse and other patterns of communication provide the basis for knowing how to read landscape, for knowing how to manage our embodied existence within it. And in becoming competent subjects we are, in that same process, inscribed as that which the discourse takes us to be:

> Discourse is not merely spoken words, but a notion of signification which concerns not merely how it is that certain signifiers come to mean what they mean, but how certain discursive forms articulate objects and subjects in their intelligibility. In this sense 'discourse' is not used in the ordinary sense. . . . Discourse does not merely represent or report on pregiven practices and relations, but it enters into their articulation and is, in that sense, productive. (Butler, 1995c, p. 138)

I was told a story in Japan about the difficulties of knowing how to read the changing landscape of the body of an emperor who had cancer. The emperor's body was discursively constructed as a manifestation of god. An urgent debate ensued as to whether the cancer was "natural" or "unnatural." If it was unnatural, the surgeons could operate to remove the cancer, since the cancer was not also part of god. If it was natural, then it was part of god and could not be destroyed. By the time the cancer had been discursively constituted as unnatural and therefore operable, the emperor had died. On this occasion, the discourse through which the body was initially defined did not provide the basis for knowing how to interact with it. Work had to be done on the discourse, to extend and develop it, in order to find the mode of action. In this example, the work of discursively constituting the landscape (in this case, of a particular body) in order to know how to interact with it is made visible (as is the slipperiness of the concept of nature).

Discourse (in the case of the human species and probably many other species) constitutes landscape, not just for the pleasure or the power of the constitutive act, but to form the conditions of our existence within it. Our various discursive strategies refer to the world around us as separate and other, "but their aim turns toward society and meaning; in Baudrillard's terms, they are our attempt to create, out of our own will or representations, the Other we choose to encounter" (Chaloupka and Cawley, 1993, p. 4).

Each landscape can be read in many possible ways—while it is something that we primarily constitute as "real," independent of the ways in which it is read and inhabited. The landscape of my verandah, for example, is read by me as a wonderful place to sit when I wish to gaze at the sea and feel the cool breezes blowing off the water. It is a place to entertain guests, to eat meals, and to talk. In this hot tropical climate, it is a central part of the house, while existing on its periphery. It is also a place heavy with dreaming; for me, a feminine, domestic dreaming associated with the verandahs of my childhood. "The untidy verandah," painted by Olivia Spencer Bower,[2] makes visible something of that dreaming. The painting shows a pattern of soft yellow light and deep blue shadow, a table covered in freshly picked fruit, apples, tomatoes, pears, a jug, and an earthen vase filled with flowers. On the floor of the verandah are boxes of fruit and an empty basket and, a little farther away, a watering can. All signal, to me, the familiar labor of growing fruit and making jam, of growing flowers and picking them, of creating aesthetically pleasing spaces.

Another such verandah appears in Drusilla Modjeska's *The Orchard*:

> On visits to Ettie's, one can go a whole day barely seeing her, just a glimpse of her wheelbarrow, or the sound of her boots as she comes in through the kitchen door for the next brew of tea. . . . [W]hile she works outside with only birds and rustling creatures for company, her visitor can lie undisturbed, given over to the half-world of her verandah. Having grown up in a country where there were no such passageways between garden and house, with beds hauled out and plants growing in, the verandah has become for me an enchanted place. Neither in nor out, it holds both possibilities and excludes neither. On that verandah with its spiders and even an occasional snake, it's as if for a moment the cry and shudder of life gives way to musings that come, rolling and inconclusive, from a secretly held part of oneself. Dreaming and only half attentive, looking through strands of jasmine and wisteria that loop like curls on a great beauty's neck, towards the escarpment, it's as if, from the vantage point of a verandah bed, that great expanse of sky rolls in over us from the very edge of existence. (Modjeska, 1994, pp. 11–12)

I imagine a small joey feels much the same about pouches as Modjeska's character feels about verandahs. It is aware of the world going on out there, which is only glimpsed in part; it can dream safely, in the place that is neither inside nor outside but both, not yet responsible for the activity around it, and yet able to glimpse the extraordinary edge of existence on the limits of its range of vision.

But for me, on this particular hot summer Saturday afternoon in Townsville in the far north-east of Australia, my verandah is a place that is too hot for me to be, and so is empty—of human habitation, that is. I sit in my air-conditioned study and look out through the window at the verandah and at the tropical palms beyond—and I reflect

---

2. To be found in the Aigantighe Gallery, Timaru, New Zealand.

on the sunbirds, the lizards, the spiders, and the frogs who have colonized that space. When I was looking for a home, it was the presence of the sunbird on a tree next to the empty verandah that settled the question of where I should live. It seemed to bid me welcome.

YELLOW-BELLIED SUNBIRD *Nectarinia jugularis* 11–12 cm
Other name: Olive-backed or Yellow-breasted sunbird
… singles, pairs, temporary groups: assertive; flits about blossoms, hovers to feed; takes spiders, dismembering them while hovering at the web. Direct flight swift, darting; mixes with small honeyeaters. Groups gather in animated display, uttering brisk calls. Tame; nests about houses/tropical gardens. Voice: splintered squeaky notes, staccato in display; loud, rising, canary-like 'tweeet'; brisk twittering song… Breeds: Oct.–March; most months. Nest: beautiful, pendulous, 30–60 cm long; with hooded side entrance; of bark, grass, leaves, spiders' web, incl. web debris; lined with plant-down; feathers; suspended from sapling, vine, low branch, sometimes over water; houses, sheds, verandahs etc. (Pizzey and Knight, 1997, p. 500)

The verandah, and my house, might be constructed in some environmental discourses as part of the "unnatural" built environment. But the sunbirds do not operate in terms of the built environment/ natural environment binary. My verandah provides spiders' webs and leafy trees and flowers, and shelter. And just as they build nests (with a hooded side entrance), so have I, as another animal in the tropics, built (or in this case, found) a house with a hooded entrance. At the same time, the green ants in my garden build their intricate multiroomed nests from the leaves of the trees that I and others have planted. The air is heavy with the rich perfume of white ginger flowers and frangipani. The brilliant blue and green butterflies drift and flutter on the air above the lily pond and swimming pool, they mate in the trees outside my kitchen window and lay eggs on the vines I have planted for them. One kind of built environment seems, in my reading of it, no less natural than the other. The ant trails constructed by the ants seem no more nor less natural than the road that leads from my house to the shopping mall. Significant aspects of the landscapes I inhabit include other people, animals, houses, roads, bike tracks, walking trails, beaches, mountains, forests, coffee shops, fruit and vegetable shops, and opera houses—this list could go on for a long time. From the sunbirds' point of view, there are other sunbirds, honeyeaters, trees, flowers, spiders, and water, and perhaps its flight paths are as clearly marked as is the bitumen road I drive on to get to the supermarket, though the flight paths may be more fluid, more postmodern.

I am not making an argument here about whether one species of animal is more or less destructive of other species than another, or makes greater impact on its environment than other species. My point is that all fauna, including humans, are embodied beings whose existence is intricately connected to, part of, inextricable from the landscapes they construct and in which they make their lives.

A fascinating act of invention can be seen in Japan. There are crows there who have taken to eating walnuts which are grown (by humans) in abundance. Since walnut shells are too hard for them to crack open, even with their powerful beaks, they have taken to dropping the nuts in the path of ongoing traffic so that the tires of the cars will crack them open. Then, since the continuing stream of traffic makes a problem for the crows in picking up the pieces of walnut from the road, they have taken to dropping them on pedestrian crossings and picking up the nuts when the flow of cars ceases. They walk on to the pedestrian crossing with the other pedestrians when the light turns green and eat their feast of walnut before the lights change back. (Attenborough, 1998)

Probably the main difference between me and the sunbirds is the fact that I'm writing this book about bodies and landscapes. Or perhaps it is that the food I eat is gathered from places I have never been to, while the adult sunbirds only eat what they gather for themselves.

Since I came to live in the tropics, I have become used to a house that is opened to the outside as much as possible (except on unbearably hot days like this one). Even in winter, the doors and windows are wide open, and all through the year the geckos live on the ceilings and walls making admirable shelters behind the paintings hanging on the walls. The geckos are particularly noisy now in late January. The parents seem to have ejected their offspring from the territories they have mapped out for themselves. As I walk around the house I come across wandering, slightly lost juveniles on floors and walls. At night I have been hearing some particularly loud territorial cheeping as they fight with each other to map out new territorial boundaries. And the frogs have recently colonized the bathrooms and my study, and for a while a green tree frog perched on my bedroom window and woke me with its primeval song each morning at dawn.

Another difference between me and the sunbird that I find it curious to ponder on is that its first landscape was not a fold of its mother's body, but the interior of an egg, warmed by its mother's body, inside of which it became a sentient being, aware of sounds and temperature and light. Its next environment was, as for me, its mother's body and the dwelling spaces surrounding her. This second landscape, for all of us, is much more changeable and, in a sense, unreliable. The image of the newly hatched chick or the newly born baby carefully enfolded and kept warm by the mother is one that is sometimes true, but just as often it is a mythic dream fueled by desire for the absent mother's body. Drusilla Modjeska begins her autobiographical fiction, *Poppy*, with the separation of the child from the landscape of the mother and with a merging of mother's tears and the rain "settling in":

The first wound comes with the cutting of the umbilical cord. The thread is cut and we're out there alone. Where? I don't know, I didn't recognise a thing, bright and light with rain pebbling the windows.

In my family there have been three generations of daughters first born, and in each case the mother wept and outside the rain settled in, as if in sympathy. Well, it was England, it's not so surprising.

When China was born to Pauline, Pauline wept and China was taken away. When Poppy was born to China, China wept, and Poppy was taken away and put in a crib covered in fine broderie anglaise threaded with blue ribbon. When I was born to Poppy, Poppy smiled and held me firm against her chest. Then she wept inexplicably, inconsolably, and I was taken away. Perhaps I was in danger of catching a chill, I don't know, there wasn't an explanation. Only the snip of metal closing. And blood.

It's a common enough story. (Modjeska, 1990, p. 3)

For the sunbirds on my verandah, the landscape of the air with its changing currents and temperatures, along with the rain, becomes the next most significant landscape after the spaces in and around the nest with its mother, its father, and its siblings. For humans, it is more the surface of the earth that holds us and binds us and feeds us, though many of us continue to long for arms that hold us safe. And we long for words, words that shape landscapes, our bodies, and the relations between them, that shape the myths that fold and hold us into their patterns of meaning-making.

The body is linked to the unconscious. It is not separated from the soul. It is dreamed and spoken. It produces signs. When one speaks, or writes, or sings, one does so from the body. The body feels and expresses joy, anxiety, suffering and sexual pleasure. (Cornell, 1990, p. 39)

Mythical histories and historical myths: Colonizing and being colonized

Another binary that I want to trouble in this book is that of colonizer/colonized. Postcolonial discourses have thoroughly disrupted automatic assumptions of the superiority and rights of groups who have taken over the lands of other people. They have also disrupted notions of the "primitive," and of *terra nullius* (an invidious concept that allowed the newcomers to declare the landscape empty of habitation, thus making it a logical impossibility for indigenous people to claim rights to their land). Postcolonial discourses have given us a strange and complex legacy in which white Anglo groups see themselves on occasion as both culturally superior and morally inferior, while colonized others are romanticized, protected, and still held, largely, on the margins. While I cannot pretend to undo this complexity, I want to be aware of it, to continually return to it in order to draw attention to it, to see if I can shift some of its troubling patterns.

In colonized landscapes in the 1990s, the postcolonial descendants of the colonizers are often constituted (by themselves and others) in terms of their moral relations with the descendants of the original inhabitants, the colonized Others. The primary moral emotion is guilt associated with an inherited responsibility for displacement of the indigenous peoples. By locating responsibility in themselves, of course, they maintain a sense of their own agency (albeit a flawed agency) and thus position those who were wronged as without agency. For those who deny feelings of guilt and refuse the moral implications of postcolonial discourses, their position is still, albeit in terms of negation, defined in relation to those same discourses: they are either guilty or not guilty—it is not possible to be neither at this point in time. For those whose moral position is one of acknowledged guilt (and responsibility), indigenous dreamings of landscape are sometimes used as a standard against which to examine their own body/landscape relations and find them lacking. To have colonized, they feel, is bad, and that which has been destroyed is arranged, in a binary logic, as necessarily good, and as other to that colonizing badness. Unlike the sunbird colonizing my verandah (or have I colonized its verandah?), the original stories of domination and control interrupt the possibility of movement towards coexistence between descendants of the colonizers and the indigenous peoples.

With only two hundred years of Anglo history in the landscape (as is the case in Australia and in most parts of the island of Hokkaido in Japan), the guilty/responsible people in Australia and in Hokkaido often revere and envy the body/landscape stories of the original inhabitants, which reach back ten thousand years or more.[3] At the same time they refuse to move themselves to the periphery, to become, even momentarily, non-agentic Others. It is, of course, very easy to be deeply impressed by the antiquity of the Aboriginal connection to the landscape, and to revere it. But if that reverence is part of a strategy (whether intended or otherwise) for maintaining the marginality of one group and the dominant hegemonic gaze of the other, then it is highly problematic.

3. Remembering of particular family stories lasts for usually not much more than three or four generations. A particularly interesting story of significance to family identity may go back for hundreds of years. Stories of body/landscape relations are embedded in stories passed down through many generations, and in print-based societies they are published and spread far beyond the location in which the original events took place. There is often, then, no direct link between the storyteller and the ancestors of the storyteller who lived in the precise location in which the story is set. The figure here of ten thousand years does not signal how long Aboriginal people have been in different parts of the Australian landscape, but the length of time over which the particular oral story that follows has apparently been passed directly from one generation to the next, all the while holding significant information about body/landscape relations in a particular place.

I do not mean to suggest that the coexistence of indigenous knowledges of body/landscape relations and the white dreamings that enfold European landscapes with Australian country are easy to make sense of.

On the tablelands of North Queensland, not so far from where I live at the time of writing this book, are rain forests and extinct volcanic craters. Robert Dixon tells of an Aboriginal story of the time of the volcanic eruptions reaching back before the rain forest was even an idea. In this story body/landscape relations are powerfully drawn. Two young men break the moral order and this leads to a breaking open of the earth, which in turn swallows up the people:

> It is said that two newly initiated men broke a taboo and so angered the rainbow serpent. . . . As a result "the camping-place began to change, the earth under the camp roaring like thunder. The wind started to blow down as if a cyclone were coming. The camping place began to twist and crack. While this was happening there was in the sky a red cloud of a hue never seen before. The people tried to run from side to side but were swallowed by a crack which opened in the ground . . ."

Dixon continues:

> This was a plausible description of a volcanic eruption. After telling the myth, in 1964, the storyteller remarked that when this happened the country around the lakes was "not jungle—just open scrub". In 1968, a dated pollen diagram from the organic sediments of Lake Euramoo by Peter Kershaw (1970) showed rather surprisingly that the rain forest in that area is only about 7,600 years old. The formation of the three volcanic lakes took place at least 10,000 years ago. (Dixon, 1972, p. 29)

It is difficult, in the face of such ancient knowledges, to imagine how recently this country was not even an "island in the mind" of the newcomers from the northern hemisphere. When I was visiting Kronborg Castle in Helsingor (Hamlet's Elsinore) recently, I came across a fireplace with brass firedogs almost identical to the brass firedogs that had sat in the fireplace of my childhood home. The castle felt familiar, even modern. The large ballroom was lined on each side with tall archways opening onto alcoves with lead-paned windows that filled the room with golden light. In another, smaller room, I came across a globe of the world made in 1640. Australia was not there, though fragments of the most northern coastline were drawn in. I experienced a bodily shock as I realized both the immediate connectedness of myself to the landscape of this castle, not just through the architecture and the firedogs but because family legend has it that one of my ancestors was the bastard child of a Danish prince. Time suddenly shifted: the 1600s were clearly quite recent, yet my ancient country was at that time unknown to my ancestors. As a child, the two hundred years since "settlement" had seemed to be an enormous stretch of time. I understood then, looking at the globe, what my indigenous friends had been telling me—two hundred years is like the blink of an eye.

And the children of the newcomers, burdened with guilt and responsibility, stutter and stumble to find the words to speak about the landscapes they have been born into, frustrated with words that seem so rich in their power to evoke the landscapes their ancestors came from and so apparently poor in their ability to speak the Australian landscape. Eileen Honan talked and wrote in a collective biography workshop on body/landscape relations of her inability to know, to read Australian forests because of her inability to name the particular detail of them:

Sitting in stillness surrounded by movement
the intricate workings of a system I know nothing about.
I can't name the trees, the birds, the insects, the lizards
How can this exist when I can't name it into being?
The wind—is it a breeze, a bluster, does it come from the south or the
    east?
Is that a wasp or a dragonfly?
My written world is filled with elders, elms, maples, oaks and acorns
Larks, red robins, nightingales.
What is that bird calling across the treetops? What is the message?

Cath Laws wrote a similar story:

It is not in her experience
This connection with land, forest, bush,
She finds no peace there
She can take in the green, the lushness,
the damp, the deepness
And admire it
As one who is passing through
Respecting it—even honouring it
But this experience—this love—this connectedness
Is not hers.
In her Imaginings as a child
She yearned for this place to exist
The secret garden
The safe place in a forest that would be hers.
Perhaps she has no right to it anyway.

Here Cath resists the environmentalist's dream of immersion in land-scape. While she articulates a childhood longing, a desire, for the kind of forest in which she could be safe and that would belong to her,

her poem ends abruptly with a statement of her lack of rights, or with what could be read as postcolonial guilt. Her poem tells how she has formed a new connection to this place that comes not from a deep untraceable desire for secret connection with a forest-garden, but from an acknowledgment of its separate existence—which is to be honored and respected, but in relation to which she remains a nomad, only ever passing through.

To be a nomad: "a way of looking which is specific . . . , a way of representing things (in discontinuous fragments, stopping and starting). It is an aesthetic/political stance and is constantly in flight from ideas and practices associated with the singular, the original, the uniform, the central authority, the hierarchy . . . without for all that ascribing to any form of anarchy." (Benterrak, Muecke, and Roe, 1984, p. 15)

Rodney Hall, in his trilogy *The Island in the Mind* (1996a), takes us back to a point in the 1600s, prior to the entry into the Australian landscape of people from the northern hemisphere and prior even to the time in which Australia as a vast island land mass had been imagined by those ancestors. In his story *The Lonely Traveller by Night*, Hall turns the familiar colonizer/colonized binaries upside down. Here we do not find subordinate indigenous passivity and ascendant Anglo invading activity. Instead we find an Aboriginal man, Yuramiru, who is an active explorer in the northern hemisphere in the mid-1600s. Further, Hall does not allow his characters to fail to communicate across the apparent incommensurability of European and indigenous Australian languages. Yuramiru actively bridges the gap between his consciousness and the consciousness of another central character, Isabella. He enters her unconscious when she is asleep, inserting the imagery and language of the Australian landscape into her dreams. He does so because he fears he is about to be killed and he needs to communicate to her his desire that she take part of his body back to Australia if he dies. Isabella writes in her journal:

I woke with the heathen word *Ikara* on my lips and the moment I murmured it his face lit up with joy. He leapt in the air and let out hoots of triumph . . . [In the dream I was walking]. All day I walked until I was out of the valley. Often I looked back. Behind me lay the outer ramparts of the mountains. They were orange and blue with flat stripes of pale green. You could not believe so strange a sight. Many times I have seen pictures of mountains, but never these impossible colours. Yet I felt peaceful while I slept and apparently not at all surprised by what I saw. I walked and walked across stony ground until, in the far distance, other mountains came in view. These looked even more astonishing. Some pink and some the colour of amethyst, as luminous as a dream within a dream. (Hall, 1996b, p. 274)

In this story, Isabella and Yuramiru loosen the tight boundaries of their separate cultural knowledges, and of their separate identities, enabling her to dream what he remembers. He enables her, too, though with some struggle, to move beyond the narrow confines of her moral (in)scription. Hall uses the concept of the collective unconscious to make sense of the fact that even when we set up boundaries in our talk and in our thinking, they are not as tightly or as safely drawn as we might usually think:

> I don't think there's ever been a time when the entire human race has not been contributing overlapping parts of what could be called the collective unconscious. But . . . you have to have absorbed sufficient of the culture in order to dream into the culture. I think that through the common humanity of things we can touch this—that we can perceive things that I'm sure are contributed to the collective knowledge by people of other cultures. (Hall, 1997)

Here, in this storying, and at this point in history, we are confronted by a particularly complex conceptual puzzle. Just what are the intricate interweavings of language and embodied knowing—for certainly neither can be said, straightforwardly, to lead to the other? Cixous, herself a child of a colonized country and a fiction writer, grapples with similar puzzles. Born in French Algeria, she has taken up the French language and uses it with powerful effects. In a conversation with Mireille Calle-Gruber about her writing, she too muses on the collective and unconscious nature of language and embodied knowledge (Cixous and Calle-Gruber, 1997). It seems to her that memory is stored as language, somewhere on a deep-surface in/on her body—that is, memory is embodied language. The retrieval of an image from this deep-surface to use in writing is not random, she says, and it is not solely to do with the individual who retrieves it.

Language and embodiment do not rest with isolated individuals— they are collective processes. Language we do already understand as collective, though we assume its meanings are limited to the speakers of that particular language, whereas bodies we tend to think of as supremely individual. But bodies and languages are not so easy to separate from each other and collectives are rarely made up of people who speak only one language, with that language being relevant only to the landscape in which it was formed. The surge of energy in readers and audiences that responds to writing that taps collective knowledge may be because the language recorded on the deep-surfaces of our bodies acts as a key that unlocks memories, unconscious knowledges, which are shared by many others. We invent ourselves through language, and at the same time and through the same process are invented. Though we may be inserted differentially into patterns of power and powerlessness, it is in our subjection to language that we become speaking subjects. As Butler (1997, pp. 20–21) says: "Subjection exploits the desire for existence, where existence is always conferred from elsewhere; it marks a primary vulnerability to the Other in order to be." The act of taking up language and using it, the act of reading the interior surfaces of our bodies on which that language leaves its trace, may seem like an intensely personal experience, yet the *effect* of language shows how profoundly collective it actually is. The individual inventions that we call selves have remarkable patterns of commonality and communicability between one and another, and a remarkable capacity to move in common.

This book is not just about finding keys to unlock cultural meanings of bodies and landscapes in order to make them visible. It is also about transgression, about finding other ways to speak and write against the grain of dominant discourses and with the grain of bodies and landscapes. It is an exploration of the power of language, not just as it seeps into bodies and shapes the very grain of them, but also as a powerful force that individuals and collectives can use to retell lives against the grain of dominant discourses.

This is a book that unsettles certainty, that undoes the fixity of bodies and of landscapes; it unsettles boundaries and at the same time sees the power of those boundaries; it unsettles narrow moral certainties and is at the same time deeply moral. It attempts to move into the mysterious, that uncomfortable, uncontrollable zone that many would rather avoid. It does not set everything adrift, but like tears, it releases some of the sedimentation of the body.

And so...

In this and each of the chapters that follow, I practice a form of embodied writing that is integral to this project. I have entered the writing not through an abstract idea of what body/landscape relations might be, but through searching the possibilities of knowing opened up in my own shifting apprehension of being embodied with/in multiple landscapes. And I have also drawn on others' writing and talk about their own embodied sense of self with/in landscapes. Each chapter can be imagined as entering another fold in landscape, and of (un)folding the possibilities of embodied beings as they move through that landscape. Just as one moves around a prism, and new spaces open up while others vanish, so as new horizons appear, earlier landscapes and possibilities of embodiment with/in them vanish. The written text of each chapter (un)folds a different space inside the prism, a different possibility of knowing, a different sense of landscape and of flesh and of the relations between them. Through entering the folds of this text, you will find yourself moving into new, and also intensely familiar, landscapes. Sometimes the experience will be primarily emotional, sometimes physical, and sometimes it will be experienced as a flight of the imagination into something not previously known or imagined. In some of these moments you will experience/remember your own embodied self-in-landscape in contrast to what you read, and sometimes you will find startling and detailed memories of your own embodied self in landscape that are similar in unexpected ways to the experiences you read about. In this sense the book is an invitation into experiencing the elasticity of your own skin, and of your own senses, as you stretch them differently in each new space. This is a writing that makes visible the usually invisible and at the same time interrogates and opens up the apparently fixed. It brings the unexpected together and so troubles familiar categories, familiar separations, and familiar connections. In some of the spaces opened up here, you may find yourself leaving behind categories you thought were fixed in your flesh, or fixed in your psyche. Some of the fixities you have come to take for granted may slip away for whole hours of reading as you immerse yourself in the body/landscapes written in this text.

This is an inside/outside place,
my house,
huge windows
perpetually open
invitations

Moonlight
sunlight
find no boundaries
traversing my bed
stroking my skin

Frogs, lizards, birds
ignore the arbitrary markers
of the window frames
and make their way
wherever they wish to go

Sunbirds fly through
exploring my cave,
feeding on spiders, eggs
collecting cobwebs to build their nests

Green frogs hop confidently
from inside to outside
across my sleeping body,
my shoulder but another hill
from which to make the next leap

Jasmine curls
around the struts of the shutters
soon it will be impossible
to close them.

Sue Gannon
(unpublished)

~2~ Writing stories of (be)longing

---

belonging: secure relationship; affinity
belong: to be the property or possession (of); to be a member; to be classified (with); to be a part or adjunct (of); to have a proper or usual place
long: to have a strong desire; to belong, appertain or be appropriate [Old English *langian* to belong]. (*Collins English Dictionary*)

THIS CHAPTER IS ABOUT (BE)LONGING. I bracket the term in this way to give special weight to *longing*. In the process of constructing ourselves *appropriately* in landscape, we long for a *secure relationship*, for an *affinity*, for a sense of being in our *proper* or *usual* place. This longing is intricately tied up with becoming the appropriate(d) body, which is *of* that landscape, which *belongs to* that landscape. The chapter is primarily based on stories told in a collective memory workshop on Magnetic Island. But before I begin the collective memory stories, I want to explore the notion of (be)longing through the stories of two individuals.

The first story is fictional and the second is autobiographical. The first tells of a moment of being enfolded in and *becoming* the landscape. The second tells of a moment of (be)longing that is troubled by a dispute over whether or not the storyteller can (be)long in the way her story suggests. This second story is told by Roberta Sykes, who grew up in Townsville. The fictional story is told by Janette Turner Hospital and is set in a rain forest similar to those no more than an hour's drive up the mountains from Townsville. These are two contrasting stories of (be)longing that defy the binaries of body/landscape and sameness/otherness. They reveal the historical and political nature of making meaning of selves in relation to landscape. They give life to the Spinozan claims that mind and body "are not two distinct substances but rather two ways in which the human understanding grasps that which exists" and "that reason, politics and ethics are always embodied; that is, the ethics or the reason which any particular collective body produces will bear the marks of that body's genesis, its (adequate or inadequate) understanding of itself, and will express the power or capacity of that body's endeavour to sustain its own integrity" (Gatens, 1996, p. 100).

Janette Turner Hospital's character, Charade, does not know who her parents are. But she does not choose separation as her point of beginning. Instead she chooses as her first memory a moment of complete and ecstatic immersion in the rain forest. It is one of many possible beginnings, but this is the one in which she (be)longs in the landscape:

[W]here, Charade wonders, is the beginning? And how does she cut her own story free from the middle of the history of so many others? In a sense she is the epilogue to several lives.

Well then . . .

Here's one beginning, she suggests, in the rainforest where time comes and goes like a bird.

The birds. To the tag end of trillions of years of decay and growth come the birds: bellbirds, lyrebirds, lorikeets, parakeets. Shadow and rotting sweetnesses lure them. On their wings is such a weight of colour that they float dazed on the green air, slowly losing height, drifting down where Charade sits crushing the mosses and ferns. Oh, she gasps. Oh.

She is five, perhaps six years old, rapt, knees hugged up under her chin. The fallen tree trunk behind her back, given over to creepers, is collapsing softly, and along its jellied spine where a flock of new saplings has a toehold—there is walnut, silky oak, mahogany—the jostling and clamouring for light is constant and silent and deadly earnest. If she sits still long enough, the philodendron will loop itself around her ankles and kingfishers will nest in her hair.

That is my earliest memory, Charade says. (Turner Hospital, 1988, pp. 46–47)

Charade sits and waits, hugging her knees. She sees in intense detail the color and movement of the forest, and in doing so weaves herself, in her imagination, into the rain forest. She names the birds and the trees; she grows in amongst the philodendrons that weave themselves around her; she *becomes a place* on which the philodendron will grow, in which kingfishers can make their nests. Like the birds, she has come to this landscape at "the tag end of trillions of years of decay and growth," and like the new saplings she grows strongly there, clamoring silently for light.

In her autobiography Roberta Sykes also tells of a child whose parentage is obscure, since her mother is white and she is black: her mother either refuses to talk to her about who her father is, or makes up stories about a black American serviceman and then denies them. Her mother is adamant that her daughters will not grow up identifying as Aboriginal. To be Aboriginal at that time in Queensland entailed a serious denial of normal rights of citizenship. But not knowing whether she is of Aboriginal descent is a gap, an absence, that haunts Roberta's life. When she is old enough to be able to explore the town on her own, she goes to a sports field each weekend, where she watches Aboriginal children playing. She tells of an old man who eventually began to talk to her, teaching her how to see, by closely observing the ways that the Aboriginal children looked or moved, which totem they belonged to. Then:

"Who am I?" I asked the old man. . . . He gazed away as if trying to decide whether to answer me or not, then he picked up the stick in his toes and drew in the dirt.

"You fella snake." He spoke towards the ground as we both leaned against the fence and watched his foot drawing, as though it had a life of its own. "Baby one, eh," he added after a pause, a twinkle in his cloudy eyes.

I watched the coiled snake taking shape in the soil. (Sykes, 1997, p. 110)

In this powerful moment, she knows how she (be)longs in the landscape. It is a precious gift, a statement of (be)longing: the small girl sees in the image in the dirt an image of who she is. The first book of her autobiographical trilogy is called *Snake Cradle*. The snake in the dust is claimed as even more primary than the landscape of her mother's body: it is her cradle, the place that holds her safe. But this gift, the image of the snake, has become a dangerous and politically fraught image. The old man's action suggested he recognized the child as Aboriginal and that he gifted her with the detail of that recognition. Nearly half a century after this remembered event, her autobiographical words have led to a strong protest from those Aboriginal people who do not think she has a right to such a story, since they cannot believe that her story is true. Pat O'Shane (1998, p. 29), for example, writes in an open letter to Roberta:

[Y]ou import the idea of the old man and the snake. That story, Bobbi, is a dead giveaway. Anyone who had an idea she was Aboriginal would want to do some research about the people from whom she believed she was born. She would have done as author Sally Morgan did: lift the covers, peel back the layers, and not be put off with half-truths and other deceits. But more than that: you would have known that in Aboriginal custom, no old man would have stopped to talk to a "lonely little girl" (a complete stranger at that) and tell her the snake story in the way that you recount it. . . .

The letter, titled "Sins of omission," takes up half a page in the weekend national newspaper.

Belonging in landscape is a deeply emotional experience, but it is also a political experience. From the point of view of some of those with long histories stretching back through time, their claims hold more weight, more emotional and more political weight, than those who cannot be sure of such long histories. Growing up in Townsville and experiencing all the racism of the north does not, from this weightier position, give Roberta any rights to belong in the ways her memories would claim. The struggle here is carried out through Roberta's body—the dispute is organized around the question of whether it is an Aboriginal body, or whether it is a non-Aboriginal (privileged) body:

> In effect, bodies are physical field sites upon which the world inscribes itself—places to which others come and make their difference, places like any other place—localised and with continuously negotiated boundaries and subregions. (Nast, 1998, p. 95)

Aboriginal politics of place, the politics that many of us support, in this instance plays itself out on a suffering body. The discourse, invented by the Australian government, opens up the possibility of restitution of land rights to Aboriginal people who can prove an unbroken pattern of body/landscape relations going back prior to invasion/settlement. A recent Australian court disallowed a land rights claim because the judge could not see that the current claimants lived out a connection to the land identical to the connection their ancestors had lived out prior to white invasion. Such a ruling on the part of the judge suggests that body/landscape relations could remain identical through hundreds of years and, moreover, could do so through a period of massive transformations in linguistic, social, political, and spatial relations. What this chapter shows, amongst other things, is that such rulings reveal a deep ignorance of the way body/landscape relations are lived as physical, emotional, political, and discursive patterns of (be)longing that are necessarily emergent through space and time.

Language and memory, the resources we draw on for telling stories of our lives and also for inventing stories of other lives, are embodied, political, and heavily saturated with emotion. Language inscribes its arc not just on the sound waves, not just on the surface/depth of the body. Language inscribes itself at the same time in the landscapes of politics and desire. Memories have the accumulated weight of associated memories and imagined possibilities. As Delia Falconer said in her paper to the Brisbane Writers' Festival (1998), "memory has weight—the weight of a photo album is greater than the photos you've put in them." The original event that we work to retrieve in words cannot be understood independently of the desires that shaped it, nor of the desires and longings through which bodies and landscapes are constituted. In Delia Falconer's (1998) words, "desire is a force field around objects" and "place is anchored by the gravity of longing." She says that "landscape in Australia is saturated by desire" and that this creates a particular fascination and dilemma for the articulation of Australian embodiment in landscape for those of us whose language and ancestry did not originate in this place: our "longings come out of somewhere else. . . . The words connected to 'forests' and 'longing' invoke something somewhere else—how does one speak," she asks, "of longing for *this* landscape?"

Memory work as it was developed by Haug et al. (1987) distances itself from autobiographical writing, which it sees as the use of particular, remembered stories to mark one specific individual as being apart from the rest, as recognizably this (and no other) person. But autobiographical writing can achieve something quite other than this in its search for writing that goes against the grain of usual ways of telling lives. More than this, it can unfurl or make possible new forms of subjectivity. Language, subjectivity, landscape, and the relations between them are organic—they unfold and shift about. As Trinh observes:

[A]utobiography both as a singularity and as a collectivity is a way of making history and of rewriting culture. Its diverse strategies can favour the emergence of new forms of subjectivity: the subjectivity of a non-I/plural I, which is different from the subjectivity of the sovereign I (subjectivism) or the non-subjectivity of the all-knowing I (objectivism). Such a subjectivity defies the normality of all binary oppositions including those between sameness and otherness, elite and mass, high culture and popular culture. (Trinh, 1991, pp. 190–91)

Roberta Sykes's autobiographical writing achieves precisely what Trinh describes here, elaborating in careful detail how "the facts" and "identity," or clear belonging in any binary category, constantly elude her restless searching. Pat O'Shane, of undisputed Aboriginal descent, respected by Aboriginal and non-Aboriginal groups alike, recently elected chancellor of a university, authoritatively redraws the boundaries that Roberta's story troubles, and she places Roberta emphatically outside the tightly drawn lines. Each stands in a different fold in the landscape. What is possible, desirable, even obvious from one fold makes no sense in the other. From where Pat O'Shane stands, Roberta has not displayed the appropriate forms of action and knowing for one who would claim Aboriginality. The folds of the landscape from where she stands are deeply knotted with colonial history and with the appropriation and destruction of Aboriginal knowledges. Her strong stand makes sense from that fold in the landscape. Roberta's story of (be)longing only makes the sense she wants in a quite different fold in the emotional and political and conceptual landscape.

In the remainder of this chapter I will explore (be)longing through collective biography stories of body/landscape relations written on Magnetic Island. Although the memories are of other places, the embodied telling of them, on the island, seems to require that I begin with a telling of that landscape.

Magnetic Island is a tropical island covered in open eucalypt woodlands, but also with drylands, and mudflats and mangroves and pockets of lowland tropical rain forest. It is the island I see four kilometres across the water when I walk each day on the beach near my house. The colours of its round wooded hillsides shift dramatically and within moments at various times during the day. Its more usual light cobalt colours change, sometimes, to a light dove-grey with a tint of mauve, or at evening, when the sea washes out, to a pale milky-blue; the hillsides are tinged with ultramarine, with a glow as intoxicating as bunches of fresh-picked violets. Sometimes it is swathed in white mist, its colours and outlines intensifying before it disappears from sight.

Traveling to the island on the ferry from Townsville takes twenty minutes. Often the ride is magical, across a glassy, silver-mirrored sea, with other islands forty miles away visible on the horizon. At other times the sea sparkles with diamonds of light so intense it is almost impossible to look at them. And sometimes it is a metallic pewter-grey. When the winds of summer blow, green waves crash up over the sides of the ferry and drench the laughing passengers riding upstairs on the deck. The ferry pulls in at the Picnic Bay jetty, a bay with flat white-sand beaches, huge, smooth, round brown granite boulders tumbled on the headlands, with tall, slender, dark green Hoop pines growing among them. A small shopping centre tucked beneath towering Moreton Bay figs offers cappuccinos, mini mokes for hire, and beer and food for those who are interested. Ferry loads of tourists land every hour or so and disappear into the forests and the remote beaches of this 5,000 hectare island. You don't see them again until it is time to get back on the ferry. The locals similarly disappear into one of the small settlements along the coastline.

Magnetic Island, for me, is a place of peace and soft tropical breezes, a place for walking through forests to deserted beaches and swimming in the warm tropical sea, for drinking champagne on the beach and talking to friends in the dappled shade of the casuarina trees, and for watching sea eagles drift through the air. It is a place of dreaming; but it is also a place where I wear my stinger suit when I swim in the sea during summer to protect myself against the deadly Chironex jellyfish and other malevolent "stingers" that breed up when the rains have fallen. And all through the year it is a place where the bush-stone curlews wail through the night, signalling to me that the place is at peace, it is safe, else why would they play so rowdily?—though I have heard that some indigenous people hear the cry as a sign of death.

This small, rocky, tree-covered island has no permanent water source, but after heavy rains, which come during "the wet," water rises up out of the hills, creating clear cold streams and waterfalls and perfect swimming holes—there for a few weeks, and then gone.

Magnetic Island: also called The Rock by the Wulgurukaba people, who lodged a land claim during the week we were there. The Rock is not just a tropical paradise, but also a place of serious political contestation over space and meaning and (be)longing. Such claims are of fundamental importance to the idea of what Australia is. As an Australian it is no longer possible to refuse to occupy a position in relation to these claims—you are supportive, or in opposition, or else you must constantly reiterate your "noncommittal."

Collective biography or memory work

We retrieve memories sometimes as words spoken, sometimes as visual images, or smells, or as tastes vividly registered on the tongue. We can struggle to retrieve memory that exists "*before* 'it is called'" one thing or another (Cixous, in Cixous and Calle-Gruber, 1997, p. 18) and in doing so arrive at something that can be recognized as truthful, though elusively so—competing with other powerful memories that hold an equally weighted truth. And always each memory is vulnerable to the landscape of desire and the discourses through which it is called up.

The kind of truth one achieves in collective biography workshops is not of the kind where it is asserted as historical fact that precisely this thing happened at this time and in this way. The participants struggle to enter into the bodily detail of what it is their body registers *now* of what it remembers of *then*. Through listening to the stories of others, through telling out loud the remembered fragments, through writing the memories down and seeing how language shapes them and saturates them with cultural patterns of meaning-making, the collective biography group searches for the kind of "truth" that comes from inside the remembered event, and also from inside the process of remembering.

The nature of the telling and listening and writing attempts to remove the participants from being cultural *spectators* and *commentators* whose knowledge lies in practiced patterns of language that only mention the body in the most general sense. Instead, language itself is understood as embodied: talk is made with the breath of our bodies expelled with muscles and shaped with mouth and tongue and vocal chords, and the sounds we hear are vibrations in membranes and bones; writing is marks we make on the page or the screen, using hands and eyes. For commentators and spectators, however, the production of talk or of writing appears to be "natural" and thus invisible—language and meaning-making get separated out from the bodies that produce them. As children we learn the patterns and meanings of our language as embodied patterns and meanings. But once we get to school, language is rarely associated with the specificity of our own bodies—we learn to speak in what Morrison (1994, pp. 13–14) calls "dead language," which she describes as a "suit of armor, polished to shocking glitter, a husk from which the knight departed long ago."

Collective biography works to find the knight, to *occupy* the language, to make it live. The kind of truth that is sought is similar to what Cixous says she finds in Derrida:

> *What I love in him as I love the* truth *itself, is the expression of the truth, the flection (the genuflection, the ingenuflection) the way his thought always forms a single body with the objects (of thought) in their flexibility, the way he never thinks as a spectator standing (or sitting) on the exterior of the trail of the world, but he always thinks the world in the world, embracing the movements, the courses, not separating himself*

from the sometimes rapid sometimes immobile dance of beings. (Cixous, in Cixous and Calle-Gruber, 1997, p. 87, italics in original)

And in our case, the dance was of our own embodied beings, remembered from childhood. The language we found with which to speak and write our memories was found in part in the detail of each other's tellings. One of my own experiences of retrieving such detail was in a later workshop, which I tell here since it enables me to write about the process from the point of view of the participants, and, as it turns out, the story is relevant to what I will write about in the rest of this chapter. The story was about crying in fourth grade. I never cried, at school or at home. Crying meant lack of character; it was inappropriate—out of place. But my new teacher had told us that the way we wrote, the way we sat, and the way we held our pens was a very personal expression of our selves, and she asked us to think about our bodies in relation to the desk, the book, and the pen. I tried turning my book around at a strange angle and wrote with the words running away from me from the front of the desk towards its back. This experiment filled me with pleasure. But the teacher disallowed it. It would not do. I must turn my book back to the correct 45 degree angle. I tried to argue with her, to tell her that it felt like a very personal expression. In desperation I even lied about this being the way everyone in my family wrote. But she would not be persuaded—and so I capitulated. I turned my book round to the right angle. And I felt as if something terrible had happened. As I sat there, squeezed into the correct posture, with my fingers cramped tight around the pen, a terrible, loud, embarrassing sob came heaving and snorting out of my aching chest. I held my breath and checked the tears and forced my body not to cry, and each time I thought I had it under control, another sob would come lurching out of me, hideously loud in the silence of the classroom.

My story, on first telling, did not make sense to some members of the group. Some heard it as a story in which I was being naughty, lying capriciously to get my own way over something quite trivial. In order to make the story make sense to them as it did to me, I had to uncover more detail, detail that no longer existed in the version of the story I had come to remember. As I told how the involuntary noisy sobs wrenched themselves out of me, I felt those sobs still lodged in my body along with the anguish that had given rise to them. I could find words to describe them that I had not found before. As each member of the group questioned me about the story, and as they each told their own stories of being in confrontation with teachers, the detailed fabric of my own experience became more vivid (both in similarity and in contrast). The collective experience of being in trouble in school that began to emerge enabled me to piece together the particular detail of my outrage and the painful feeling of the sobs, to smell again the dusty smell of the wooden desks and floor and the pungent smell of the ink that we wrote with. I could also begin to make sense of the story from the teacher's point of view. My experimentation on that day was not what she wanted from me or from anyone else. I had misread the landscape of the classroom, which she had the power to define. For my part, I was engaged in a bodily/emotional struggle to (re)constitute myself as good student, as one who is recognized as knowing how to (be)long, as knowing how and when it is permissible to be creative and different.

> Nietzsche posits reason as the effect, the outcome or the product of painful work on the body—work which is performed in specific social and political contexts. Reason and ethics are here understood as the outcome of inscribing the body with pain in order that it might develop a memory, an internalised sign system, a code of which behaviours to suppress and which to cultivate. (Gatens, 1996, p. 102)

Cixous, talking about writing, includes many of the features of collective biography in her description of what it is that generates her own "poetic" writing, that is, writing that reads the possibilities of knowing from her body, rather than philosophical writing whose reference point lies outside any specific body. She talks about the beginning point of something both unexplained and yet concrete, and how it goes through moments lived by herself and by others, crossing many "zones of our histories." She talks about how she seizes the moments, "still trembling, moist, creased, disfigured, stammering" and in doing so chooses what she calls a poetic rather than a philosophical path:

> When I begin to write, it always starts from something unexplained, mysterious and concrete.... It begins to search in me. And this questioning could be philosophical: but for me, right away it takes the poetic path. That is to say that it goes through scenes, moments, illustrations lived by myself or by others, and like all that belongs to the current of life, it crosses very many zones of our histories. I seize these moments still trembling, moist, creased, disfigured, stammering. When I write a book, the only thing that guides me at the beginning is an alarm. Not a tear [*larme*], but an alarm. The thing that alarmed me at once with its violence and its strangeness. (Cixous, in Cixous and Calle-Gruber, 1997, p. 43)

Memories drawn on for collective biography work do not exist in some pure, veridical state, awaiting the means of revelation. They are not written on the body in indelible and minutely legible ink. Politics, desire, patterns of language use—each play their part in constituting how we read our own bodily (in)scriptions, what we find there, what we search out in some prior-to-naming space in the depth/surfaces of our embodied beings.

It is useful to contrast the memory work of collective biography with those therapy workshops where memories are used as proof of past "forgotten" outrages. In some workshops, for example, women are encouraged to remember experiences of childhood sexual abuse, the assumption being that the memory of abuse is held in a veridical form in the unconscious and that the task of the therapist and the group is to facilitate its retrieval. Through such workshops abusive memories are "retrieved" and then used as proof that the horrifying event actually took place. But research on memory suggests that such veridical storage is not how the memory actually works. Memory is endlessly creative, working afresh sets of images and stories that may come in part from present discourses or desires, from the memories of others, from dreams or from imagined events—as well as from the things that actually happened.

In contrast, the use of memory work as research strategy, in the way that it is used in collective biography, draws attention to the words used and makes visible the way the stories are retrieved, in part through listening to the patterns of meaning-making in others' stories and in the kinds of questions that are asked and answered. It also reveals how the truth is struggled after in the task of finding words with which to write the story in detail. Collective biography works to reveal how words may occlude the embodied detail in favor of culturally normative or desired or politically appropriate explanations. Collective biography teaches participants to see how language may obscure the detail they want to tell, and it teaches them to work with language as poets. Collective biography works with the participants to enable them to see and feel and tell and write the specificity of bodily experience, and to recognize as well the constitutive and collective effects of particular storylines, of ways of speaking and of writing.

The week that we spent together on the island was actually part of a longer course run by Lorri Neilsen and Sharn Rocco, which encouraged "the exploration of multiple literacies and ways of knowing: the visual arts, musical expression, kinesthetic/rhythmic, sensory, as well as verbal forms of meaning making" (Neilsen, 1998a, p. 1; see also Neilsen, 1998b). I had invited my postgraduate students to take part, and the stories I was given to use in my research were almost all from my own students. Those who gave me permission to use their stories and whose stories are included here are Sue Gannon, Eileen Honan, Lekkie Hopkins, Cath Laws, Helen McCann, Rosemary McLaren, and Paula Smith. Each morning all the participants worked on collective biography, and then in the afternoon we dispersed into different activities all to do, in some way, with writing or embodiment.

Sue Gannon, who was writing a thesis on women and writing, wrote a poem after the workshop expressing the alarm she had felt at her initial inability to grasp what "embodiment" was and how we might remember and talk about it. She writes about what the collective biography process was for her, how we threaded our stories onto each other's stories, and how the particular images that came up in the storying finally brought her, with startled pleasure, to an understanding of the connection between words and bodies. She begins the segment of the poem quoted here with the detail of her insertion/submersion in(to) the processes I had set up, revealing her pleasure in the orderly way in which I had framed the work. She also reveals her almost (to her) absurd willingness to authorize me to use her stories for my research, and her abject uncertainty about her capacity to know or understand what it was that I wanted of her. She is caught up in the landscape of student/teacher binaries, handing all authority to me, in this early stage of the workshop. Through the work done at the workshop, however, she was able to recast her thesis as a poetic piece of writing, poetry having become, for her, the most desirable way of writing clearly and directly from the body:

(Gradual)
Submersion

On the rock
(as opposed to
in the kitchen
in the tower)
A clear agenda,
a question for every day
(Elaborations,
Examples)
Someone else's purpose
Bliss
Of course with your approval
She's ready to sign the authorization now
And she hasn't even written anything

She wants to know
Should we come with a story in mind already?
What exactly do you mean by 'landscape'?
What exactly is an 'earliest' memory?
Are we allowed to . . . ?
Can we . . . ?
Is it legitimate to . . . ?

The first morning
She writes important words
on the back of a page
discursively constructed
determinism (albeit by <u>lang</u>. not class e.g. Marxism)

Once we start talking
Stories spill out
Lap over each other

Wash us into other stories
We give our gifts,
memories,
to each other

I don't quite understand 'embodiment', she worries

Until the taste of nectar on her tongue
Blue bubblegum on pink flesh
Warm hot piss streaming through clenched thighs
Sour damp sheets
Heartbeats of fear
Mrs. Snake
the
(wicked)
Banksia men
Water and sand swirling me over and over
I'm out of control
the salt sting inside my eyelids
I'm drowning
Vomit in the back seat of a car
Please stop
I'm going to be sick
Cold knees
She's gone to London to visit the queen,
said Christopher Robin to Alice
The weight of soft ripe figs in my hand
My strong legs running
Now look at me! I can do it!

She worried though—
Worried at the words,
A terrier for perfection
Oh no, not another cliché
Is this an explanation?
What if I just drop the first paragraph
She rushed home each day with her story
No you can't have it yet.
It's not right

Aha the good girl syndrome, says Eileen
Will they understand?
Have I remembered it properly?
Is this the right memory?

As Sue's poem tells, in preparation for each session I had given the
participants detailed instructions along with excerpts from the writing
of Australian novelists such as Janette Turner Hospital, Rodney Hall,
and Sam Watson, whose stories include evocative explorations of

body/landscape relations, and whose texts I explore here, in this book. I also gave them excerpts about writing from authors such as Toni Morrison and writing about collective biography (Davies et al., 1997). Some of the participants had already taken part in that earlier collective biography, and Sue was using collective biography in her thesis on women and writing.

Each day we read and talked and wrote around a different context: landscapes of home, of water, and of forests. In the afternoons we swam in the sea, walked through the forests, talked about theses in progress, went to body/dance/voice/writing workshops, and some of us played with paint. Each morning we began by remembering stories and telling them to each other. Often we had already remembered the particular stories we wanted to tell, but as we listened to each other's stories more of the minute detail of how the moment felt, of the reactions of others, of the landscapes in which they took place, would click into place like small shining pieces of glass in a turned kaleidoscope.

After telling our remembered stories, we wrote those stories down. As each participant finished writing, I worked with them on the texts they had written.

Thinking deeply
Waiting
Where does this thought come to us from: from the body
It is the place that writes

What is it called
To follow the course: of the blood
Of the wind etc (Cixous, in Cixous and Calle-Gruber, 1997, p. 42)

The discussion and the writing and reading took place on the spacious high-set verandah of a house set amongst lush gardens and towering eucalypts: the soft wind cooled our bodies and the birds chattered in the trees while we wrote and talked: "*of the blood/ Of the wind*": the written words and the reading of them were inseparable from the space/time in which they were written. In following the course of what each participant had written, I entered into the flow of their words, to live in my own body the experience they were writing about. Intuitively I read the words that were written, and if they prevented rather than facilitated my entry into the embodied experience, if the words prevented me from knowing the embodied detail, then I looked more closely at them, I searched for the clichés, the words that have been overused, which had lost any specific embodied reference. I also searched for "explanations," for culturally approved ways of "making sense" of something that abandons the specific detail once the "sense" has been made. It was specificity of embodied experience that we sought in the writing. Rather than words such as "I was upset" (an explanation), participants found words such as "Running across the oval, heart beating from the rage—a huge hot red anger pushing me forward. My whole body bursting—the rage causing my knees, my legs, my hands to shake and shiver—my head bursting with the pain." As Cixous says:

> The most impassioned, the most passionate in us is the quantity, the flood of extremely fine and subtle affects that take our body as a place for manifestation. It begins in this way, and it is only belatedly, and to go quickly, to sum up, that we give general and global names to a whole quantity of particular phenomena. In *My Pushkin*, Tsvetaeva says in passing: it begins with a burning in the chest, and *afterwards* it is called love. Now writing deploys itself *before* 'it is called'. (Cixous, in Cixous and Calle-Gruber, 1997, p. 18)

Writing in collective biography seeks this before-the-naming, before the explanatory words that parcel it up as meaning one thing or another, peel the detail away from it, allow it to go quickly, to be summed up or explained away. This is not to say the original event is prediscursive, but that it is lived in the body in ways that practiced forms of telling often make inaccessible.

Often, at the end of the two hours, the participants were still not satisfied with the words they had found, and so they took them home to work further on them, to get the detail right. ("She rushed home each day with her story/ *No you can't have it yet/ It's not right.*")

When all the stories were written, they were read out loud to the group, and then again each morning, reading out loud the rewritten stories became a valued moment, the gift of listeners who would hear the memory come to life in the detail caught in the written/spoken words, bringing the story to life in their bodies—in the speaking of it; in the hearing of it.

> [T]he materiality of the voice cannot be denied, its substance is a vibration which penetrates the bodies of those listening or present. (Muecke in Benterrak, Muecke, and Roe, 1984, p. 21)

In this description of what we did during the two hours each day, working on the collective biography, I have told you so far about the island, about the verandah on which we sat, about the subject in which the workshop was embedded. But I have not mentioned the emotional landscapes in which some of us found ourselves caught up in the spaces between the workshops. For much of the time the participants were in a state of pleasure and delight, talking and walking and swimming together, enjoying the beauty of the island and the spaces inside and outside of which we were living. But the politics of space and desire also created tensions in the landscape that troubled the idyllic picture I have drawn. There were some of us, for example, who wanted to start on time, and some who were tuned into "island time" and were always "late"; there were some who had paid extra money for the privilege of a single room, and some who found the privilege intolerable and entered and colonized the space that the "privileged" wanted to keep private; there were some who saw the week as an exercise in building community, and some who saw that as oppressive and controlling; there were some who happily accepted the task of communal cooking, and some who felt threatened by the fact that they had no control over what they ate; and there were some who left keys in "obvious" places, and some who objected to being locked out. These tensions were also part of the talk during the week, though not in the workshops, and we tended to discuss them quite differently than we usually might, describing and analyzing them in terms of our embodied selves in landscape. They were part of the process of tuning into the multidimensionality of embodied being, to the emotion of it, and to the political and contested nature of it.

I have divided the collective biography stories that follow into three groups. The first group consists of stories in which landscape is the desired space in which the body is immersed in a harmonious blending of embodied being and landscape. These are stories of longing and belonging, of (be)longing. The second group of stories tell of being out of place, of losing one's footing in the landscape, of being lost and at a loss. These are very painful stories and they highlight and lie in sharp contrast to the stories of (be)longing. The third group of stories tell of individual struggles to become embodied appropriately, to develop ways of moving, thinking, understanding that enable the storyteller to become the competent subject, the subjected being, who will not lose her footing in the landscape.

Stories of ecstatic immersion—landscape saturated with desire

The interweaving of selves in landscapes of other selves, in the formation of what Trinh calls the plural I, begins before birth. At that time, we are literally held and grow in the landscape of our mothers' bodies in a plural I: motherandchild. After birth, the landscape of the mother may continue to be longed for. The first awareness of (be)longing in the landscape of the mother's body is the first collective biography story told here by Helen:

The young mother sits with her firstborn baby daughter on a cane lounge in a sparsely furnished room. She holds her baby on her foot, balancing her by holding her hands outstretched. She swings her foot up and down, then slowly, sensuously swings her backwards and forwards, smiling as she sings.

The baby girl laughs in pleasure at the game, and in the glow of her mother's gaze. Looking up into her mother's face, she sees the soft waves framing her face, her head surrounded by a roll of hair. She basks in the warmth of her mother's happiness, her smile and her singing. The solid smooth curve of her mother's knee rises above her, while she sits, precarious and excited, but balanced and secure—smoothly, lazily swinging, held by her mother's hands, the focus of all her mother's love, careful attention and intense pleasure.

The child's embodiment in this moment is first located in the sensation of swinging, but that swinging is inextricably linked with held hands, the mother's sensuous movement, the mother's smile and her singing voice. Her eyes see her mother's face, her hair, her knee. The body sitting astride the foot is not described in detail: the intensity of her awareness is primarily in the landscape that holds her; what the story tells us about the child's embodied self is that it hears singing, it is held, it is laughing, and it is basking in the warm gaze. This is probably a rare memory of intense delight. There is nothing that alarms the child in this moment "with its violence and its strangeness" (Cixous, in Cixous and Calle-Gruber, 1997, p. 43).

Sue tells a story of fusion in landscape in her grandmother's garden. Here it is the detail of the taste of nectar on the tip of the child's small tongue, the feel of her skin brushed by the air, and the feel of her grandmother's hand that brings to life the embodied being in this garden-landscape:

In the summer when the rest of the grandmother's garden is warm and dry and sunny, the "jungle" behind the garage is a dark cool place.

Nanna Ida takes me there when I am very small by the hand when she waters the special damp-loving plants that need watering in the evenings. She takes me with her when she picks the figs she makes into grey jam. She's a bit like a witch when we're in the jungle together. She's tall and sharp and bony not like my other round and cuddly Nanna. Her hand is cool and damp and her fingers are sinewy and grip tightly my own small hand.

I like to go there alone and everyone knows they can find me hiding there. It's so quiet and still. My skin is always cool and moist and open to the air in there in the darkness. I sit still on the mossy wet stump and breathe the fresh green dark air. The tiny flowers that grow at the base of the fig tree are purple cups of nectar. I pick them one at a time and poke my tongue gently inside to lick out the sweetness. I'm so still and quiet and I wait there hoping that fairies will come.

This is a landscape deeply (in)scribed with (be)longing. It is heavy with desire. It is a place the child can be alone, yet known by others to be there. It is also a hybrid place, a place of mixed ancestry, a place in which the feel of the air and the taste of the flowers may well be the same as it was thousands of years ago, and at the same time it is a place made by witches who came from across the world, bringing their ancient language and longings with them. The child's immersion in the garden has similarities to Charade's immersion in the rain forest. Each is connected to the lives of others, and each securely finds, alone, a sense of themselves in place. Each child finds in the cool damp space a form of embodiment, of solitude and ease, of (be)longing. Charade's embodiment is such that the forest grows into and around her, her boundaries dissolve. In the garden, the child's embodiment is made up of fresh green dark air drawn into her body, of her skin cooled and made moist by the air, of body held by the mossy wet stump, of drinking the sweet nectar from purple cups. She imagines, she longs for, the presence of fairies, the imagining of whom is made possible by the language of her mother and her grandmother and all the mothers before her.

Rosie tells of a moment of wonder induced by light on leaves. The narrative voice in this tale is not "I," but the voices of children telling and showing each other how to be in this landscape, how to come by this way of seeing, this way of being, cradled in the landscape. She does not write, for example, "the stones hurt my feet" but "the stones hurt your feet" and "first you close your eyes and look upwards"—as if the words of other small children are still traced on her body as vividly as the images of trees and light and water:

To get to the creek we walk down a long gravel track that once was a road. The stones hurt your feet. The overgrown track leads to the remnants of a small wooden bridge. It is summer time. Hot, dry, heat haze, cricket singing late January, West Australian bush summer time. The creek bed, dry now except for small rock pools where baby frogs play, is a magical place. To get there you have to climb down a rock wall of huge granite boulders and then over silver grey jarrah logs. The rocks and logs are all there is left to remind you of the bridge. The sand is soft, damp, grainy. The colours of autumn squelch up through your toes. The smell of fig trees, lining both sides of the creek, is musky and thick. The trees are large and gnarled and twisted and very old. Heavy with fruit they lean towards the centre forming a fragrant green roof over our heads. Puffs of hot easterly wind ripple every now and again, causing the roof to dip and sway. You can lie in the sand, wriggling your shoulders and bottom until you feel like you are being held. It is lovely. First you close your eyes tight and then look upwards. Through the gently moving leaves you can see bits of blue and white. And then brown and more shades of green from the giant sugar gums standing on the edge of the paddocks. If you hold your hands, like a funnel in front of your face and imagine hard enough, it's like looking through a kaleidoscope. Shafts of blue, gold and red flash in diamond patterns on the edges of the leaves.

The child's body and the bodies of her playmates are held in the embrace of the sand, her sight is held in the embrace of trees—in the sight and smell of them—and of the sky. In this story, too, a thread reaching back in time is created by an old bridge made of ancient jarrah logs, by old twisting fig trees forming a cathedral-like canopy, and by old, river-worn, smooth rocks.

Embodiment in landscape is made and remade. It is made out of the possibilities found through language and through the particular materiality of place and the possibilities for embodiment held there. The threads of history shift and change and overlap. Continuous being is not passed down from generation to generation intact, but made again and again out of what is possible for this child, these children, in the spaces in which they find themselves.

Stories of alarm, of separation, of being out of place

Stories of being out of place, pulled out of one's place in the landscape, are held in strong contrast to immersion, to being in place. Rosie folds these two elements together—alarm and separation are told inside a story of being enfolded and cared for:

Small pink body. Naked. Blonde hair—soft like baby's breath. And blue bubblegum ATTACHED TO *the tiny folds of my labia. How did it get there? There is only the knowledge of me as naughty child—*ANNOYED *parent—tut tutting—and place of body where this sticky substance was not supposed to be. Dark laundry—light glistening on dusty louvred windows—stone laundry trough and cold grey water, Solyptol added to help dissolve the gum* AND *mother picking at my blue sticky lips—*
Then being left
Alone
To detach this substance from my body.
Small hand
dipping in and out of Solyptol-smelling water.
Cold dark grey trough
little fingers pulling at strings of blue
Rolling strands into little balls
and dropping them onto the floor
sensing shame
Then awareness
of the "new" but unacceptable part of myself.
Separate = me? but not me
Then mother—tutting again—less angry now
Soft warm arms lifting—towel rubbing briskly at tender lips.
Then her lips dropping a kiss—
transparent enveloping love.

The child is intensely aware of the detail of the strange landscape in which she finds herself: in cold grey water, in the Solyptol-smelling laundry tub with light glimmering through the dark, dusty louvered windows of the laundry. She finds herself acutely aware of her small embodied being in this strange landscape, but uncertain now about what is to be included in the region of her legitimate embodied self.

In her disapproval and abandonment and then re-embracing love, the mother traces the child with a new knowledge, a knowledge of the landscape of her body as having regions and subregions, some of them loaded with emotion, unacceptable, alarming, acknowledged only in strange dank landscapes.

In each of these stories the child's body is traced with words and with actions, and with perceptions that give it new substance. But the experience of being out of place may not derive from words. Lekkie's story tells the anguish of a landscape that does not appear to be safe, even though others find it so. Other children skip along, unafraid, increasing the child's sense of isolation and separation. The child is unable to find the step, the movement, the words that will render the situation safe, familiar:

The planks of the jetty hold two fears for me: splinters and gaps. The wood is weathered and grey, and huge splinters lie in wait for little bare feet. The gaps between the planks are wide, too wide for little feet, and there, as I look down I feel that sudden lurching, sickening pull towards the deep green lapping sea below. I know that the other kids are skipping along this same jetty towards the boat, nimble footed and carefree. I feel uncomfortable, scared, out of my place.

Danger on the jetty comes with a feeling of being pulled towards the deep green lapping sea through the gaps in the boards, where the sea is read as active and dangerous, able to pull the child towards it. And it can come from not knowing the regions and subregions of the body and how to read them. Danger lies in the places where we have no known way of locating our body in the landscape. That landscape, in a story told by Helen, is a day-care center made up of a sea of laughing, screaming children:

She finds herself in the middle of a sea of children, running, pushing past her, yelling, calling out to each other, but not to her. What is she doing here? Why have her parents left her in this terrible, grey frightening place? The other children all seem to know how to have fun here—they laugh and scream as they slide down the slippery slide; they play in groups in the cubby house; but no-one asks her to join them and, confused and afraid, she does not know how to join a group herself. She walks around aimlessly, alone, looking in amazement at all the other children, in her own little space of silence in the midst of the noisy movement around her.

Throughout the long, never-ending day she frequently goes to the door to see if her parents are returning. She puts her hands on the bars covering the entrance and gazes out desperately but there are only empty grey corridors. By the time they finally arrive, she is numb and spent by the effort of dealing with the day. She cannot speak or cry any more—there is only a sense of relief that her ordeal is over, that she is at last safe again.

The child-care center was a place of tears and of alarm, a grey place, a noisy place, a place in which there is nothing/no one to enfold her safely. Her intense longing is to be elsewhere, to be re-enfolded in the safe landscape of her family. The landscape of laughing and screaming children is unreadable to the small child. She cannot locate herself within it. She is not in her place. She knows she should work to locate herself here, but she is confused and afraid and does not know how to become competent in this landscape.

I heard the sunbirds chattering and screeching on the verandah—the babies are out of their nest on an early flying lesson. Then silence. They are gone. Did the carpet snake get them? (BD)

Even familiar landscapes become strange when the others in them vanish. Homes can be locked and abandoned and so become utterly unfamiliar and strange—a cause for deeply registered bodily alarm, for being *out of place.* Eileen tells a story of running home from school in a rage, rushing to get away from an environment filled with alarm—home to a space that was safe:

Running across the oval, heart beating from the rage—a huge hot red anger pushing me forward. My whole body bursting—the rage causing my knees, my legs, my hands to shake and shiver—my head bursting with the pain. When I got to the main road I had to stop, look for the traffic—heaving in gulps of air, talking to myself, muttering out loud repetitive murmuring curses. Down to Esdale St. and when I turned the corner starting to run again—hurtling down cutting across the front yard down the driveway—the cement paving blocks of home—up the step—STOP! The door is shut—Mum's not home—where is she? Good—by the time she gets back I'll be in bed with the blanket pulled tight up over my head. Then the handle won't turn. It's stuck—push and turn—push with my whole body up on the door step pushing with all my weight. And then a cold quick dawn of remembering. She's not here, she won't be back—someone has locked the door—I didn't even know there was a key.

Sick—I felt a sick emptiness in the pit of myself—I stood there in front of the locked door shivering.

I have to intrude here, into the surface of this tale, in which I have left out my embodied writing self for some pages now. I can't write what I want to write about this particular story without bringing myself visibly into it. When this story was read out on the verandah on the island, I was amazed and impressed with the child who could allow her anger expression, who could allow the anger to propel her out of the controlling landscape of school walls and rules and authoritative adults. Now, writing in the Auckland airport, in transit back to Sydney,

I'm amazed all over again at the power of her anger, her heart beating, her knees shaking, her gulps of air, her curses. I am envious at the release of anger and compare it with the tight control I imposed on my body in the writing lesson, when my body betrayed me with its noisy sobs. And then I am appalled all over again at the sudden STOP at the door, the refusal of entry, the betrayal, the finding of herself with no place. While I never came home to a locked house, it was often empty. I would wander through the many rooms searching and calling for my mother, not even sure it was "really" my own home until I had found her. The story of the locked door is, for me, an alarming story, a story of tears, a story of inexplicable loss of the landscape of the mother, the denial of entry into the spaces of the home, the loss of (be)longing. It is an unbearable story that catches me in it each time I read it, as if I could learn from it how to let rage rush through my body and propel me forwards—yet the transformation of rage into sick, shivering emptiness returns me to my preference for my overregulated and controlled body, despite its knots of arthritic pain that are due, I am told, to a body not able to "let itself go" when it feels angry.

Stories of being abandoned can be passed down for generations; so deep is their trace on the one who is abandoned, they become tracings for their children and their children's children. The final story in this section, told by Paula, brings together the story of a great-grandmother who was abandoned as a child, and the great-grandchild sitting safely in the forest, hearing the story again from her grandmother. Here the forest is inscribed both with safety and with danger. The grandmother's words lull the child into safety as she hears about the dangers faced by her abandoned great-grandmother:

The family members sit around the small fire in the forest clearing. Emma watches the smoke curl up into the clear mountain air. The gum trees smell that welcoming eucalyptus, made stronger in the burning. Her Gran holds a mug of billy tea as she tells Emma again the story of her mother. It is a story Emma can listen to again and again, an account of a ten-year-old girl left in Bathurst a century ago, by her father, who died on the ship on his way back to India. That story now filling with trees and forests, becoming circled with Gran's voice the light of the flames, the security of the log on which Emma sits.

Danger is understood in relation to safety. Safety is experienced in contrast to danger—awareness of one rarely exists without some awareness of the other. The child's safety now comes in part from the family circle around the fire, and the repeated pattern and sound of the words, but also perhaps from the knowledge that her great-grandmother survived such a shocking moment of abandonment.

Stories of bodily competence, of working to be appropriately embodied in place

Given the shock to the body of being out of place, of having no landscape in which it can belong, and given the ecstatic well-being contained in the stories of (be)longing, it is no surprise that so many of the body/landscape stories told in the workshop were of heroic struggles to become appropriately embodied. Being born into a particular landscape gives no guarantee of belonging there. The stories tell of a struggle towards appropriate(d) embodiment, through which the child can be re-cognized, even if only momentarily, as belonging as a masterful subject to whom subject status will be accorded. Butler, elaborating on Althusser's definition of subjection, writes of this process:

> The more a practice is mastered, the more fully subjection is achieved. Submission and mastery take place simultaneously, and it is this paradoxical simultaneity that constitutes the ambivalence of subjection. Where one might expect submission to consist in a yielding to an externally imposed dominant order, and to be marked by a loss of control and mastery, it is paradoxically marked by mastery itself. . . . [N]either submission nor mastery is *performed by a subject*; the lived simultaneity of submission as mastery, and mastery as submission, is the condition of possibility for the subject itself. (Butler, 1995a, pp. 14–15)

In the first story here, the child, Sue, notices the detail of the aunt's misshapen foot and her strange walk, and she recognizes with a burst of power and energy that this deformity is not hers, that her body can run separately and differently from that of her aunt:

I've just turned three last week. My grandmother's sixtieth birthday. A huge family gathering from all over Gippsland and Victoria. Everyone's brought picnic food—egg and bacon pies, cold meats, boiled eggs with curry mixed in them, too hot for me.

Mossvale Park huge green lawn but shaded by giant trees with picnic tables underneath. All around is thick forest and pathways leading from the picnic area into the thick trees and ferns and trickling waters I can hear.

I am on a path with my Mummy and our Aunty Lovey. I'm walking right next to her legs. I've got plastic sandals on for summer but she has the funniest shoe and foot. It is black and shiny and has a clobby sort of bottom across the whole shoe. Someone has told me that she has one foot shorter than the other. Up the sides of her legs are pieces of shining metal extending up from the shoe up into her dark skirt. She has a big stick that she walks with to help her but she still walks in a funny way, swinging one hip out and her bad leg after it. So much that I have to keep out of the way of her leg and her stick. I'm fascinated. I know I shouldn't ask questions but I don't really know why. I feel so powerful and my legs are so strong. I run ahead back into the picnic area.

Butler writes about the emergence of the subject requiring a complex combination of differentiating oneself out, as the child does here, an exclusion (of oneself from others), again as the child does here, and argues that the sense of autonomy of the subject is achieved with the concealment of the dependence that is inextricably bound up with the breaking away:

> In a sense, the subject is constituted through an exclusion and a differentiation, perhaps a repression, that is subsequently concealed, covered over, by the effect of autonomy. In this sense autonomy is the logical consequence of a disavowed dependency, which is to say that the autonomous subject can maintain the illusion of its autonomy insofar as it covers the break out of which it was constituted. This dependency and this break are already social relations, ones which precede and condition the formation of the subject. (Butler, 1995b, pp. 45–46)

Sometimes a moment of (be)longing takes us by surprise. As we engage in (subject ourselves to) ritual and collective practices organized by others, we can find ourselves separated out, transfixed, in an ecstatic state of transformation, of realignment. Lekkie tells of a child who is not at all aware of working to become appropriate—her intense focus on her surroundings can actually be seen as a failure to attend correctly, according to the prescribed forms, and yet the depth of her personal response is entirely appropriate:

We wander out into the bush chapel to pray and sing, twenty eleven-year-olds shaking off sleep, drowsily sensing the light and smells and damp of early morning.

We stand in a semi-circle around the big rock with the white wooden cross on it. We sing, or pray, I forget which. One moment I am part of the group. The next moment something shifts. The sparkle of the sunlight glinting on a dewdrop on a leaf catches me in the eye, and suddenly it's just me in this space, enveloped by, part of, this clearing, these leaves, this rock, this cross. My heart expands. I belong here.

The child's desire transforms into (be)longing in the landscape, separated out from the others, connected through the light in the dewdrop, to the rocks, the cross. Her heart grows larger and she is merged in the landscape in which she finds herself. The moment infuses the child with wonder, transforms her body (something shifts), and she is realigned with the landscape, (be)longing in it, appropriately subjected, a subject with expanded heart, secure in her (be)longing.

The child's (be)longing may not come in an instant of powerful (re)cognition and differentiation/separation. It may be labored over as she struggles all day to learn to swim in the cool dark water of the river. Helen works to embody herself in the landscape in a way that she knows will mean that she (be)longs, not only in the warm gaze of her family, but as one who already knows how bodies should be(have) in this watery landscape. Her autonomy is labored over; she works to differentiate herself from that child who cannot swim, who is not enti- tled to (the illusion of) autonomy. She separates herself off from her family (though not so far that she can't see them if she wants) so that she can (in)scribe her body, her musculature, with the correct forms of (be)longing in the Australian landscape:

The water is river-dark, cool in the late afternoon, satiny smooth on her skin. All day she has thrashed her arms and legs, trying to keep her head out of the water. Not afraid of the invasion of this clear unsalty water into her eyes, nose and mouth, but wanting to master this sought-after skill—she is teaching herself to swim.

The family on the green grass beside the river fade into the background of her consciousness, enough to know they are there if needed. The white trunks of the gums with branches drooping into the water flash into her vision every time she urgently lifts her head for a breath. Face into the water, mouth closed, don't breathe, see the browny-yellowy underneath of the smooth water surface, thrash arms and legs, try to get the rhythm. Without warning, all the movements work together, not smoothly, but enough to lift her head, take a gasped breath—water as well as air, but enough—then do it again, again. She stands up in the waist-high water, balancing her feet on the smooth stones underfoot, turns to the watching parents and calls out triumphantly "I can swim! I'm swimming!"

The child announces herself triumphantly as an appropriately embod- ied subject, as one who can be (re)cognized as autonomous subject, capable of mastering invaluable skills of survival and pleasure in water.

The final story is also about swimming and water, but here we have a longing for the sea and the salty sunlit water. The child, Cath, sepa- rates herself even further from parents and the orderly patterning of the day by the sea and immerses her body in the salty embrace of the waves, at the same time thinking through how she is to competently manage herself in this space:

The smell of salt—the taste of salt—wonderful. Blues—so many blues—deep, then green, the sunlight coming through the top of the water as she has been put on the bottom by the tumbling of the waves—a milky green. No fear. Sand in the costume—many coloured and bubbled with elastic. But she works out how to get this out of her costume by lifting the bottom and the front. She will stay here for- ever. She won't go to lunch as she won't be allowed in for an hour afterwards so she stays in. She has to keep her eyes open to see the blues—to take in every- thing—to feel the tingling in her skin—it feels so warm but not hot. Her eyes are starting to hurt so she gets a hanky to tuck in her costume so she can wipe her eyes. A wave dumps her—she takes out her hanky to wipe her eyes but it is wet.

She feels really surprised at first and then a slow understanding of why it didn't work. She then feels dumb. So she won't tell anyone—she just puts up with the stinging as she has to stay in there until she's made to come out and go home.

Cath reveals the child's inner dialogue, a conversation in which she achieves a distance from the ordering instructions of her family embedded in the landscape of the beach. She has other work to do, work that the orderly embrace of the family will disrupt. She needs all day, alone in the sea, to explore the movement of her body through water, to solve the problem of sand in swimmers and to search for the solution to the problem of stinging eyes—of course she cannot keep her eyes shut because it is primarily the kaleidoscope of blues and greens, along with the smell and taste of salt and the warm tingling of the skin, that transports her into immersion in the watery landscape in which she becomes the embodied being who can (re)cognize herself as autonomous and competent.

And so...

In Chapter 1 I suggested that the grain of ourselves is not so separate from the landscapes in which we are enfolded. The separation is an artefact of discourse, an artefact that is in need of troubling. In this chapter I have extended and elaborated the ways in which being embodied, and taking oneself up as a speaking/writing subject, takes place through a simultaneous separation from and immersion in the landscape, through bodily (in)scription, through an already existing set of actions and discourses that make being embodied, becoming a subject, possible. Because language practices are so often removed from their original embodied source or derivation, the recovery of early moments of embodiment through discourse and through the already given (re)cognized practices requires special strategies of retrieval, such as the work of collective biography. Such strategies have been used in this particular collective biography to make the obvious naturalness of the body, its evident separation from landscapes, open to inspection. The body is (in)scribed, but not in any final way. The body in landscape, the body as landscape, landscape as an essential extension of the body, is worked and reworked, scribed and reinscribed. The physical, discursive, emotional, political, and social landscapes in which we are subjected and become speaking subjects are both solid and coercive *and* fluid and shifting. We work hard at our subjection, we take enormous pleasure in our subjection, we suffer extreme pain through our subjection—and through being subjected, we become appropriate(d) beings in the landscape and, in that same process, beings who can (re)appropriate its meanings and patterns, (re)constitute bodies in relation to landscapes, (re)signify what we find we have become. As Butler writes of the relation between subjects and discourse:

[I]f the subject is a reworking of the very discursive processes by which it is worked, then "agency" is to be found in the possibilities of resignification opened up by discourse. In this sense, discourse is the horizon of agency, but also performativity is to be rethought as resignification. There is no "bidding farewell" to the *doer* "beyond" or "behind" the deed. For the deed will be itself and the legacy of conventions which it reengages, but also the future possibilities it opens up; the "doer" will be the uncertain working of the discursive possibilities by which it itself is worked. (Butler, 1995c, p. 135)

What the collective biography, the fictional and the autobiographical stories collected together here, shows is the *lived* complexity of that relation between the powerful (in)scribing effects of discourse in the shaping of body/landscapes. They reveal as well the fluid, multidimensional, political, and social nature of that (in)scription. But more than that, these stories deeply trouble the illusion of bodies and embodied beings as independent of, or dominant over, the landscapes through which they take up their being.

FOLDING

The folds in the earth's surface
the hills and valleys of my childhood—
ancient eruptions and erosions.

The curve of a wave
lifting itself above me, fills with light
swirls over and around me, and is gone.

The fold of arms holding
a small child's body—
each the other's landscape.

With/in the intricate involuted folds
of my internal/external body—
words and images take root.

Writing, I trace these folds
I touch them intimately—
and unfold.

Unfold
in laughter, in *jouissance*, or rage—
or slowly, like the petals of a chrysanthemum.

Bronwyn Davies

~3~ Australian men talk about becoming environmentalists

THE DISCOURSES OF ENVIRONMENTALISM are not peculiar to Australia or to the West, or even to men. But in this chapter, written in collaboration with Hilary Whitehouse,[1] we explore the take-up of environmental discourses by a small group of men living in the northeast corner of Australia. What these interviews allow us to do here, in this chapter, is to examine the complex relations between a particular discourse, environmentalism, and a particular set of landscapes in the tropical north of Australia, as they both constitute and are constituted by the men in our study. Before we begin, it is important to give some indication of the cultural and political elements of the landscape with/in which environmental discourses in Australia are taken up. In the following story of traveling into the far reaches of the Australian desert, Robert Dessaix touches on some of the most salient features of that landscape. He describes traveling from his safe, familiar city landscape and moving farther and farther away from anything he recognized, towards a place called Patjarr in the Gibson desert:

[F]rom my upstairs verandah at home what I see is a row of terrace houses with familiar iron lacework, people coming and going whose stories I've heard, tiny front gardens full of plants I know—wisteria, roses, fuchsias, daisies—in fact, I've watched them being planted and watered. In the distance, above the iron roofs, I can see the jagged, living city—cranes, tower-blocks, glass and concrete monoliths, all swarming with life. Everything's signalling to me, everything's jostling to assert some meaning, to semaphore some message (subtle, brazen, devious, comic) about the lives of the people living there. And all the spaces in the city are minutely measured, too, squared off, rectangular. I've paced all those quadrilaterals out, I know exactly the time it takes to walk or drive from this corner to that, how many metres a diagonal short cut saves. Out here in the desert—nothing. Just shapes and colours . . .

---

1. The interviews used in this chapter were undertaken as a joint study by Hilary Whitehouse and Bronwyn Davies and are part of a larger body of work on environmentalism being carried out by Hilary for her doctoral program, as well as this book. At the time these particular interviews were carried out, Bronwyn was also involved in a study of masculinity, and so some of the questions asked of these male environmentalists were to do with their experiences of masculinity. All interviews in this chapter were carried out by Hilary. The interviews in this chapter were also used in B. Davies and H. Whitehouse (1997), "Men on the boundaries: landscapes and seascapes," *Journal of Gender Studies* 6(3): 237–54, but they have been taken up differently in this chapter.

. . . I'd had to fly across half a continent to Alice Springs, watching the greens turn to olives and browns and then to a curious raw sienna streaked with purple. No people, just a palette of colours. Then from Alice Springs I'd flown westwards another four hours across swirling salt-lakes—blue-white-brown—and mountain ranges scooped up out of the earth almost recklessly. . . . Perched in my seat in a single-engined plane . . . I felt like a beetle about to swoop down and land on the back of some tawny animal slumbering in the dust—skull, backbone . . .

Then we headed north right into the desert itself, out into the astounding green of it, along a road recently bulldozed through the mulga and scrub. For hour after hour we rattled in our truck across creek-beds and sandy ridges, across dreaming tracks and past hidden waterholes. All I see is a blur of red and green. I feel a gnawing apprehension. I do not belong here.

We pass a sign saying NO THROUGH ROAD, but that's the only indication of a mind at work. Not a shack, not a track, not a fence-post, not even an abandoned ice cream wrapper—just bushes I can't name in red sand, some speckled with pink. Millions of them . . .

In the morning, when we drove off even further into the unknown towards the waterhole at Patjarr, I could feel my consciousness fraying with the strain. Was there no end to these empty wastes which were *just there*? Nothing is *just there* in the city . . .

. . . When we came to the mouth of the gully where Patjarr lay, we clambered down out of the truck—Philip and some of the people from the out-station: Pulpuru in her red and black beanie, some bearded men with rifles, a small boy or two. There was no fuss, no crackling in the air, although this place was the focus of their spiritual energy, and virtually no outsiders had ever been ushered to its mouth.

Standing on the flat amongst the high, whispering spinifex grass, you don't at first notice why this is a blessed place. You see the gully ahead of you, the lower side on the left orange-red with a scattering of desert oaks and the higher, shaded side on the right almost black in this brilliant sunlight, but you don't see what makes Patjarr a blessing: almost at your feet, gashing the grassy plain, is a deep, green ribbon of water. The dank smell of it—shocking on this bone-dry gibber plane—seeps into the nostrils. Little knots of anxiety start to dissolve.

[Avoiding the hill on the left, which belongs to the women, and following the water, they come to oblong stones standing on end and know they can go no further]. We gazed further up the gully, across the green-blue water into the shadows on the bluffs on the other side. When the breeze ruffled the water, the shadows lit up with thousands of tiny lights like a swarm of fireflies. Were those more marker stones we could see on the other shore? We could never go there to find out. What happens there, what is experienced there, what the water, rocks and trees there mean, we could never know . . .

I'd come alive in new ways in the desert. A blankness in me had been vividly filled in. Something about those days in the desert had enlarged my sensation of being alive. Yet not comfortingly. In fact, a sort of bleakness had seeped into me—not a sadness or a desperation, but a kind of melancholy that never goes away: many of us know, learn about, remember, love, respect and feel attached to the land, but we can't belong to it in the way the people I'd met belong to Patjarr . . . (Dessaix, 1998, pp. 151–66)

In Australia, the built landscape is (in)scribed in ways that mimic the built landscapes of the northern hemisphere. The buildings, roads, dams, power lines have all appeared in the last two hundred years. Though they are not based on a set of aesthetic principles that belong specifically to Australian culture, as Dessaix describes, the embodied being of many Australians is taken up with/in such landscapes. The landscapes, which are not built landscapes, and which have been inhabited and (in)scribed with meaning for many thousands of years by the indigenous people, are a source of deep fascination and longing for many nonindigenous Australians, but not of belonging. As Robert Dessaix writes, there is a complex combination of fascination and longing, of fear, of connection, of separation, and loss. Postcolonial discourses trouble the easy appropriations of the past and require a separation from and respect for indigenous people and their relations to the land, which leaves nonindigenous people with what Dessaix describes as "a kind of melancholy that never goes away." He talks about the way "many of us know, learn about, remember, love, respect and feel attached to the land" and yet believe that the indigenous people have a connection that we cannot have. "[W]e can't belong to it" he says, "in the way the people I'd met belong to Patjarr . . ." (Dessaix, 1998, pp. 151–66).

The Australian environmentalists interviewed here talk about their own culture as an alien imposition on the landscape, and the landscape as something that can be known and connected with in ways that are not readily understood in Western constructions of body/landscape relations. At the same time, they know that they cannot take up as their own the ancient discourses of the indigenous people, since that would be an unacceptable form of appropriation, and as Dessaix points out, they may well not be able to do so anyway. Environmental discourses are what they do have legitimate access to.

While some environmental discourses try to break down the culture/nature binary, it is nevertheless the experiences of "nature" that the environmentalists in this study seek out, and "culture" that they seek to escape from. At the same time, the movement in their talk is away from environment as that which is *external to and surrounding* the self, to a sense of self as *coextensive* with nature.

Environment: 1. external conditions or surroundings esp. those in which people live and work. 2. *Ecology.* the external surroundings in which a plant or animal lives, which tend to influence its development and behaviour. 3. the state of being environed; encirclement. (*Collins English Dictionary*)

In this chapter we explore some of the shifting patterns of (in)scription of the male body that take place when these men take up environmentalist discourses as their own. We were particularly interested to talk to male environmentalists because the change in bodily inscription in becoming an environmentalist seemed more dramatic for men and therefore more visible, more able to be talked about. Central to that take-up, we found, was the constitution of themselves as having a different relationship with the "natural environment" than *other* men, and in particular, macho men. They see themselves, in contrast to such men, as "part of the natural environment": they seek what Robert Dessaix suggests is only possible for indigenous people with their particular cultural knowledges and their ancient connections with/in landscape. We explore here the intricate layers of meanings lived out through these environmentalists' bodies as those meanings disturb but also constitute and maintain male-female and culture-nature binaries.

In relation to the culture/nature binary, the traditions of Western philosophical thought have positioned men in the ascendant "culture," where culture means access to a rationality that transforms and controls an unformed and unruly "nature." This chapter provides an interesting twist on an argument made by Ortner, that men's alignment of women with nature is based on the assumption that nature is "something that every culture devalues, something that every culture defines as being of a lower order of existence than itself" (Ortner, 1971, p. 72). That assumed superiority of men over women and nature, she writes, rests "on the ability to transform—to 'socialize' and 'culturalize'—nature" (p. 73). Ortner's sweeping claims position her, probably unintentionally, with those who believe that the ability to transform nature should be taken as the defining feature of relations between humans and nature. After all, it is only some people within any one culture who devalue nature, but in Ortner's definition these people become the defining feature of their cultures ("every culture devalues . . ."). As the environmentalists in this chapter show, cultures are multifaceted and capable of profound shifts in the way body/landscape relations are understood and lived.

No doubt there are, as Ortner claims, some (or many) men in every culture who devalue nature and women (and who see them as more or less the same thing). Robert Drewe's novel *The Drowner* provides an example of this way of seeing. The novel is set in the Australian desert. One of the central characters is an engineer who sees his ability to transform nature, to bring about a different order as the powerful defining feature of dominant man. Another central character, an actor and a woman, sees quite differently. The engineer, who has come from England to Australia to bring water to the goldfields, says to the actor, his wife:

"There are no streams in the goldfields. No rivers."
"A minor geographical point."
"Not at all. That's the whole reason I am here. The complete absence of streams in the desert is why we are in this place, why we are sitting here on this ferry now."
"The drama is the important thing."
"*Drama*. You've never considered what it is that I do, have you? What engineers do?"
She looks at him steadily. Her face is expressionless and the dark masks her eyes. "Tell me what it is you do Will."
He takes a deep breath and speaks very slowly. "We change the order of things. And that is as dramatic as life gets."
She stands up then. A strange smile is on her face. "An ant changes the order of things. A cabbage. Even an actress." (Drewe, 1996, pp. 205–206)

But there are also men within each culture who see differently from Drewe's engineer. From these environmentalists' point of view, it is not "men" who devalue nature and who seek to transform it, but *a particular kind of man* who is not like them, and from whom they are at pains to distance themselves. Nor did we find Ortner's apparently inevitable link between women and nature in the talk of our environmentalists—the elevation of nature did not bring with it an elevation of women onto the same plane, though it did bring with it beliefs about treating women in nonmacho ways.

It is often assumed by those writing about the culture/nature binary in relation to human bodies that it is "culture" that is inscribed on the "natural" body, as if nature is always passive and culture active, as if that which we take to be "nature" is not also capable of powerful action and transformation. Falk's characterization of the inscription of human bodies, like that of Grosz (cited in Chapter 1), maintains this binary between passive-nature and active-culture, with nature disappearing once any transformative act has taken place:

From [a] broader perspective it may be argued that the human body is never found in its "natural" state except for a short period after birth perhaps. . . . Every human culture has specific techniques for bringing up the new-born human body in accordance with the specific codes for the body's appearance both in its static and dynamic representation. . . . The body is an unfinished piece of art to be completed. It must be transformed from nature to culture. This transformation is realised by inscribing membership of the community in the flesh. (Falk, 1995, p. 95)

Such distinctions are enormously problematic. It is not just humans who transform their young into specific patterns of individual and group existence, any more than it is just humans who transform the spaces they inhabit. If transformative acts are definitive of culture, then culture cannot exist in a binary other to nature. Further, the transformations that these environmentalists describe come from "culture" insofar as their environmentalist discourses can be said to be generated through a set of cultural or discursive practices. The reinscription of their bodies that they set out to achieve, however, is one that moves away from what they understand as "culture," and that attempts to (in)scribe the body as nature.

The discourse with greatest salience for these environmentalists is that of environmental ecology. In the last decade environmental ecologists have begun to reject the division of the biosphere into (male) human and nonhuman (Lovelock, 1991; Lovelock, 1995; Margulis and Olendzenski, 1992; Wilson, 1984). David Suzuki's *Declaration of Interdependence* expresses the essence of this shift. He defines a world in which the boundaries between humans and nature can no longer be understood as the defining (and separating) feature of what "we" are. Instead, he says:

> We are the earth, through the plants and animals that nourish us.
> We are the rains and the oceans that flow through our veins.
> We are the breath of the forests of the land, and the plants of the sea.
> We are human animals, related to all other life as descendants of the firstborn cell.
> We share with these kin a common history, written in our genes.
> We share a common present, filled with uncertainty.
> . . .
> At this point in our relationship with Earth,
> we work for an evolution: from dominance to partnership;
> from fragmentation to connection; from insecurity,
> to interdependence. (Suzuki, 1995)

In this chapter we draw on the voices of eight Australian men from Hilary's interviews with environmentalists. These men live and work in the tropics. They have experience of spending many years of their lives in landscapes and seascapes that are often imagined in romantic terms by people living in more temperate zones. Joseph (age 38), Graham (37), Bruce (32), and Hamish (36) are marine biologists who have spent many hours working in the Great Barrier Reef and in other tropical waters. Bruce describes some of his work thus:

I've enjoyed working in sometimes difficult environments and things. I mean remote locations and that. I've always loved diving. We used to spend a lot of time in the Whitsundays just camping on islands, a friend and I, doing . . .

inventory surveys, on fish and corals. We'd just go around counting fish and corals for the Marine Park Authority. They were always great sorts of trips.

Terry (22), Arthur (42), and Nick (38) are citizen environmentalists and community campaigners who have traveled widely over northern Queensland, both for leisure and work purposes. And Tom (38), whose major interest in landscapes is aesthetic, moved to northern Queensland from Sydney after a holiday there ten years ago. He said:

I took a holiday and I travelled up as far as Cairns and the thing that I vividly remember about being up in this area was the blue oceans and I've even got photos, just of the blue water. When you come from Sydney, you are so used to the green colour or a brown colour and . . . here there was the blue oceans and I thought, that's it! I just decided that this was the place to go and being here I've found obviously what I wanted. I don't think it was conscious, I just think I've luckily stumbled to the area which is in sync with my thinking.

We asked these men to talk, in particular, about their experiences in relation to the landscapes that matter to them. We draw here on examples of their talk of the land and the sea, looking in particular at the interplay of masculinity, masculine bodies, and seascapes, and at the boundaries between land and water.

Dry land and water

Tropical landscapes can be described as in-temperate zones. While the winter weather in northern Queensland is nothing short of spectacular, the ferocity of the heat in the months between November and April makes huge demands on people's physical and emotional resources. Temperature readings in degrees Celsius, while high by temperate standards, are still misleading, and they give very little indication of the real stresses the human body is under. Very high humidity, the dazzling glare, and the intensity of the sun's power as it beats on bodies must also have their effect. People sweat, their skin goes brown almost unintentionally from being out and about. Pools of water are too hot to swim in. Step outside, out of the shade and into the glare, and the light and the sensations of glare in the eyes and such high wattage hitting skin is close to painful. The sun is described as "having a sting in it." Premier Wayne Goss's government lost the 1992 referendum for daylight saving in western and northern Queensland because at the end of a (summer's) day, people just want the sun to go down, they want it gone. The air at night is tranquil, balmy, bearable. In the absence of sun, the sky is luminescent, indigo. The moonshine is beautiful and benign.

Robert Drewe, in *The Drowner*, writes of the experience of his engineer, newly arrived from England, first seeing the dry, harsh Australian (west coast) landscape:

This is a landscape of such stark space and beauty that reason can only try to defy it. Small boys kneel on the ferry jetty burning ants with magnifying glasses. From these tiny squirming fires rise little plumes of smoke and the acrid smell of hot varnish. A dog barks all day at a stationary goanna with a blue tongue. A laughing bird shakes a snake five times its length in its beak. Pink trees with the delicate texture of moist flesh sprout from the sand; to touch their soft trunks leaves fingerprints. And all around the city bushfires burn, defining the sky and the heat.

This is a landscape to make him curt and undemonstrative in return. White flowers, white sand everywhere, the sun glinting off the limestone and oyster-shell footpaths, can bring on headaches. So the eyes of newcomers are constantly guarded and squinting against the glare and its flickering surprises. (Drewe, 1996, p. 190)

Much of northern Queensland is characterized as "dry tropics." There are vast areas of country where rainfall is intermittent and sparse. The wet tropics are to be found on some portions of the narrow strip of coast east of the Great Dividing Range. West of the mountains, the landscapes are unforgiving. You have to be tough to live out there. And northern Queensland men are known to be tough. Terry describes the men who live in these dry, hard inlandscapes where men have conquered the tasks that confront them:

North Queensland men are hard, and they're hard because they've worked hard and they've had hard experiences and they've had hard times and they've lived hard, they've played hard, and they've done hard tasks and they've conquered these hard tasks and therefore they have the right to be hard in character because they can back themselves up with these tall tales about their hard living, and a lot of this hard living goes on in hard landscapes. Hard areas where the sun shimmers off the land in the distance. . . .

Oh, you feel very dry. You feel very emotionally dry as well. You feel pretty awestruck because you're a long way from the ocean, you're a very, very long way from the ocean, so it's like being trapped on land almost. When you're on the coast you can have this emotive sense of being in control of the land and the water. You know, you've got the land to one side and the water to the other side of you and you can develop this emotive sense of being able to pass between the two or at least when you walk along the coast you can feel that there's a bountiful lifestyle along the coast. Whereas if you go into the desert you're stuck on one tangent. There's just this idea of the land and it's all around you . . . with this dryness in the air around you that's making your lips crack and you're sort of just out there really.

The inland men do not conquer the land, according to Terry, but they survive, and that in itself is heroic. It is the dryness of the land that dries out their emotions. Land where there is no water is land you cannot have a sense of control over, but you can, heroically, control your own body, though the land affects that as well (drying out your skin and cracking open your lips). But if you bring water to the land, then you can be in control, since you have given it life. Terry says of his experience of water in dry inlandscapes:

They've dammed up five estuaries of the Leichhardt River system and you get these very large lakes and so that's where you get the body-of-water feeling, you know. I think it's important in life to be near a body of water. I don't understand why but you get that electric hum off it. . . . Water is life, you know.

In *The Drowner*, when the water arrives, it changes people: "The deluge had somehow changed the emotional climate. Unlikely people became intense and passionate and unrealistically optimistic" (Drewe, 1996, p. 231). At Patjarr, the water makes the land sacred.

A love of water and the sea is a theme running through much of the talk of the environmentalists in our study. They find pleasure in water and are active in their enjoyment of it. Joseph describes his relationship with seascapes as a "love affair." In warm water "I just feel totally at ease . . . I need to have water in my life. I find it very difficult to go for long periods without a swim." Tom finds the shifting boundary between sea and land both energizing and calming. He says:

If at times I would be stressed I would go to the beach and walk along the ocean, and it's amazing . . . how energizing it can be. So you can take all your troubles of your life with you and you still have done nothing but walk. But you've had a chance to look at the ocean and find calm, I guess.

The other men

One of the constant tensions in the men's talk of their embodied selves was between macho or dominant masculinity, which they were both repelled and fascinated by, and more feminine or spiritual or politically correct forms of masculinity that they desired. They talked about a stereotype of macho masculinity, which they were at pains to construct as other to themselves or, more specifically, as other to the environmentalist selves they were in their talk with Hilary. They nevertheless talked about the ways in which the distance they wanted to maintain from such masculine selves was constantly disrupted.

"Macho" is described in their talk as an undesirable form of masculinity, wherever it is practiced, within urban or "natural" environments. Macho is characterized as other men using landscapes as sites for a piss-up and superficial male bonding, other men throwing their beer cans (or tinnies) into the bush or the ocean, other men who are neither cognizant nor respectful of the lives of others, human, plant, or animal. In contrast, when men's relations with nonurban landscapes and the inhabitants of those landscapes are personal, reflective, and admiring, then this is constructed as desirable masculinity. Similarly, within the social world, undesirable masculinity is constructed as a position without care, respect, or understanding.

Macho man, we would suggest, is the predictable product of dominant discourses that encourage men to think of themselves as wielders of power and of language in civilized society; as dominators of women and children (and also of weak men); as beings who can exert mind over matter, ignoring the body, its emotions and its pain, and at the same time promoting "natural" urges that are valorized by powerful members of the worlds they live in. Dominant discourses encourage men to dream of becoming like celebrated individualistic hero/gods (such as the latest football or Olympic star or the president of the United States, or the Christian God).

Nick describes getting caught up in macho talk and even macho patterns of desire through being part of the gay scene. When he "came out" as gay, he thought he would find many other men like himself, misfits who had never achieved and did not want to achieve dominant forms of masculinity. To his horror, he discovered that he was as different from other gay men in the rural Queensland city that he moved to as he had been from heterosexual men:

Moving into gay men's world . . . was really disappointing. Like when I finally did the, um, telling my parents and all that sort of stuff and raced off to embrace my new brethren, it was sort of like recoil immediately because there were all these men sitting 'round bars spit-farting and saying cunt all over the place and being racist and sexist, and so for me it was like, moving into this world which I thought, okay, after all these years, this is where I'm finally going to fit and, and it was just really appalling. Like it was suddenly, you know, walking in with open arms visually and um, and suddenly realizing that you were embracing the hydra.

Much as Nick was horrified by the talk of the men in the gay community when he arrived, he is afraid of becoming like them since it is impossible to hold oneself apart all the time, always being the (boring) one who is politically correct, aware of the damaging implications of whatever is being said. Low population densities mean the gay community is not large in northern Queensland. If Nick speaks his "belief systems" all the time he risks being "boring," or worse, socially isolated. He talks about using macho discourses and keeping his fingers crossed to protect himself when he does so:

There's a level of distress at which I hear myself changing my language, or changing the way in which I live my belief systems. Some examples are either being silent when people start talking about cunts and coons. . . . But then I also hear myself doing stuff that's similar. . . . I can be speaking stuff and thinking "I don't actually really like this but this is the way you play." Because at some levels I like this particular person, or this group of people are really essentially quite nice people and they're intelligent and well, you know, you compromise a little bit and yet I don't like compromise at all.

HILARY WHITEHOUSE: So there's a tension there between what you really ethically feel and what you can or cannot say.

Yeah, for example, things like, a particular type of guy and it might be, "Oh he's a real daddy, isn't he," and I will say that now too but there's this part of me which says, it's really a bit off. . . . You know, I buy into all that stuff and I say those things now, not necessarily too overtly. But there's those contradictions and I think it's almost like crossing your fingers when you say it, you know, like yeah, cross my fingers . . . because I don't really mean this and I actually have an understanding of what it actually means to be saying this and I don't really like it, I'm just fitting in, so "please excuse me universe." Because what happens is, if you start . . . people's response to that is, "Oh God, you know I was only joking," or "I'm only having a bit of fun," or "Oh you're just so boring," and people just find it all a bit tiresome to be continually reminded that what they've said actually represents an abuse of a particular group of people or is offensive to them, you know.

The same contradictions and shifts between desirable and undesirable patterns of masculinity emerge through the men's talk of their experiences within landscapes and seascapes. After Joseph agreed to take part in this project examining masculinities in relation to environments, he told Hilary in a telephone conversation of a nightmare he had in which he had featured as the ultimate macho male, out in his boat fishing, the radio blasting away drowning out the noises of the water, drinking, throwing his tinnies overboard, rubbishing the sea. He was at some pains in his relating of this dream to convince Hilary that he was not this macho dominant male, telling her she was not to find him as that in their talk, though even in saying so recognizing the irony and humor in his nightmare story.

In the interviews Joseph tells heroic stories of himself as a younger man, diving off the New South Wales coast and handfeeding Bronze Whaler sharks, something he did for a couple of years. He describes the experience as "so exciting it was almost an addiction," but he also takes considerable care to distinguish his way of feeding the sharks from what he sees as macho and unacceptable modes of doing so. Of one of his own shark-feeding sessions Joseph said:

You'd just come out of the water and there'd be so much adrenaline buzzing around that it was very hard to settle down for days afterwards. In retrospect I suppose it was always dangerous but we were fairly careful in that there were always just two, possibly three of us. I think the main thing was not to panic because at times they [Bronze Whalers] were quite big and we had sometimes up to a dozen circling around, just waiting to be fed. These things would come in and if you didn't have something to feed them you'd have to put the tip of the hand spear on their nose and sort of push them.

He compares this with the others he sees and disapproves of as feeding the sharks in nonspiritual and macho ways:

I don't think I'd be all that excited about doing it now. I'd do it, with the right people. To me it was a fairly spiritual thing, too. I see other people doing it now in some of the dive schools, on trips to the outer reef, and it becomes a very macho thing to do. To go and get a group of drivers, say four or five divers, and put them in a group and then have other divers go and string up some fish and watch the sharks come in and eat them. Eat the fish. It's, to me, the macho side of it. I don't feel comfortable with that and I don't feel comfortable with that when I go out and spear fish either. I've been in situations where at work one of my friends asked me to go and monitor a spear-fishing competition and it was really, it was a real macho, what I'd consider a real macho event. All these guys going out and it was almost like the whistle sounded and they're all just charging off to go and spear whatever they could, to come back and then compare the size of things that they'd got and the number and all that sort of stuff. I've never been interested in that side of it. It's always a much more personal thing.

Bruce is not sure how to describe his nonmacho self. He says:

I've never considered myself to be masculine, um, I always felt that I had a fairly strong, the element that ruled my life was a female or a negative, whatever you want to call that.

HW: It's what you want to call it.

That element, all right, let's call it a female aspect all right, and I was always immensely proud of that particular aspect in me, of the types of attributes that I call intuition and sympathy, I suppose, to the environment, or sympathy with the environment or belonging to the environment, was something that was a female aspect and I never felt that I belonged really to any masculine, boys' type things. I mean, I'm not into those going to the pub, slapping each other on the back, piss in each others' pockets type things. I never ever felt like I belonged. I always felt distant from all of those things but I think that I'm like that in any environment probably.

Here, being an environmentalist requires qualities of intuition and sympathy, and *(be)longing* in the environment. Male bonding in the landscape of the pub, getting drunk, slapping each other on the back are the forms of masculinity that Bruce sees as antithetical to the (fe)male environmentalists' embodied self.

One of the most extraordinary (to us) of the stories told by the men was one in which a group of young boys engaged in male bonding and drunkenness in conquering the bush. Arthur says:

We chose the bush . . . because of the privacy, obviously, because you couldn't be seen. The other thing is, it was like pitting yourself against, you know, you're out there against the environment and you're a man and, I mean, this is an embarrassing confession, that one of the things I did, and I remember doing this, I was really pissed and I dug a hole in the ground and my mates came along and I was rooting the earth . . . and they said, "What are you doing?" and I said, "Oh, I'm fucking Mother Earth." I haven't thought of that for twenty years now.

Arthur later described these early experiences as embarrassing to talk about because of how he has remade himself as an environmentally caring adult and as sympathetic with the feminist cause. But his insight is an interesting one. As a young drunken boy wanting to conquer nature, his act of copulation was one which, he later explained, combined love of nature as well as conquering nature. Arthur also talks at length about the men he sees and hears of, who attempt to achieve domination over nature by trying to re-create themselves as frontiersmen. He describes some businessmen he observed from Darwin who went to Kakadu National Park, whose performances of going bush placed them unequivocally in the category of other; they didn't even pretend to know how to get it right, relying on "imperialist" invasive images of penetrating wild landscapes:

They loaded one truck with booze and one with a generator and a refrigerator and went up to go Barra fishing. . . . [I]t's that desire to live out the mythologies created in the frontiersman. [It's] a very sad and bastardized way [of doing it] because they didn't even have a fishing line to pretend that they were doing this frontier stuff. They just had the booze and so there wasn't even any attempt to even confront nature.

HW: And why do you find it so appalling?

It's not even a decent facade. . . . [T]hey could have stayed in the pub and done that, but they had to tell someone "we went to Kakadu and got pissed."' "That was what we did." . . . Of course they have absolutely no way of accessing the environment apart from maybe . . . pissing on it, shitting on it, vomiting on it, or generally fucking it. . . . [T]hey don't want to tune into it. They can't even see that it exists . . . it's sort of an imperialism almost, of bringing their way of being . . . into the landscape that's outside of my way of knowing the landscape.

The importing of pub masculinity into Kakadu National Park was seen by Arthur as deeply distressing. The ways of being that were appropriate to Kakadu were ignored, not sought out, lost on these men, who fouled this natural place with their "out of place" imperialist behaviors.

Language and embodiment

Just as these environmentalists struggled with dislodging dominant forms of masculinity from their practices, so too they talked about the difficulties of dislodging the pervasive and dominant division between nature and culture. To the extent that discourses are labile and volatile, and are taken up in a palimpsest of overlapping meanings, then it is inevitable that in practice contradictory discourses will not be able to be held completely separate and discreet. The adoption of a new discourse is not a simple rational process in which a new understanding displaces the old, or even partially overwrites the old. Rather, the new discourse provides a text that is and becomes action with powerful but often unpredictable effects: "a force or energy which creates links between objects, which makes things, forges alliances, produces connections" (Grosz, 1989, p. xvi).

Bruce talks of his struggle to adopt environmental discourse and to move beyond old binaries. The effect of the new discourse is not one of reconstituting his body in new and appropriate ways. New connections are made, an energy is created, but the pattern of take-up is not perfect and complete:

Generally people think of the environment as being out there and society is in the house and the social life, and I suppose that's a binary, but it's important all the way through, I mean, particularly as a kid. . . . [F]or people of my generation the environment was always something that was promoted as being the rugged outdoorsy type thing, the wildness, rather than the view that I'll probably espouse now, but I don't know how truly I believe it, or I mean, I believe, but don't know how deeply it is entrenched. It is that you are part of the environment and the environment is everything.

Bruce "espouses" a view that we are "part of the environment and the environment is everything," echoing the ideas encapsulated in Suzuki's *Declaration of Interdependence*. He no longer accepts the binary view he was brought up with, where the house and home are culture, while "nature" is outside the boundaries of home and of social life. Yet he worries that the views he espouses may not be as deeply "entrenched" as he would like, and he does not know how "truly" he believes what it is that he says. It is as if his environmentalist talk does not (yet) come from embodied knowledge—it is somehow not yet "deeply entrenched" in/on the depth/surfaces of the body. Perhaps one does not ever *become* an environmentalist, but is in an intermittent state of *becoming*, of forging alliances and producing connections.

> [K]nowledge is more a mode of being than of having, not something we possess but something we are or become. As Monique Schneider notes, in attaining knowledge we do not gain an acquisition, as if something new were added to the inventory of our possessions, but rather we exist differently. (Yovel, 1989, p. 159)

The men talk about a number of strategies for finding ways of knowing with their bodies what it is they espouse as environmentalists. They talk of their efforts to distance themselves from their individualistic social selves, to move into and become part of natural landscapes, to disrupt the physical sense of separation between body and landscape. Joseph explains that this is easier to do in warm places where the temperature and humidity differences between the skin and the air or water are not significant. Bruce talks of willing himself into "an alpha state" when diving. Graham talks of his body "atomizing" in warm oceans. Joseph, free-diving in waters off Cape Cleveland, stares into the living eyes of groupers in an attempt to comprehend their existence, to move himself away from human towards fish knowledges of existence. But these are not experiences they talk of in relation to the spaces of home or work. Home and work remain places to *escape* from. In this way the boundary between nature and culture is kept intact as a spatially meaningful distinction: one escapes from culture into nature. In contrast, the culturally inscribed body can be reinscribed as natural. In troubling the binary they talk about their desire to redraw the boundaries, to remap themselves, to create different ways of being. They actively seek out experiences of (be)longing, of immersion in landscapes and seascapes where the tightly bounded self, separate and distinct from the desired spaces, is lost. Bruce explains that on return to the workplace, this reinscription of the body serves him well in his work—he can see things differently and more clearly:

I find science generally being extremely reductionist and it does tend to break things down to a greater degree than what I like. . . . [I]t prevents the ability to . . . connect, to hook into that connective feeling of just being, I suppose, to be part of is the phrase I would use. . . . It's a connectedness thing, like I'm part, I am no longer me operating in the environment, it is me being a collective part of the environment, and that's, I suppose, the overwhelming feeling that you have that gives you the buzz I suppose. . . . I feel connected to the environment again by being immersed in something that's bigger than me, that's got no respect for politics or for society's values or . . . It's free and connected, I suppose is the way I say it. It's to me, it gives me inspiration, it gives me strength to come back. Yeah, I suppose it defocuses you from your everyday myopic view of where you're going, to having a more bird's-eye view on life and seeing your life in its totality, and generally occurs at times that you have been particularly focused, so to me it's a great refocusing mechanism. . . .

The embodied environmentalist experience in this example is valued for its pleasure (the buzz, the sense of connection) but also for its effect on the self returned from the natural environment, since it returns as a more competent self in the workplace. The bodily (in)scription in the sea carries over into other landscapes, not so much as a bodily way of being but as facilitating or refocusing ways of seeing in the workscape. It is almost as if this environmentalist's body is in subservience to, and facilitative of, the more important "mind" (perhaps even the rational dominating mind?).

The sea is thus constituted as "other to" the demands of stressful work lives. Bruce talks of finding a "happiness that comes from being connected" in the ocean, in contrast to a work life he describes as full of "different politics, different conflicts or issues, things that have to be done." He says that he needs to go out on regular dive trips because "if I operate in the social context too long I find that I become extremely fragmented." Reefs and warm oceans are places for respite, for renewal, for creation of the new, but creation of the new that comes back to the workplace environment, restored to continue as rational man.

Arthur describes the sea as an oppositional site to that of capitalism, a place where he can go when his work catches up with him and overwhelms him. He describes the sea as life-saving. He can find a refuge in it that restores his capacity for life. He tells of a time, for example, when he was close to suicide and went out on a boat trip with a friend. While it is a story of escape from culture, it is simultaneously a story in which he gains control, becomes a hero:

I was just on the verge of suicide where I was being threatened at work and having my livelihood taken away from me and devalued as a human being when I went out in the boat. . . .

HW: All right, so you used it as breathing space.

Yes, that's a really good metaphor for it. It's breathing space. It's a way that I can be part of something else that I want to be part of, rather than these things that I have to be but at the moment don't seem to have any control [over]. So even though when Alistair was asleep and we were sailing across the ocean, I wasn't going through my head, "Oh how shall I resolve this issue?" What was going through my head was the wind and the salt spray and whether or not I could keep the boat on course, whether or not I could trim the sails good enough, whether I wasn't going to drown and turn the boat over and disgrace myself in front of my mate who'd entrusted me with his yacht, and those were the things. Yeah I think it's very much the breathing space, the shitting space if you like. The space to get away from the trappings that come with employment and fast-living space and the capitalist state. Because very much I see this non-human environment as being the total opposite of capitalism.

Joseph also reveals in his talk the elision of the reinscribed environmentalist's body with dominant masculinity, in particular the individualistic hero-god. Like Bruce and Arthur, he also holds the culture/nature binary in place by seeing culture as a place to escape from. Joseph talks at length about his connection with the sea, beginning with his love and fear of surfing as a young child, then later as a young man riding surfboards, and finally as a diver, becoming one with the watery, terrifying depths. His descriptions of how and why he engages in these practices include ideas of challenge and danger, of conquering fear, of ignoring pain:

When I go diving out here, it's a number of things sort of make me go. One is just the escapism. It's just being, getting out of town. Just feeling the spray and the wind on your face and going out. It's exciting going to, to new places. It's that real sort of sense of adventure, not knowing what's there. But often when you get there, it's almost like, especially if the water's not all that comfortable, like if it's not clear you don't know what's there and often that is a real, it becomes, it's almost a matter of psyching yourself up to go in. The hard thing is if you actually go in and you're confronted by something. And out there the things that really frighten me are the things like big groupers that live out there. And they do, they come in and front me in the gloom. And often you're feeling uncomfortable from the start and then suddenly there's this huge mouth or something right beside you, it's a big grouper that's just glided in, or you hear this big bang of a grouper flaring its gills out at you or the flick of its tail as it goes past and that's terrifying. I just absolutely shit myself. But I still go back. I'll still go back, back down and I don't know what, what makes me do that. It's, it's almost like . . .

HW: You didn't [come] up to the surface and say, no, I'm too afraid to do it again?

No, because like I, I, I had, I have gotten out of the water at times but most of the times, even, like even when I was diving off Byron Bay and there were sharks and stuff, I would still stay in. Umm, within reason, like if they weren't coming in and sort of buzzing you, if they were around, I'd still stay in. And, it's almost like you, yeah, just want to experience the—whether it's the terror or what I don't know.

HW: Do you need to keep going back in the water even though you're terrified?

Yeah, well, that's, I can't, I don't know why I do that. Like when I go down and spear fish, I do it for a number of reasons. One is I really like eating fish, right. Umm, I like just looking around in marine environments, just seeing what's there, umm and just like with surfing. It's very exhilarating if you're down there and you see a big school of fish, it's probably a little bit like surfing in other ways too in that it's very physically demanding, you really get to know your own limitations because you're taking a breath and then diving down, sometimes quite, quite a reasonable depth and just staying there, and you have to be relaxed because otherwise you can't stay for very long. So often you're fighting off this, this sort of need to breathe, just trying to be relaxed and to stay down there or otherwise you miss so much. If you don't stay there for a certain time it's just like bouncing off the bottom, you're not going to see much. So, the fitness side of it appeals to me, the excitement is definitely there. It's, umm, it's very relaxing, it's always an adventure because you just don't know what's there, and it's rewarding in that you get, umm, you get to eat all these amazing things, like fish and lobsters and a range of different things. But it's also an escapism because you're just away from everyone. But I think for me the main, the main attraction is the excitement. It's definitely the excitement, umm, the exhilaration of, I suppose the going down, spending time just, just hunting. You're there, you're looking and suddenly you see something that's quite, you know, like a big mackerel, just comes in out of the gloom, or a, or suddenly a coral trout materializes out of something or other. I would be just as excited seeing it, and often sometimes if I see a school of fish I'm mesmerized and I'm not thinking about actually hunting them, but then when I, when I sort of become focused, I think right, get it. It's yeah, it's the anticipation some-times of not knowing. You might spear them and then get back to the surface and you're not really sure if you've still got it. Then it's a long swim back to the boat, you know, struggling to get this thing in, and so there's lots of different aspects for doing it. But I can't, I can't describe this, this need to go back. It's almost like you're challenging yourself to confront your fears because, I don't know, it's dangerous. And yet I still do it. You'll have to come out, I'll show you.

Joseph's environmentalist body is evoked by the pleasure of seaspray and wind on his face, and by the relaxing mesmerizing effect of seeing a school of fish. But his description also fits with the male hero-god: he escapes from culture; he moves into the exciting unknown; he is con-fronted by fearful others and overcomes his fear; he uses his reason to know when to leave a dangerous situation; he is a hunter; and he takes pleasure in the use of his physically fit body in a challenging situation.

This elision with the heroic elements of dominant masculinity does not rule out or override the search for personal environmental prac-tices that are less hegemonic, less intrusive on the lives of the others (on other species, other living things). This searching is based on a longing for connection. Joseph describes the practices through which he achieves connection ((be)longing) in the sea:

When I see any big sort of marine organisms it's almost like you can feel their presence. I always wonder about things, like where have they come from, what does it involve, you know, what do they do. We only see such a small part of their lives. And I often wonder about where they go at certain times and what they're doing. But to actually be in the water with them it's a—especially when you see their eyes—they, they look at you, it's something that really sort of goes right to the core of you.

HW: So you can recognize the otherness of fish. They have other kind of dimensions and lives we cannot see?

Yeah, because we're only there for, like, I suppose it's just by accident that we run into them in their environment, but there's a whole part of their existence that we know nothing about and that's the thing that really intrigues me about it. It's funny, getting back to this thing with water, like sometimes, like say if I was out off Townsville today, sometimes you'd just be swimming for hours. It's not unusual if I go out to spend somewhere between five and seven hours in the water, just swimming. And, so, you're swimming around for a long time and most of the time you're not seeing anything and suddenly you'll encounter something and it's a, yeah, it's a real experience now. I don't know if you can say that's a real spiritual experience, but sometimes I feel as if it is because it really overwhelms you when you see something, especially when it's got real grace, sort of elegance under the seas and then it's just gone.

Joseph's story is one in which he recognizes, while he is in the sea, the limitations of his own capacity to see and to know. He happens upon life-forms who have a whole existence he cannot know about. He talks in particular about the moment of seeing their eyes, as if in this moment there is a recognition of their power to see and to know, and to know what he cannot know. The all-seeing godlike eye/I is abandoned, handed over to the marine organism, and a realignment or transformation takes place at the core of his own body: "the eye of the law is replaced by a multiplicity of little eyes; everyone is on stage; no one is outside" (Conley, 1991, p. 22). He achieves a new form of subjectivity, "the subjectivity of a non-I/plural I, which is different from the subjectivity of the sovereign I . . ." (Trinh, 1991, pp. 190–91). Joseph uses the same term as Bruce to describe what happens to him. He is "overwhelmed" *(overwhelm:* to overpower the thoughts, emotions or senses; to overcome with irresistible force, *Collins English Dictionary).* In this space and at this moment, Joseph casts off the inscription of himself as rational dominant man. He is rewritten, reinscribed (he scribes himself) as one who recognizes the power and mystery of other life-forms. He is in awe of it, and his busy dominating mind is overcome with a force he cannot resist—does not want to resist. He (be)longs for that moment in the sea with the graceful and elegant creature who gazes at him, and is gone.

But Joseph does not abandon, while he is in the sea, the right *also* to be a predator, a powerful life-form in his own right. He is in awe and he is one with the creatures of the sea, but he does not romanticize this to mean that all life-forms are humanoid, and that to eat them would be an unnatural act, like a form of cannibalism. Like other animals, he must eat. He is careful, however, to distinguish his own act of predation from the displays of macho bravado that he observes amongst other groups of men:

When I look at other people out in their boats catching fish, sometimes I see this
real sort of macho thing where there's lots of guys 'round there and they're all
catching, you know, they're winding in fish and everyone's drinking and I
don't like that side of it, at all. The side that I enjoy is when I'm actually in
there, diving, and I see these fish. Most of the time you don't get a high percent-
age of the fish because they're quite timid, so you really have to go in and stalk
something and often that means you have to lull these things into a false sense
of security and that involves just being very relaxed, no sudden movements,
sometimes looking as if you're trying to swim away from them so that they
actually then come to have a look thinking that you're swimming away, so
there's all these different techniques. I do feel like I'm in there hunting but at
the same time I have, I feel like I have a real respect for the things that I'm
chasing as well and I don't just go in there and blast anything. I only take the
ones that I would like to eat, and I don't take lots of them, I just go and get a
few. So, this idea of men going out fishing and just catching and catching and
catching just to almost satisfy the blood lust is not really what I'm about. I take a
few but it's, again, it's a much more personal thing. It, it's hard to describe. . . . I
got a big barramundi a couple of weekends ago. I came back and I had a
huge barramundi, it was about thirty-something pounds, quite a big one and I
felt quite sorry that I had actually killed it. I was excited by the prospect of hav-
ing all this fresh barramundi to eat, but I was a little bit sad that I'd actually
killed this big fish. And it's funny some of the thoughts that were going through
my head when I was cleaning this fish . . . this fish has come from a very small
larval stage and has made it through unscathed this number of years to get to
this size only to meet me and then, I've killed it. I felt a bit sad.

Joseph talks about his ability to move beyond the category "human"
towards that of fish. To be able to outwit the fish underwater one
must also think like fish. But when he returns to the landscape of his
home, bringing back from his immersion in the sea his prize of fish to
eat, the chatter of environmental and masculine discourses starts up in
his head, with all their tensions and contradictions. He cannot help
boasting about the size of his fish. Yet perhaps he should not have
killed this fish—it has all of these amazing scientific properties, it has
survived so long, and now he's killed it. He has moved back, through
guilt, into being the one who is responsible—and therefore the one
with the right and the obligation to be in control. And so his moment
of conquest and of pleasurable (be)longing in the ocean turns, in part,
to sadness and partial regret. Perhaps he would not feel such regret if
he was constituted with/in the same discourses as the southerners in
Italy, whom Dessaix (1998, p. 187) describes as "in tune with their
instincts and passions, letting them flower for good or evil, refining
their animality but only to heighten their pleasure of being human, not
to extinguish it."

Learning to experience oneself as not bounded and separate, not
fundamentally an individual with the right to dominate and exploit

what is other to oneself, is a complex task, which these men describe themselves as able to achieve sometimes. They are capable of experiencing moments of immersion in what they construct as the natural world. They are capable of deconstructing the culture/nature binary in their embodied beings, and in their body/landscape relations. When they place themselves in oceans, they lose, in that time and in that place, their individualistic identities. Graham describes his body as "atomizing" in tropical oceans, as having no boundaries. The delineated self disappears into the warm ocean body. He says:

If you go scuba diving for instance . . . you lose your body . . . you become a part of the sea and . . . you almost become atomized and split apart. . . . It's probably as close as I'll ever get to, you know, spiritual behaviour as this . . . feeling that in fact you're no longer in this frail little body, but you're actually a part of all this and that you extend out.

The word *spiritual* is drawn on many times to describe this loss of boundedness, to describe the reinscription of oneself as connected to and part of landscape or seascape. "Spiritual" is not used here in a binary other to the body, but as a means of describing a particular kind of embodiment. Terry explains the connectedness in terms of his reading of indigenous body/landscape relations. Indigenous people, he says, are not only spiritually/bodily connected to the landscape, but their spirituality is linked to environmental practices that are respectful of and caring for the land:

Most indigenous cultures . . . just have this full-on spiritual connection with their land. But it's not just a spiritual connection, the functional connection is right down to they only take what they need. They don't cut down the tree because they want to see past it, they walk around the tree.

Tom describes the connectedness not in terms of spirituality but in terms of love. He compares the experience of seeing light through the trees in the forest and smelling the forest and feeling the air to a chance connection with another person who remains part of you always, in your memory:

If I'm walking through treed areas I look at the light through the trees, I look at the games the light plays with your eyes, the smells, the sounds, the temperature. You can usually feel it; I suppose because I don't talk, I just let my mind do all those things, I allow all the stimulus to come inside and then play with them in my head. . . . It's like, how do you describe love in those different levels? I mean, you know that you love something or love someone, because you can feel it and when you're out there with nature it's the feeling, it's the warm inner glow, if you've got to give it some words and even that phrase doesn't give it the right connotation. It is a feeling thing inside and it's the same as when you are with

a person and you just connect and it might be that you've connected for a con-
versation over coffee with a stranger in a café in a foreign country for fifteen
minutes and you felt like you've known them forever and you walk away and
that meeting will always remain in your memory.

Unlike previous descriptions of abandoning the external boundedness
of the body and moving outwards to become part of the surrounding
spaces, Tom's description is of his boundaries being penetrated by the
environment, and by the feeling of love. He draws the images and feelings onto the deep surfaces of his body and holds them there as part
of himself—as embodied memory.

Terry's connection is with the wind that buffets the external surfaces
of his body and at the same time penetrates the inner emotional surfaces and calms them down. His own moods and modes of being are
brushed and altered by the wind, which he invites by wearing clothes
that attract the wind:

The wind is moody. The wind is a very moody thing that, it buffets you and
you know sometimes when you're very sad you feel that tickling of the breeze
that will take the hotness off your face you know. If you're feeling unhappy and
flushed or something and a good breeze will give you that cooling and it'll take
the flush away from your face and then you can get a calmness in your mind
from that. At other times the wind is pushy. You have to fight against it and it
gives you that dramatic feeling or you can walk up a hill against the wind. I
really appreciate the wind. I wear lots of baggy clothes because I like to have it
catching and fluttering in the wind. I like things that flutter in the wind. Except
for that sort of plastic bunting that you get over used-car yards.

And so...

The network of material and discursive practices in the lives and stories of these men includes, inevitably, not only environmentalist ideal-
ism, but also stories of heroic individualism and of escape from
drudgery, the domestic, and the everyday. In the text of their interviews the men in our study move through and between a palimpsest
of environmental and masculine discourses. Environmental discourses
are taken up and lived in ways that have profound effects, which shift
their patterns of perception and ways of being. These sometimes push
up against and disrupt more usual (masculine) perceptions and modes
of being and at other times leave them intact either as irrelevant in
that particular time/space, or as melded into and part of the new
material and discursive practices.

These environmentalists have found a variety of strategies for troubling the surface of rational dominant masculinity and of coming to
(be)long in landscapes in embodied ways that give them much pleasure and complement their take-up of environmental discourses. But

"nature" has many meanings, as does "masculinity," and there are many contradictions between them. One way of managing these different meanings is to make discursive and bodily practice specific to particular folds in time and space (such as "the pub" and "Kakadu"). Another way is to merge and meld elements of one discourse and the related set of practices with other discourses and practices. These men constantly *separate themselves out* from other, lesser men, who are macho exploiters of women and environments. But the individualistic hero image is not easily let go of. Each man escapes from culture and other men in a journey of renewal and return. Each one finds himself vulnerable to the practices and discourses of the culture he finds himself in—vulnerable to becoming "like them." Each works to achieve experiences in which environment is no longer that which surrounds the self but is also the self, an experience that is exciting and *overwhelming*. But that coextension is not laid down as a permanent and exclusive inscription: their (in)scription in each different fold of the landscape coexists in/on the depth/surface of their bodies with the (in)scriptions that take place in other folds; the folds created by politics and other discourses, the folds of the sea and the wind.

RAIN

I can hear you
making small holes
in the silence
rain

If I were deaf
the pores of my skin
would open to you
and shut

And I
should know you
by the lick of you
if I were blind

the something
special smell of you
when the sun cakes
the ground

the steady
drum-roll sound
you make
when the wind drops

But if I
should not hear
smell or feel or see
you

you would still define me
disperse me
wash over me
rain

Hone Tuwhare
(O'Brien, 1997, p. 91)

Part 2 ~ (In)scribing body/landscape relations: Japan

IN THIS SECOND PART OF THE BOOK, I explore body/landscape relations as they are talked and written about by Japanese students, academics, and environmentalists. I also write about my own travels in
Japan, during which I attempted to enter into the meaning of body/
landscape relations in a landscape entirely unfamiliar to me. By entering into the folds of Japanese landscapes, and the folds of meaning-
making of Japanese writers and poets and the Japanese people I
encountered, worked with, and interviewed, I found ways of seeing
aspects of my own constitutive practices that had been invisible to me.
As well, I found myself unfolding in these landscapes, in ways that
were, in part, appropriate—or to put it differently, I became appropri-
ate(d) with/in the landscapes of Japan—albeit in fragmented moments
of bodily comprehension. This second part begins with Chapter 4,
which is based on a collective biography undertaken with a group of
Japanese students studying in Australia. It is based on the stories they
wrote of being embodied as Japanese within the specific landscapes of
their childhoods. Japanese culture and language have a long history in
the landscapes of Japan, and although some aspects of it are questioned by some of the participants in Chapters 4 and 6, the alienation
from "culture" in the stories of the Australian environmentalists and the
problematizing of usual ways of speaking and writing that were developed in the Australian collective biography are played out quite differently here. Chapter 5 is based on the journal I wrote about my
embodied experience while traveling for a month in Japan. It explores
the embodied experience of being in an unfamiliar landscape while at
the same time wanting to come to know it within the terms made relevant by Japanese writers and the various Japanese people I encountered on my travels and in undertaking my research. Chapter 6 is
based on my interviews with environmentalists and people interested
in environmental issues in Japan. These interviews took place on the
island of Hokkaido. This second part of the book seeks to take you,
as reader, into the folds of Japanese landscapes in such a way that
they become imaginable from within those folds.

~4~ Remembering Japanese childhoods

BEFORE I VISITED JAPAN I began working with a small group of
Japanese students in a collective biography project. We met once a
week during term time in the period leading up to my trip and again
in the remaining months of the academic year after I came back. The
discussions I had with this group enabled me to attempt to enter the
Japanese landscape in its own terms, to know it from inside itself
rather than only as an outsider—though of course I was also and
always that. I realize I am setting up a problematic binary here—of
insider and outsider. What I did not want to do was to tour Japan and
bring my own already formed judgments to bear on it, as David
Suzuki and Keibo Oiwa (1996) were accused of doing in the reviews
of their book *The Japan We Never Knew: A Voyage of Discovery*. In
reading words or reading landscapes, the reading can be an imaginative act through which one can move inside the text, or it can be
more a surface act, as someone looking in at the writer/inhabitants.
The work we did as a collective biography group enabled me to gain
a sense of some of the multiplicity of Japanese body/landscape relations from the point of view of those who have lived them. The students, too, were in a sense looking from both inside and outside: they
made visible their own experience of body/landscape relations through
contrasting how they had been in Japan with how they were in Australia. Through listening to my stories and seeing my struggle to understand what they were saying, and through listening to each other, they
developed the art of remembering the detail through which their experiences could be made tellable and recordable.

At the same time, it was in the works of those writers who knew
Japan both from inside and outside that I found the words that
brought Japanese culture to life in my own imagination. More traditional books, such as Inazo Nitobe's *Bushido: The Soul of Japan*,
seemed to present a knowledge whose surface was, for me, smooth
and impenetrable. In contrast, Kenzaburo Oe, who spent most of his
life in Japan and who now lives in America, Alex Kerr, an American
who spent part of his early childhood in the East and who has spent
most of his adulthood in Japan, and Leonard Koren, who lives in both
America and Japan, seem able to break open the surface and allow
what is there to become visible, thinkable, imaginable.

At first the students in the collective biography group found Japanese
ways of being embodied in landscape extraordinarily difficult to articulate. Through the process of working together over that one-year period,
however, growing up embodied as Japanese, in Japanese landscapes,

became something that could be talked and written about in detail. Although we read Japanese poetry, novels, and short stories, we read them not as authoritative, but rather as jumping-off points for our talk and our writing. One of the many strategies we adopted to arrive at this point was to pick out phrases from a modern short story, "Kitchen," by Banana Yoshimoto, and to turn these into a poem that encapsulated "this is what I hear this story to be about." Since these phrases could not be fitted into tanka or haiku, new forms were developed. This breaking of the unquestioned assumption that poetry can only be written inside a strict format, along with the development of a new strategy and purpose for writing, led to a stream of poetic writing, and an expression of delight from Masako in particular that she did not know she could write such things.

There were four students in the group. I began with Masako, who was studying for an M.Ed and whose parents I later visited when I was traveling in Japan. I asked her advice on how best to proceed, and she suggested that we limit the group to a small number to ensure that the participants would feel comfortable enough to talk freely and without shyness and embarrassment. She asked two other students to join us: Seiji, who was undertaking a Ph.D. in marine science, and Hiroko, who was in her second year of a B.Ed, having already undertaken her final years of schooling in Australia. Their families still lived in Japan. Masako and Hiroko began with the assumption that all Japanese people are fundamentally alike. In contrast, Seiji, who had worked in other parts of the world as a marine biologist before coming to Australia, did not believe there was any such thing as a typical Japanese person—he had more in common, he said, with some of his Australian friends who shared his birth sign (the Ox) than he did with any Japanese salaryman. When Seiji left the group, his Ph.D. completed, Masako invited Kaori, an exchange student from Hokkaido, to join the group.

Our task was to find ways of telling and writing life stories that would reveal the discursive patterns through which Japanese body/landscape relations are lived. When I explained at the outset that one of the outcomes of undertaking a collective biography is that the participants can see for the first time the collective nature of being, along with its discursive construction, Masako and Hiroko were bemused. How could one set out to discover what was already obvious? Their commonality and their construction through language was something they took for granted. Seiji was very skeptical about the idea that so few individual stories might reveal something called "Japanese culture," because it ran against his understanding of good "science" and against the multiplicity he could see in Japanese ways of being. He found it difficult to understand that I would not be looking for the "truth" in the content of what they said, but rather that I would be looking at the ways in which the available discursive practices had made possible the ways of being that they experienced. I had not invited them to join the group as authorities whose task it was to speak *about* their own culture. I did not wish to hear any received wisdom nor explanations about why Japanese people experience things as they do. I wanted them, rather, to learn to read their own bodies and the bodies of their childhoods, and thus to *speak and write as embodied beings* capable of observing their own embodiment as they had experienced it in Japanese landscapes.

With these puzzlements and misgivings, the group began the work of storying on which this chapter is based. The point of our storying became, through such talk, a search for the ways in which their "Japaneseness," in terms of body/landscape relations, had been taken on by them as (partially) shared yet difficult to describe ways of being. At first it appeared that the fabric of Japanese selves could only be told through the words of the poets, or the words of those with authority to speak and write, and through specific cultural patterns and practices of Japanese life. Making those words and patterns and practices storyable through their own particular experience of them seemed a daunting task.

At first the students' stories were very brief and seemed, to me, impenetrable. I could not find the way to enter imaginatively into the spaces and experiences that they talked and wrote about. I asked question after question about how things felt, what they looked like, revealing in my questioning the kind of detail that was needed, for me, to bring the story to life. Sometimes I told stories from my own childhood to enable them to see not only the kind of detail I might draw on to enable them to imaginatively enter into growing up in Australia, but to see what they might need to tell to make their experience imaginable to someone who had not been there, who could not imagine for herself what a Japanese autumn moon or the interior of a Japanese house might look like. In one of the early sessions together we read some traditional Japanese poetry that I had come across in reading Kawabata's speech given when he was awarded the Nobel prize:

Winter moon, going behind the clouds and coming forth again,
  making bright my footsteps as I go to the meditation hall and descend
    again,
  making me unafraid of the wolf;
does not the wind sink into you, does not the snow,
Are you not cold?
(Kawabata, 1969, p. 69)

The time of the snows, of the moon, of the blossoms—then more than ever we think of our comrades. (Yashiro Yukio, quoted in Kawabata, 1969, p. 69)

Kawabata wrote in elaboration of these poems:

When we see the beauty of the snow, when we see the beauty of the full moon, when we see the beauty of the cherries in bloom, when in short we brush against and are awakened by the beauty of the four seasons, it is then that we think most of those close to us, and want them to share the pleasure. The excitement of beauty calls forth strong fellow feelings, yearnings for companionship, and the word "comrade" can be taken to mean "human being." The snow, the moon, the blossoms, words expressive of the seasons as they move into one another, include in the Japanese tradition the beauty of mountains and rivers and grasses and trees, of all the myriad manifestations of nature, of human feelings as well. (Kawabata, 1969, pp. 68–69)

Masako observed that reading such words made her feel very happy and that she did not need to have seen the moon or the snow that the poets wrote of to feel that particular happiness. To read and know the poem was enough to feel a deep contentment. I was deeply puzzled by what she said. Was it that the landscape itself was nothing and that her body/landscape relations were taken up entirely through the words of others? Some insight into my inability to understand what she was saying to me came later when we read a contemporary poem by Keiko Kato:

Michinoku—
a thousand ricefields growing green
where he once walked.
(Lowitz, Aoyama, and Tomioka, 1994, p. 68)

When I first read this I assumed, without even realizing that I was doing so, that "he" could be anyone I imagined him to be. My task of reading was to bring the poem to life with my own images, concocted out of my own experiences. Although I could not imagine Michinoku, not having been there, I could imagine misty Japanese hillsides covered in bright green rice fields, from pictures I had seen and from the rice fields I had seen when traveling by train through the Japanese countryside. And I could, without any conscious effort, imagine a rather mysterious man who had walked there long ago. I had succeeded in making the poem come to life—for me, just as I had learned to make poems about the English countryside, which I had never seen, come to life in the poems of my childhood. The students explained to me that this reading missed the point of the poem altogether, since I did not have access to the implicit knowledge available to any Japanese reader. The "he" who walked there was the poet Basho. They also knew a great deal of visual detail not made explicit in the poem—not detail imported at whim as I had done, but detail intended by the poet and introduced into the poem through shared knowledge of the imagery and what it carries with it. They knew, for example, that "growing green" would signal late spring when the rice shoots begin to turn green in Michinoku, and that this is therefore a poem that evokes all of the emotion and sense of being that is appropriate to a late spring landscape in Michinoku. They also knew about Basho, what he had written, where he had walked, and what it would have looked like when he walked there. As it turned out, I had a print of the poet Basho hanging in my bedroom, and suddenly I was able to imagine what it might be like to bring the poem to life with such certainty. This was an important moment in the development of my capacity to hear what the students were telling me. It brought about one of those startling shifts in perception that feel as if the pathways of the brain are rearranging themselves. I was in awe of their rich, shared knowledge of place and of the history of place, which I had not really been able to imagine until that point. The detailed translations that I later engaged in with Professor Tanaka, when traveling in Japan, enabled me to enter into, at least partially, the sharing of rich implicit knowledge of place.

Gradually, as I worked with the students, I began to imagine what it might mean to read oneself and one's embodiment through the seasons, and to know through the slightest allusion to the seasons in each poem, or piece of writing, what sense of embodiment might be brought to the reading of it. Hiroko drew up a chart of her embodied sense of the seasons:

Spring	Summer
nice and warm (from the winter's cold) cherry blossoms season many animals and insects are coming out lots of green, pollen laughing, smile (green, blue) full of energy	sunflower, a straw hat, hot, hot, hot pool, sea, gigantic columns of clouds shaved ice on my sore temples! Shining, summer holiday long days (blue, orange, yellow) rainy season, good for crops, slug in a bathroom
Fall (Autumn)	Winter
(brown, red) not too hot, and not too cold. Nice to live feel calm, dreary In general, reading, eating, studying season Beautiful leaves which turn red Sky—cirrocumulus, great sunsets (red) feel lonely but calm	(white, gray, black) look fat, making snowman, cold getting white, snowball fights dark and silent getting dark early hot-pot season! (so often) (look out for fire!) at night Can't wake up, don't want to get out of bed in the morning Beautiful sky, white breath, stars

We began our story writing by talking about our earliest memories of home. What early memory could we each find that might evoke the first self-awareness of being an embodied being in that place? We told stories and listened carefully to each others' stories and asked questions to draw forth the kind of detail that enabled us each to imagine the situation being talked about. Before the next meeting we each chose at least one of the memories we had talked about and wrote it down to be read out to the group at the next meeting. I wrote of a moment alone by the fire in winter:

> *Cold winter's night*
> *curled up by the fire,*
> *wood paneling glows in the soft light,*
> *brass firedogs stand sentinel;*
> *my back grows warm and I dream.*

I probably would not have thought to mention that it was winter if it had not been for our discussions about the seasons, and I might not have chosen a winter story if we had not read poems about cold and snow in Japan. Seiji also began with cold and winter and he also chose a moment of aloneness, in contrast to Masako and Hiroko, who wrote about each of their family members and their feelings towards them. Seiji's story locates itself in the pattern of seasons. Unlike the poets Yashiro Yukio and Kawabata, for whom the seasons evoke above all the awareness of and even yearning for others, Seiji's story begins with his family, but it moves to himself alone embodied in landscape. The detail he puts into his story brings us with a startling vividness into the experience of the small boy in that specific moment of awareness of embodied being, alone in the landscape of a Japanese house on the north coast of Honshu Island:

The northern coast of Japan where I lived with my family has cold and humid winters. It snows a lot. The houses are built using very big columns and heavy beams to sustain the weight of snow on the roofs. We stay at home under dark winter skies waiting for the spring to come.

When the snow melts, everything changes and becomes green.

In summer, all the roof tiles reflect strong sunshine in the hot dry air.

I remember an afternoon of a summer vacation of primary school. I was lying on the tatami mat. Nobody was at home. Very quiet. All the fusumas (sliding doors) were open to let the fresh air go through the house. The wind brought a strong smell of summer grass and loud cry of cicadas.

I was listening to the old-fashioned clock tick-tock.

Seiji's description of his childhood garden in late summer also carries the same vivid detail of embodied self in landscape. In this story the child's embodied sense of summer pleasure and shared laughter is weighed against a sense of change and loss:

A walnut tree, a pear, a jujube, a cherry, a couple of mulberries and many other kinds of trees were in the garden.

In a late summer, with my friend, I climbed on the roof of a hut, in which, I was told, my grandfather, who died just before I was born, kept a goat. Now my grandmother's chickens were there.

From the roof, we could reach the branches of the mulberry, which had plenty of fruit. When we ate it, the fruit colored our mouths bluish-purple. We laughed a lot looking at each other.

I had a white mongrel dog, called John. For unknown reasons, the dogs in my neighborhood tended to have Western-type names. I can't remember any of these, but my dog was John even though she was female.

When a garage was built in the garden, the walnut tree and mulberry trees were cut down, which I found when I came back from the University one day.

John died a long time ago, too.

Seiji's story ends with the cutting of trees and the death of his dog and a sense of time stretching a long way between then and now. The strong sense of loss of the landscapes of a Japanese childhood echo the sense of loss expressed by many of the people I later talked to while traveling in Japan.

The next set of stories that we told and later wrote were of first memories of venturing outside the house and garden, of being embodied away from home. We discussed the routine and clockwork plan that enables Japanese children to walk to school together as a group. Each child knows, to the second, when the group will arrive at her or his house, at which point they join the group and walk on to the next child's house. Masako and Hiroko had no memories to tell of these walks—they were uneventful and repetitive, allowing no movement outside the group in the transition from home to school and back again. Seiji, again, had a different experience to tell. He and his group did deviate from the expected path laid out for them. His discoveries in those deviations (including the very interesting discovery that he and his friends might be different) he now reads as holding the key to his later life's choices:

The kindy and the primary school were far away from my house. It was more than one kilometer. It usually took more than half an hour to get there and another half an hour to come back. It's a long way for small kids.

The road goes in the middle of rice fields, grape and pear farms, and hills covered with thick woods. I usually walked with my friends.

In spring, we sometimes caught mud snails in the stream. The school uniforms and shoes got all muddy. I kept the snails in a glass jar at home. They grew quite fast grazing green algae on the surface of the glass. And one day they produced baby snails. They are viviparous, more precisely, ovo-viviparous. It surprised me a lot because I thought they would lay eggs.

When we were not wading in the stream we explored the bush. In summer, I often found a couple of types of berries.

I sometimes got poisoned by a lacquer tree. It is very annoying. But surprisingly, one of my friends was extremely resistant to the poison. Once I complained about a rash on my skin, he wiped his face hard with the leaves of a lacquer tree. He didn't have any problem even after that.

Being outdoors was an important part of my early life. There were many reasons for me to decide ten years later to go to study Biology at university.

I'm afraid that today's kids don't have time to spend outdoors because they are too busy studying at private schools.

Seiji's stories are wonderfully ambiguous. They are written in free form. Yet they are each clearly located in the tradition of making seasonal change the underlying organizing device through which one knows oneself in the Japanese landscape. And closely linked to these changes are the relationships with his "comrades," with whom he muddied his school uniform and shoes and caught mud snails in spring, and with whom he ate mulberries and laughed in the late summer. At the same time, his stories contain a sense of difference, of separation from the group: awareness of self alone on the tatami mat, of selves who respond differently to things like poisonous lacquer trees. Then the third story ends with what by now has become, for me, a familiar Japanese refrain: the fact that children in Japan no longer have the time or opportunity to experience life outdoors.

Seiji blames the attendance at private schools for the children's loss of the kinds of experiences he treasures in his memories of childhood. Hiroko provides two wonderful descriptions where her embodied being in the landscapes of such schools does not sound like the kind of loss Seiji envisages:

The abacus school was placed only five minutes from my house, and it was on my course for taking a walk with my dog. Not every day, but twice a week, I went to that school to learn abacus after school around four o'clock. I usually went there by bicycle with my friends, and sometimes by myself. I always took a green vinyl rectangular bag which the school gave me as a welcome gift, when I joined the school. Of course the name of the school was written on the bag.

My long abacus always peeped out of one end of the bag and the handle of the bag was stretched, and it looked a little funny. But it was the same for other students, so I could easily know who was on the way to that school, from the green vinyl bag with stretched handle, and the end of the abacus.

The abacus school was a private school named Taura-jyuku, and it was built just for learning abacus at that time, so it wasn't a large building. It was wooden, and had two stories. The outside of the building was painted white,

but inside was natural wood color, which was dark brown. There were many
trees around the school, and a very small playground in front of the building.
There was a car road near the building, but it wasn't too bad because the other
side of the road was a rice field (now, it has changed though).

When my friends and I arrived to the school, we always ran up to a huge
dog, said "hello" and patted her. She was outside the school, and had her home
just under the window of my classroom.

Before we came inside, an old wooden shoe shelf was waiting for us.
Because we often spent so much time with the dog before the class started, it
was very difficult to find a nice (nice means "complete") pair of slippers, when
we tried to come inside, so, we used to have a little funny battle in front of that
shoe shelf. And the shoe shelf was always watching it quietly.

Even if I could win the battle, I didn't feel comfortable to see other friends
who couldn't get a pair, so finally, I gave my slippers to them. The battle was
just for fun time before the class.

Once I came inside, I always smelled the special smell of the school. Which
was shady, old wood, calm, peaceful . . . (I don't know how to explain the smell
properly) . . . some students didn't like that smell, but I felt very comfortable
when I was in that building. Especially in summer, it gave us really nice shade,
cool floor, and air . . . so I sometimes went there earlier, and just sat in the pas-
sage, and pretended to sleep. There was still strong sunshine outside, but inside,
there was nice wind, cool passage, and some students' talking was heard from
somewhere. It sounded like a lullaby. Very relaxed. I really liked that moment.

By the way, I often said "hello" through a small window, to an old woman
who sat inside a reception room, and then I would run (actually not run, but
sliding, like, skating on the ice, I liked to skate on the waxed passage with my
socks) into the classroom.

My abacus class was on the ground floor, just next to the huge dog's house,
except a wooden wall, with a large window, was in between.

All tables and chairs were made of wood, and those were covered with lots of
graffiti, lots of small holes and carvings (scratched into the wood) which had
obviously been made by students with their automatic pencils. Those tables were
arranged in many rows, and my seat was always in the first row, just in front
of the teacher. Once I entered the room, the special smell was stronger, and I
could hear the busy sound of using the abacus: "pachi pachi pachi pachi jyatt,
pachi pachi pachi pachi. . . ." I walked through between the tables very quietly,
to my seat.

Only the sound of using the abacus, the teacher's unique coughing, and
sometimes the dog's barking was heard.

The quiet moments at the end of this story, hearing the busy
sounds of the abacus "pachi pachi pachi pachi jyatt, pachi pachi pachi
pachi . . ." as she quietly enters the room, then the teacher's cough and
the dog's barking, carries much of the same emotion and sense of
intense awareness of self in landscape as Seiji's first story on the
tatami mat. And leading up to that are many other small, exquisite

moments of embodiment: noticing the funny stretched handle of the abacus bag, with the abacus peeping out, but recognizing this as a badge of belonging with other students from the abacus school; the shoe shelf waiting for the students and watching quietly; the shady, old wood, peaceful smell of the school building; sitting quietly in the passageway feeling the cool wind and hearing the lullaby of students' voices; skating in socks on the waxed wood floor of the passageway. And here, too, are moments of a sense of difference: giving away the nice slippers so others can have them; seeing that some others do not like the smell that she finds so soothing; going quietly, late, into the class after everyone else is seated.

Hiroko's second story of private school is of a calligraphy class. This time she uses a poetic form, though without conforming to any particular poetic structure. She explores the embodied conflict she experienced between the requirement that she acquire her own individual style and years of learning the disciplined forms through which calligraphy should be done:

At the same place, at the same time
I was sitting
On a brown-green tatami mat
My knee was bent properly
I rose my face up
My back was straight like a wooden stick

I breathed in the air of sumi[1]
The unique taste of the air
It was spreading slowly
from my nose all through my body
I started to grind an ink-cake
without a word
My heart was calm, high concentration
Or was I just pretending?
I don't know
but it had been many years now
It should be perfect

I asked my teacher,
"What do you think of my calligraphy, Ms.?"

She said, "Look at your copybook more carefully, and try to copy it neatly. OK?"
"What do you think of my calligraphy, Ms.?"

She said, "Well, you should pay more attention to the speed of the brush, and the shading of the ink. Do you know what I mean?"

---

1. India ink

I went back to the tatami mat
My shoulder was getting sore
My arms were heavy
I felt that I had pins and needles inside my legs
My figure was getting slightly ugly

"Now, Ms. What do you think of my calligraphy this time?"

She said, "Hmm, you are on a right track, but you have still got a long way
to go. Putting feeling into the characters is more important than form. Show
your spirit through your calligraphy."
"Well, Ms., but you said . . ."

"Shh, also, you have got to develop more relaxed handling of the brush, too. OK?"
". . . . . ."

How can I show my own spirit?
Within a strict rule of writing
How can I relax?
Within a completely shaped figure
With my pricked legs, sore shoulders, and heavy arms
How many papers did I waste?
How many years did I spend?
To understand the soul of calligraphy

I pretended not to feel anything
Kept my back straight, and sat again properly
I felt nothing
I didn't remember even if I was breathing or not
While I was writing again
I felt nothing

"What do you think of my calligraphy, Ms.?"
The answer was, "It's not too bad, getting better!"
I was surprised.
She expected me to show my spirit.
I had nothing to show
But she said it was good.
What does that mean?

Write on a white paper
With a brush, and black ink
That's all
It's very simple, but very complicated
Now I know
That in Japanese art, and Japanese beauty
It's all about conflict!

Hiroko's calligraphy story explores the coexistence of correct form and feeling-spirit. Seiji's and Hiroko's stories both hold in tension the facets of self experienced as members of a group and as individuals, which is also expressed as the tension between tradition and change in Seiji's stories, with change tending to be associated with loss. At the same time, Seiji welcomes the freedom to question what he sees as oppressive in Japanese culture. Hiroko's stories, in contrast, show both the freedom to question and the trust that even though she does not comprehend how it can be, she is learning, through her conformity, something deeply personal. One of Masako's first memories of moving outside the safe confines of her family home also holds tradition and change within it, but she does not associate the change with loss. Her first story is of a photo she found of herself:

One day when I was looking at my photo album, I found me climbing a huge tree in some of my pictures. These were taken when I was two or three years old. So I asked my grandma, What am I doing???

She told me there was an enormous tree (approximately thirty to forty meters) near my house. People were really afraid of the tree because they believed if they touched it, some kind of "curse" would be put on them. The tree was surrounded by a big fence.

Of course, I didn't know how sacred it was. Since I loved climbing trees, I really enjoyed climbing the tree EVERY MORNING!!! One day my grandma found I was climbing the tree, which made her so scared. She feared some "bad luck" would come to me.

But I wonder how come she took my picture???

This photo and its story holds all the tension between tradition and change in Japan. Here is a sacred tree carrying the mystery of ancient knowledges, declaring itself to the grandma as dangerous and untouchable, and here is Masako, the small child, celebrated as she climbs it. The celebratory act of taking a photo of her, representing her as individual, intrepid climber of dangerous trees, is there in the fact of the photo; the ancient knowledge, which made it such an extraordinary and recordable act, is there in the grandma's stories, which she tells to Masako. Masako's second grandmother's story contains the same tension. In this story there is no resolution or balance between tradition and change: the fears that arise from the traditional knowledge, which was used to protect Masako's grandmother during the dropping of the bombs, is carried around in Masako's body as a constant threat of attack whenever it is dark and she is alone:

My dark-phobia has never been cured, which has bothered me since I was a child. If I am alone in the dark, I feel like something is attacking me, including not only human beings, or ghosts, but also pillars, walls, or ceilings, etc. They are all my enemies. I know it sounds irrational; however, I cannot get rid of that feeling.

My phobia began with my grandmother's bed-time spell. She always turned the light off, sat beside my bed, and started casting a spell. The spell said that if some mishap happened during the night, please help Masako. I couldn't get the exact meaning; however, it sounded very fearful to me. The darkness escalated those feelings.

My grandmother often talked about her experience of the war at bedtime. I was deeply impressed by her story about giving birth to my mother. At that time American troops dropped bombs from the sky, so people were scared of turning the light on. If the Americans could see the light, they would attack. In that situation, my mother was born. A little while after my mother was born, my grandmother held her, but she held her upside down.

I always listened to my grandmother's story imagining me being in that scene. It was so dark, just the flame from the bombs shone on the houses. How dreadful it was. It was not a fantasy contrast, darkness and light.

Darkness is associated with a fearful feeling. I still feel uneasy, sleeping without the light on if I sleep alone. Straight after going back home I turn all of the lights on. Waste of energy, I know. But it seems to me I need light to survive.

Kenzaburo Oe, the celebrated Japanese novelist, understands these ambiguities as an unresolved East/West binary, which he experiences as a "deep felt scar":

> After a hundred and twenty years of modernization since the opening up of the country, contemporary Japan is split between two opposite poles of ambiguity. This ambiguity, which is so powerful and penetrating that it divides both the state and its people, . . . affects me as a writer like a deep felt scar. . . . (Oe, 1995, p. 117)

The scarring in Masako's story comes from a terrifying combination of dark traditional spells and the dropping of American bombs endangering her mother, newly born, and her grandmother. Japanese embodiment must always carry some ambivalence towards the West and its powers. Yet Masako's life trajectory is one of change, of movement towards the West, first to Tokyo and then to Hawaii and now to Australia, where she hopes to stay. At the same time, her connection to her "comrades" and to the *Matsuri* festival are experienced by her as "in her blood":

I grew up in Iwata in Shizuoka. It is such a tiny city that the population is about 8,000 people. Most of my classmates of Iwata-Minami high school went on to a university in big cities such as Tokyo or Osaka after graduation. We, the country folk, can't help experiencing culture shock there, especially when we are teased being called inaka-mono *(countrymen) because of our dialect. So we try to wear fashionable clothes and moreover make a big effort to use standard Japanese so that we are not humiliated.*

In short, we want to stay away from Iwata as much as possible and try to become urbane. So we seldom go back to our home-country, Iwata.

However, Matsuri will bring us back to Iwata. On Matsuri days every year, we go back Iwata to join in Matsuri Then we march around the community putting our arms on others' shoulders. We are shouting for encouragement along with the festival music. It is full of excitement.

Traditionally, during Matsuri days, we are allowed to do what we can't do normally, like getting drunk and sitting on the public roads, using someone's toilet without permission. The police have to overlook such things. In this way, we Iwata citizens enjoy two days of Matsuri very much!

For sure this Matsuri has a very long history. It has been held on the same day and in the same way since it was started. Everyone living in Iwata and coming from Iwata—from kids to old people—always looks forward to Matsuri and is proud of this festival. Joyful feelings of this sort are ingrained in our hearts: never gone no matter where we live.

Why is it that Matsuri holds us so tight? (or, draws us so strongly?) Matsuri has a spiritual essence, which is beyond generations and the times.

Every year I feel a tingling with excitement at the time when Matsuri days are coming. Such a feeling might be in my blood as other Iwata citizens are.

For Masako, then, the traditional Japanese ways are a site of deep ambivalence. They repel her and they draw her near; they lodge in her body as an experience of fear; they are in her blood as a tingling sense of joy. She has detached herself by moving to another country, but every year she feels herself drawn back. Seiji, in contrast, felt he had succeeded in detaching himself from Japan's traditions. One of his strategies for detachment was through political analysis of the use of Shinto religion to harm the Ainu people and to rest all power in the emperor.

When I was traveling in Japan I noticed yet another form of ambivalence/ambiguity. Japanese people seemed to move between very high praise of Japanese people ("we Japanese" the sentence would begin) and abject criticism of their hopelessness in the face of the advancement of developers. I found one stark example of this abject self-criticism in the book by Suzuki and Oiwa. Katsuichi Honda, a Japanese journalist, describes Japanese people as incapable of individual action and thought. He links this lack of individual consciousness and conscience to the failure of the Japanese to properly care for the landscapes of their country:

I call Japan a *medaka*[2] society, where thousands of little fish are in one school all going in the same direction. There is no leader, no common logic. They just watch what their neighbour does. If he turns they all

---

2. *Medaka* are small fish that have been a favorite research animal for Japanese scientists.

turn. Neither theory nor logic nor ethics underlies or informs Japanese behaviour. Quite simply, a Japanese looks around and does what others are doing; that is the principle of action. That's why Japanese have trouble with theory, logic and ethics; they cannot argue or debate. Particularity, idiosyncrasy and individuality are hated and discouraged. That and Japanese environmental problems are closely related. (Honda, in Suzuki and Oiwa, 1996, p. 43)

There is a sense in which what Honda says is true. The group is experienced as within the self; oneself and the group are not distinct entities; the highest moral good does not rest in individual conscience but in the conscience of the group (Rosenberger, 1992). But it is only in Western binary forms of thought that this would be seen to rule out the existence of the individual as a moral being. In binary thought, "individual" and "group" take their meanings in opposition to each other and cannot easily be understood in concert. The individual may feel helpless in the face of the authoritarian rule of the emperor system and of Japanese institutional life. Who would not? But such helplessness can coexist with a strong moral knowledge that comes from being embedded in the group.

A person's capacity to affect or be affected are not determined solely by the body he or she is but also by everything which makes up the context in which that body is acted upon and acts. When the term "embodiment" is used in the context of Spinoza's thought it should be understood to refer not simply to an individual body but to the *total* affective context of that body. (Gatens, 1996, p. 131)

In each of the following two stories, the first by Hiroko and the second by Kaori, the presence of moral, aware persons, with a capacity to affect and be affected, who are intricately aware of their embeddedness in the context of family and community, can be strongly felt:

As Mie prefecture is blessed with marine resources, and as one of my father's hobbies was fishing, my parents often took my sister and me to the sea. So in my house, there are many pictures of us with the sea in the background.

When we started to drive, the sky was still dark. Sometimes we could even see the moon and stars clearly in the sky, and the air was a little cool even though it was in summer. My parents always told us to go to bed early, so that we didn't sleep in in the morning, but my sister and I couldn't sleep, because of excitement. I just couldn't stay in one place quietly. Those nights were so special for me because I could stay up late with my parents who were doing things at midnight—that was so very interesting to me. I felt that I could see another world. So finally, we gave up on sleep, and began checking my clothes, sun cream, hats, towels, snacks to bring, and everything, again and again, and then went down to the ground floor. My parents were still awake, my father was checking fishing rods, hooks, reels, lines, and sinkers sitting in front of the closet, which I really loved.

The closet was placed at the very corner of my house. The door always opened with a creak, and when I opened the door, the air inside the door always smelled like the sea. While my father was working, I sometimes opened the door, and saw his fishing tackle, touched them, and played with them. I just really loved to do that.

However, my mother was making obentou *(Japanese lunch) and cold tea, and packing everything we needed to spend a whole day under the strong sunshine. While my parents were talking about the weather, I always worried. They listened to the weather forecast on the radio and special phone line, but it was sometimes wrong.*

The final decision was always given by my father. He went outside for some time, then came back into the house. He sometimes told us we won't go fishing that day, even though the sky had nothing wrong that I could see. Of course I was really really looking forward to going, so I tried to change my father's decision. But even if I won, and we went to the sea, it was always going to rain, or the sea was rough. My father's weather forecast was so accurate.

On the way to the sea, my sister and I were always singing many songs in the car, so we didn't need to turn the car radio on. We just couldn't sit down quietly. We stopped at the same old fishing-tackle store, and bought some different kinds of lug worms, small shrimps, and some ice. My father and the shop owner were friends, so he often gave us a discount. He was old, but his skin color was healthy dark and looked so brave and strong. While my mother and my sister were eating ice cream outside the shop, having a rest, my father was talking with his old friend, getting and exchanging new information about fishing and secret spots. I was listening beside him, or looking around inside the old shop. It wasn't a big shop but it had a very nice atmosphere and air. The small lug worms were so cute, but I felt a little bit sad when I imagined that we would use them only as bait. The sky's color was getting light grey or soft blue by then, but the wind was still carrying early morning air.

I personally don't prefer air conditioners. I always opened the window of the car. When we tired from singing, I watched outside. I liked the feeling, when I stuck my face out of the window, and felt the fast wind. It was so fast I sometimes felt my hair might be all gone when the car stopped. When I could catch and smell the sea wind, I started getting excited again. Waiting waiting and waiting to see the sea from the car, and from the mountain. Then the sea appeared. All of us gave a shout for joy, then said, "We have come back here again."

By the time we reached the fishing place, the sun had completely appeared, and was getting brighter and hotter. My father preferred offshore fishing, however, my mother is a bad sailor. So we often used a raft. My mother and my sister couldn't bait a hook with lug worms, so it was my father's and my job and I was really proud of that. The raft was moving along the wave very slowly and I wished I could cut the rope and go somewhere from there.

On the raft, there was no way to hide from the sunshine. So I wore a hat, and a towel was around my neck. As my father knew the spot, we could catch

*many fish. Time flows very slowly on a raft. I could hear only the sound of
calm waves and waves breaking against the raft, a seagull's singing, and
sounds from the mountain. We ate my mother's special lunch on the raft, took
a little nap, and fished again. That's all we could do on the raft, but I never
got bored. I was really satisfied.*

*When we caught a little young fish, my father always told us to return them
into the sea and also if we already had enough fish to eat, then we should stop
fishing, or if we caught them just for fun, we should also return them into the
sea. I was little, but I could understand why he said so.*

*The sky color was turning to beautiful orange and red, then slowly getting
dark. On the way back home, I was very tired, but happy. The car window was
still opened. I didn't feel fast wind, but little warm and slow. Finally, I shut the
window as less noise was heard from the outside if I did so. Then I slept deeply
in the car.*

*My father's way of eating fish is amazingly beautiful. According to him,
when we eat animals, we shouldn't leave anything as far as possible. That's the
way to respect and to show our gratitude to other animals that we killed.*

*Before or after we had those great fish, my mother always gave some of the
fish to our neighbors, and our cousins. My father's parents' house often gave us
rice and vegetables as they had a large rice field, and a garden. My mother's
sister's house often gave us many different fruits, as they were working at a big
market. My cousin's home always gave us meat, when my sister or I came back
to my home. My mother told me it was because when her husband went to
Saudi Arabia for his job, only my family wrote a letter and sent him a box of
Japanese food and she still remembers that, so she always gave us something
when someone in my family came back. My mother often told me how important it is to keep good relationships with neighbors.*

Then, all of us were really tired, so everyone could go to bed early this time.

Hiroko's story of going to the sea has the same beautiful attention
to small details as her earlier stories of going to the abacus and calligraphy schools. We can see the small child at the cupboard with the
fishing tackle, in the small shop peering with excitement at the lug
worms or gazing at the dark face of the old, brave, strong shopkeeper.
We can imagine, with her, the feeling of all our hair blown off, see
the color of the sky changing, feel the wind carrying the early morning air, and feel the excitement of the first glimpse of the sea. We feel
the authority of her father and his knowledge of the weather and the
sea but also the energy of the small child refusing to sleep and resist-
ing his reading of the skies. We can feel the pride of the small child
who can thread lug worms on hooks when her sister and mother cannot, and we feel her sadness at the same time for the poor lug
worms. This is a story of self experienced and moral understanding
gained through the day at the sea. The child sees and smells and feels
the details of her landscape at home and at the sea, and on the trip
in between. She hears and understands the importance of returning

small fish to the sea, of eating fish beautifully to show them respect and gratitude, and of giving gifts to those people who are members of her community and are generous in their turn. The outburst from the journalist, Honda, seems extreme and superficial in its understanding of the Japanese sense of self and place when held against this beautiful moral tale. Honda tells us the impenetrable surface story of one aspect of the Japanese sense of self in landscape—a *medaka* in the sea—whereas Hiroko takes us inside to the detailed physical, emotional, and moral sense of her embodiment in landscape when her family went fishing at the seaside.

In case Hiroko's experience should be taken as marking her off from other Japanese people, I include Kaori's stories of her father in each of the four seasons. Unlike Seiji, Hiroko, and Masako, Kaori was from Hokkaido, where the landscape and the climate are different from Honshu. Masako and Hiroko listened with amazement and delight to Kaori's stories because they had never heard of many of the things she talked of; she confirmed and disrupted, at the same time, their belief that all Japanese are the same:

Hokkaido has four distinct seasons; spring, summer, autumn, and winter.

In spring in Hokkaido, between March and June, it is still cold, sometimes we have snow even in May. My father always feels spring is coming earlier than any other families do.

One day when it was warm, he went to the mountain near my house. There was some snow left even though it was spring. I used to go with him, rather, he often took my younger brother, sister, and me to the mountains and river. The reason we went to the mountains was to look for wasabi (a horseradish) and sansai *(a kind of plant). We walked up the path pushing aside the bamboo bushes. It was very hard to walk through them because I was much shorter than them. My father was going ahead as if he knew the way to exit the bush. We were following him desperately. I was often wondering whether I might get lost and die. However, we never did got lost in the mountains. My father might have known everything about mountains. We came out from the bush at last. There was a marshland in front of us. I could see a stream and some plants along the stream. The sunshine came through the trees above us. A comfortable wind was blowing. My father stretched and began walking again.*

We followed him. I tried to find something that my father would be happy with, but I couldn't find anything. I just picked some flowers. My father was walking slowly and then he stooped down to pick up some sansai *which was covered with weeds. He told us that he picked them there last year as well. After a while, I felt thirsty and so did my brother and sister. We didn't have anything to drink. So my father suggested to me that we drink the water from the stream. I hesitated to do so at the time, but he was drinking the water without any hesitation. I drank a little. It was so nice, much better than tap water. He also showed us a plant that looked like a green bar. He peeled it and gave it to me to eat. I took a bite of it. The taste was similar to a lemon or grapefruit but I* can't remember the name. He didn't pick too many of them. He left small ones for the next time. He did the same as the animals. Animals only eat what they need. My father knew what we should do with nature to keep it rich. Actually, the marshland which we visited has never been damaged by human beings. According to my father, people who often visit the mountains to pick plants for themselves never tell others where to find them. He said that it was a rule of the mountains among people who love nature. On the way home, we picked the leaves of dandelions to eat for dinner.

Summer in Hokkaido is very short and it isn't hot compared to summer in Honshu.

One day when it was very hot, my father took us to the river to go fishing. The river was not deep enough for us to play there. My father was fishing for a while but he didn't catch any fish until that evening. We were getting bored just playing by the river. He then got into the river and walked to the opposite bank holding a net. He called us quietly to come there. He told us to hold the net near the big stone and we didn't know what was going to happen. As soon as he moved the big stone, lots of dojo (loaches) rushed into the net. We were so excited and we tried to do the same thing but it was very hard. My father then cooked dojo for dinner.

In autumn, it is getting cooler. The color of the mountains was changing to yellow. We were going to go home from the next town. One day, while he was driving a car, he sometimes glanced at the mountain just beside the road. He muttered to himself, "some mushrooms . . . ," and then parked the car around there. He went toward the mountain. He knew that the mountain had lots of trees for mushrooms. Actually, there were many kinds of mushrooms in the mountain. It is very difficult to distinguish which mushrooms can be eaten. But he could do it. He smelt them and checked their colors and he worked out which to eat.

Before I was born, my father and mother went to the mountain one day in autumn. My mother was pregnant, with me. It was nearly time to give birth to me. He didn't worry about that very much. So he took her to the mountain to pick mushrooms.

After a while, in the mountain, my mother felt labor starting. My father stopped picking mushrooms and took her to the hospital. She entered hospital from that day and I was born a few days later.

We had much snow in winter, especially in my home town. When I was an elementary school student, we went to the foot of a mountain at midnight at the end of the year. It was like a special event for children. My father told us about this event. My father and my cousins and I left our home at midnight. We walked for a while. Nobody was on the street. It was snowing quietly. There was no sound except our breathing around us. It was absolutely dark. Our feet sank into the deep snow. We took some oranges and a shovel. We stopped at a place which had nothing but snow. The snow was grey because of darkness but sometimes shone, soaked in the moonlight. We started to make a kamakura (a snow house). It took a long time to make it. He told us inside of the kamakura was much warmer than outside. We ate oranges inside after we made the kamakura.

He always says, "I will become sen-nin *(a hermit) and live in the mountain." I think he could do it.*

*He keeps his routine life, he gets up at the same time every morning. He goes
to work at the same time. He sometimes brings injured doves or owls. On the
other hand, he kills mice which live in my house to keep our house. And then
he tells us the proverb, "The house with mice is a good house. When the mice
are gone, the house will be taken by fire or some catastrophe will happen to the
house."*

We see in Kaori's story the now familiar embedding of being in the
movement of the seasons. She takes us to the mountains to taste fresh
snow or spring water and tells of the excitement of catching loaches.
We are amazed with her at the cleverness of her father in knowing
where the mushrooms are and which trees they grow under. And in
winter we hear the silence of the nighttime snowscape where only the
breath is audible. And again there are moral elements to each step of
the story. Do not take more than you need, value landscapes that
have not been damaged by humans, and understand the importance of
caring for doves and owls.

When our meetings ended, each student wrote a reflection or a letter on what the group's meetings had meant to them. I end this chapter with the letter written by Kaori from her heart:

Dear Professor Davies,

*It was a great time for me to talk with you about Japanese culture and
many ideas. For me, it was very difficult to tell you my ideas in appropriate
English. However, you listened to my poor English carefully and generously.
Also, this session was very helpful to develop my English and also my behavior
as a Japanese person. Thank you very much for giving me such a nice opportunity. Before I came to Australia, I felt uneasy that I am Japanese. I thought
many people had different prejudices against Japanese people, so I was not
proud of myself in terms of my nationality. Moreover, I had never thought how
Japanese people behave and think through their lives. Through these workshops,
I found that you really understand Japanese culture and Japanese ideas. I was
very happy at meeting such a nice person. I could experience precious time with
you. This experience cannot be given anywhere else.*

*To tell my country's culture is more difficult than telling another culture. I
should understand Japanese culture and then other countries' cultures. When I
become an English teacher in Japan, this is very important, I guess. I didn't
know what Japanese culture is before you pointed out different ideas between
Australian and Japanese people. We have different ideas amongst Japanese people but we have many common ideas and customs as well. My home town is in
Hokkaido, and I found gaps between Masako, Hiroko and me. At the same
time, I realized I had believed that we Japanese people had the same ideas and
opinions. While I was listening to their stories, I found new customs I had never
experienced in my life. It was very interesting.*

I should apologize to you that I might not be helpful for your researches, but please let me help your researches even after I go back to Japan. I can send you real Japanese ideas and original things from Hokkaido, Japan. If you have time to visit Hokkaido again, I have to take you to the mountains with my father. I miss my home town with its rich nature. I can tell you many stories about Hokkaido and Japan.

I will never forget your kindness and smiling face. Thank you very much for everything.

Yours sincerely,

Kaori Tanaka

And so...

Kaori's letter touches on some important points about this collective memory work and my part in it. Unlike when I worked with the Australian students, I did not have a taken-for-granted knowledge of the language and culture that could allow me to find clichés in the students' writing and work beyond them. But through careful listening and reading, I could work with them beyond the clichéd assumptions of Japan as a *medaka* society in which the individual is totally submerged in the group. I did not do this through contradicting their knowledge (which I was in no position to do), but through careful listening and questioning and through the development of strategies for talking and writing that enabled previously unexpressed detail to be spoken, written, and examined. Through engaging in activities they had not previously imagined possible, they discovered ways of writing in the workshop and ways of experiencing themselves in detail outside some of the clichéd descriptions of Japanese society. And I, in listening to them, felt that I came to see beneath the polished surface of the official versions of what it means to be Japanese. Of course, a sense of oneself as having done so must always be treated with caution, and so I took great pleasure in Kaori's statement that I had seemed to her to "really understand Japanese culture and Japanese ideas."

In the Japanese education system, appropriate embodiment is explicitly taught and learned, and with it comes a secure sense of belonging. The longing does not need to be emphasized here, as belonging is not ever in question. The illusion of freedom, such as the one given to me at the beginning of my writing lesson (which was actually a lesson about correct embodiment), is not offered. The individual is given to understand that it is only through disciplined attention to the details of the culture that their own spirit can be expressed. Japanese language and poetry have a long history of connection to and telling of Japanese landscapes and of embodied being with/in them. Through learning the poetry and the literature one becomes embodied as Japanese. But there have been significant disruptions, such as the questioning of the emperor system, of the oppression of the Ainu people, and, of course, World War II. And, perhaps significantly, a change in patterns of living, which means that small children tend to experience only the controlled landscapes of interiors. There are glimpses of these changes in the stories in this chapter. Their effect on understandings of body/landscape relations will be further explored in Chapter 6. But first, I will take you with me on my journey with/in Japanese landscapes, and tell you my faltering attempts to embody myself in those landscapes, in terms of my sensual experience of being there, but also in terms of my taking up, to the extent that that is possible, some of the Japanese concepts relevant to body/landscape relations. At the same time, I examine how my experiences there enabled me to unfold and look again at old (now newly strange) sedimented knowledges of embodiment. This next chapter is almost entirely taken from the journals I wrote while traveling in Japan.

Muffled in white breath—
voice of the
heart.

Koko Kato
(Lowitz, Aoyama, and Tomioka, 1994, p. 68)

~5~ Traveling in Japan

Part 1 Honshu

The first part of my journey in Japan was on the island of Honshu. My plan was to join Masako's family in Hamamatsu for the kite festival, followed by some solitary explorations of the ancient cities of Nara and Kyoto. Then I would travel to the northern island of Hokkaido to meet up with Professor Osanai and his colleagues and begin to interview people with an interest in environmental issues. My travels in Hokkaido are included in Part 2 of this chapter, and the interviews in Hokkaido appear in Chapter 6.

As I set out, two related concepts that I had come across in my reading were keys that I used in my search for embodiment in Japanese landscapes. These were *wabi* and *sabi*, two concepts often run together as one (*wabi-sabi*). I had talked to my collective biography group about these concepts and, as Koren (1994, p. 15) would predict, they agreed they were important concepts for understanding Japanese embodiment with/in landscape, but they could not easily define them. Seiji, as an environmentalist, did not see them as relevant to the experience of "nature," but only to special historical buildings. What Seiji made clear was that while I might be searching out a particular Japanese way of seeing, which was probably not available to me as a speaker of English in Australian landscapes, it was not a concept that informed every Japanese person's way of seeing. In providing the formal definitions, then, and in describing my search for the embodied experience of them, I am clear at the outset that it would be a serious error to think of the concepts as essential to any Japanese person's experience of landscape. The concepts, rather, give me no more than a point of entry, an imaginary line into (be)longing in Japanese landscapes.

Wabi, according to an authoritative encyclopedia, is defined as "an aesthetic and moral principle advocating the enjoyment of a quiet and leisurely life free from worldly concerns. . . . [I]t emphasises a simple, austere type of beauty and a serene transcendental state of mind" (*Kodansya International*, 1998, pp. 514–15). Although the concept was originally related to the idea of loneliness and lack of comfort, it was later developed as "making poverty and loneliness synonymous with liberation from material and emotional worries and by turning the absence of apparent beauty into a new and higher beauty" (p. 515). In its incorporation in the tea ceremony, the tea ceremony masters associated it with the spirit of Zen and stressed the importance of "seeking richness in poverty and beauty in simplicity." The essence of *wabi,* according to the encyclopedia (p. 517) is found in this poem:

I see neither cherry blossoms
Nor tinted leaves:
Only a modest hut on the coast
In the dusk of autumn nightfall

What the words of this poem, in particular, evoke for me is the kind of attention to detail that I and the students had sought in the collective biography workshops. The emphasis is away from romanticized landscapes and from spectacular and orchestrated cultural happenings, and dwells instead on a simple, detailed moment of seeing.

Sabi emphasizes loneliness or aloneness. It "points toward a medieval aesthetic combining elements of old age, loneliness, resignation and tranquillity" (p. 516). *Sabi* is also related to the tea ceremony and to poetry. "Underlying this aesthetic was the cosmic view typical of medieval Buddhists, who recognised the existential loneliness of all men and tried to resign themselves to, or even find beauty in, that loneliness" (p. 517). The following poem, which is given as an example of *sabi,* was written by Basho (p. 517):

Two blossom-watchmen
With their white heads together
Having a chat

In both *wabi* and *sabi* the landscape is central to the meaning given to human existence, but it is not a landscape empty of people—rather, the one who sees, and those who are seen, are not left out of the lifescape created in the words. The watchmen can be imagined because both the reader and the poet have watched the movement of blossoms in spring: the hut in the autumn dusk can be imagined in its simple outlines because we know the moment of color disappearing at nightfall.

In the stories that follow, of my travels through Japan, the elusiveness of *wabi* and *sabi* becomes more and more evident as I struggle to learn the communal nature of embodiment in Japanese landscapes. Although the Japanese people I talked to tended to agree that *wabi* and *sabi* are central concepts in understanding Japanese body/landscape relations, they did not appear to seek out such experiences in the course of their everyday lives, nor did they seem to imagine that I might want to do so. Such experiences tend to be seen to belong more in the lives of poets, and to be associated with reading their poems, or in special practices such as the tea ceremony, rather than in the life of a visiting professor of education who is interested in environmental issues. The years of disciplined education, such as that

described by Hiroko in her calligraphy class, and the repeated partici-
pation in cultural events such as the *Matsuri* festival described by
Masako, make possible an embodied knowledge that I can never
share. They are appropriate(d) beings within their culture. And while I
can *long*, I cannot *belong*. In what follows, I explore the embodied
experience of traveling in landscapes unknown to me, with all my
senses open to what I find there, with the hope of learning to experience, in an embodied way, the knowledge I had begun to glean from
novelists and other writers, and that the students had revealed in their
stories of childhood. The concepts I set out with I regarded as conceptual buds, as primitive folds in my consciousness that might unfurl
a little if only I were patient enough.

Hamamatsu

My first stop in Japan was Hamamatsu, where I was to attend the kite
festival. Masako had recommended this as the best introduction to
Japan. She had arranged for Keiko, her sister, and Iguchi-san, her aunt,
to meet me at the airport in Tokyo and for Keiko to take me to
Hamamatsu. My first immersion in Japan, then, cared for, first of all,
by Iguchi-san and Keiko, and then by the Onoda and Suzuki families,
was of secure connectedness and belonging. When we were finally
installed on the fast train to Hamamatsu, I was so exhausted I immediately fell asleep, as I had just traveled from Sweden and lost the eight
hours that would have been nighttime. As a result, I missed seeing Mt.
Fuji and so missed the first opportunity to have an important Japanese
experience.

Keiko and I walked to the hotel, which was close by, and checked
in and Keiko left me to rest. Three hours later, in the lobby to meet
me were Masako's parents and Keiko and Mrs. Asano, who was our
interpreter and a friend of the family. I managed all my greetings in
Japanese and we went out to a Japanese restaurant. The food was
exquisite, as was the wine, but I was completely overwhelmed by the
amount of it all. We sat around a long Japanese-style low table.
Onoda-san (Masako's father) called out instructions to the waiter to
bring more and more and more food and wine. Three different glasses
of wine were placed in front of me to see which I liked and I was
the center of attention as they instructed me to try each different kind
of food. They were generously approving of my dexterity with chopsticks (and of the Japanese I had managed to learn). As I took each
mouthful of each new dish (e.g., raw cuttlefish, raw cuttlefish eggs,
raw beef (!)) and my face registered surprise or amazement or pleasure, they all laughed with amused delight. But I was anxious about
having to eat so much. I think Onoda-san might have read my hesitation as not liking the food—because we then went on to a sushi bar,
where he ordered vast quantities of food again—a whole crab, freshly

caught and cooked, miso soup, and I can't remember what else. Overwhelmed by jet lag I was finally taken back to the hotel to sleep.

Next day Mrs. Asano (who is Taiwanese) and Keiko picked me up to take me to dinner. Because we were not due at the Suzuki household until six o'clock, I was taken out to experience Japanese afternoon tea at a restaurant. This included fruit, pickles, and bean soup, and green tea. I now knew I was in trouble again. I couldn't eat it all, and we were on our way to dinner and I'd already eaten enough. Looking around the coffee shop I noticed there were mostly elegantly dressed Japanese women. They all left a large amount on their plates. My belief that I should eat food to show appreciation of it seemed oddly out of place.

When we came out of the restaurant Onoda-san was there in his car to take us to the Suzuki home. We drove down a maze of winding streets, so narrow I could not believe they were two-way streets. The houses were side by side with no garden between, yet each house seemed to have found spaces to grow pots of flowers and trees. The Suzuki house was exquisite in its attention to detail of wood and tile and screens and tatami mats—a beautiful example of architectural simplicity inspired by the principles of *wabi*. When I took my shoes off at the door, I made the awkward mistake of putting my foot down on the entry floor instead of the tatami mat, but I was being watched attentively and was gently and politely shown how to behave. I felt like an oversize baby learning, through the careful attention of others, how to organize my body correctly.

[In Zen practice] the body, not language, is the repository of knowledge and technique. (Koren, 1994, p. 81)

Once in my stockinged feet I was taken to the dining room. A large Japanese table filled the room, with tatami mat floor and cushions for sitting on. I sat in correct Japanese style but was told that was too difficult for me and I should not try to do so. The table was laden with food. Onoda-san's eighty-three-year-old mother was there, his brother, his brother's wife, his niece, his wife, and his daughter Keiko. Mrs. Asano was there to translate. Again I was given sake and beer and wine all at once and plied with vast quantities of food. Again my reaction to each mouthful was the center of attention. The food was prepared with loving attention to the aesthetics of taste and sight. We began with cold food and then moved on to food cooked at the table. At one point Suzuki-san's best friend rang to gain permission to visit briefly. This was against the rules regarding the recent death of the grandfather, but he had prepared a special dish for me and wanted to come and present it. He arrived amongst much joy and laughter and placed his dish of a whole raw fish in the center of the table and sat down to join us. He and Suzuki-san were both dressed for the festival, which was to take place that evening.

In preparation for my joining in the festival I was presented with a *happi*, a special coat for the ceremony, with the special signs and color of the Suzuki's community group and a number to indicate that the *happi* had been properly paid for. I was also presented with a new *happi* of my own that was the special *happi* for outsiders, and they dressed me up in it for the dinner (headdress and all). I then presented them each with the hand-painted scarves I had brought from Australia, which they seemed to like very much. As the dinner progressed and I relaxed, I said how much I liked to see the grandmother as part of the family. I explained how Australian grandmothers often live alone, as my mother had, and that it was so much nicer to see her amongst and loved by her family. She was so happy with my speech that she came around and sat next to me to have a photo taken with me, wearing the scarf I had given her. We established that if my mother was alive she would be the same age—eighty-three—and the grandmother shook my hand for a long time and looked into my eyes, and everyone laughed and clapped and told me she was now happy. For the last weeks she had been grieving very deeply for her husband, and had scarcely ceased from crying. She was very beautiful—silver hair cut short and smooth brown skin—she looked so much younger than my mother—except when she stood up to walk she was bent right over.

Later I was dressed in the local community's *happi* and taken out into the narrow street to wait for the community troupe that would be passing by. Each troupe, consisting of about forty people, moves in a prearranged pattern through its own community, tramping along with small marching steps and beating tin drums and blowing tin whistles. We waited with eager anticipation for them to arrive, sometimes hearing the noise of another community's troupe and thinking it might be ours. When they finally appeared in our street, they stopped near us and Suzuki-san's friend pulled me into the throng, holding me tight and showing me what to do, how to move, how to crush into the circle, how to stamp my feet, raise the lantern, and shout out the words of celebration. *Yoisho!* One part of the group chants one word and the other part replies with another. Then the group marched on and we visited a neighboring family who offered us green tea and special festival sweets.

Later we walked to one of the many houses where there was a new son to be welcomed into the world by the community troupe. Gathered around in the street outside the house, members of the community who were not in the troupe were waiting for them to arrive. Each family with a son knew exactly what time the troupe would arrive at their house. They had prepared an enormous feast. There was a wooden cask full of sake, which smelled and tasted of the wood, a beautiful smell, and vast quantities of food. When the troupe arrived I was again drawn into it by Suzuki-san and his friend. This time the troupe surrounded the baby, who was held high by his proud parents, and we stamped and sang and shouted and beat drums and blew whistles in a frenzy of energy. The parents looked ecstatic as they held their baby up high and we celebrated his existence. We all then sat on the street and ate and drank (more!) and talked. The community seemed very happy to include me, and those who could speak English came to talk to me. It felt very good to be there. The food was beautiful, the family was happy, and I experienced being part of a community in a way I could not have imagined, even at home. I managed to relax and eat, sitting out there in the street in the cool, dark, lantern-lit, people-filled night, my body finally finding its way to join in the excess and the collective excitement of this first night of the festival.

The next day was the kite-flying ceremony. I was to be dressed in all the right *happi* and footwear, which would allow me to participate as a member of the community. For each son born in the preceding year, a kite must be flown and it must fly high if he is to be healthy. The kites are huge and take about six men to carry them and are anchored by a thick rope on a reel like a lifesaver's reel. At the kite-flying site there were hundreds of thousands of people. Each community was dressed in its own colors with its own signs. There were 170 communities. Because of the crowds, communities with small children often walked along with a rope held by two adults to which the children could hold on so they did not get lost. There were lots of stalls selling food freshly cooked on the site. Each team had four different sizes of kite, allowing them to choose the right one for the particular wind conditions. There was a lot of excitement but it was a dull, cloud-covered day and there was not enough wind. The kites would get up so far and then crash down. When it is windy the kites often get tangled in the sky and a battle ensues as to who should give way, each kite pushing against the other to see who is the strongest. Since it is often the case that neither will give way, policemen are on duty on a high stand ready to arbitrate when the dispute cannot be settled by the kite flyers.

We had a picnic lunch under the trees—the men had hangovers and were drinking already. They pointed out to me that it is only on holidays like this that they drink so much. When it was time to leave the kite ceremony, they were going to take me back to my hotel but as luck would have it I had left my hotel key in my bag at the Suzuki house, not understanding the arrangements. So I was taken back there, where the whole family was gathered for the Buddhist ceremony for the departed grandfather. I was left in the kitchen with Mrs. Asano, who explained to me that each week for seven weeks the priest comes to the house and a ceremony is held to help the grandfather on his way to Buddhist paradise. The ceremony is strictly a family-only ceremony, but Mrs. Asano suggested I would be allowed to look from the doorway. Quietly and as unobtrusively as possible, we went to the door, and the decision was quietly taken to welcome me in.

The priest was kneeling down before the bright glittering shrine to the grandfather and the family was seated on the floor in a circle around the room. The priest was dressed in spectacular robes and chanted a long sutra, which he read from a small white book, turning the pages from left to right. He punctuated his chanting with notes struck from a metal bowl on the shrine. In his hands he held a string of wooden beads that he rubbed together. I watched and listened to this extraordinary event, electrified. It seemed so far outside of anything I had ever imagined. My body was painfully tense, and so I shut my eyes and took a deep breath, and listened. To my amazement, the sounds of the sutra were suddenly uncannily familiar: I could have been listening to an old Aboriginal man singing in the vast and open landscapes of the desert. What had seemed distant and strange was suddenly strangely familiar. Boundaries marking off Japan from the West and from indigenous Australia dissolved as I sat there and listened. How many hundreds of years ago had connections been made that were now lost to conscious knowledge? And were these connections peculiar only to my hearing of them, or might others hear the same thing?

When the priest was finished, each member of the family went to the shrine and lit an incense stick from a candle, hit the bowl to make it chime, bowed with hands in prayer position to the image of the grandfather, and then left. Onoda-san showed me what to do. Later it was decided that I had legitimately participated in Masako's place.

At night we went out to look at the procession of huge carved wooden floats, or *dashi*. Each *dashi* is pulled along by a team of men. The intricate carvings on each of the floats were very beautiful. There are 170 floats—one for each community. Everyone in the community is expected to contribute to the cost of their float. Each community vies with the others to make their float more beautiful. One man told us his float had cost a billion yen—equivalent to the cost of three houses. Each float has a band of small girls in it who play drums and Japanese violins, or *shamisen*. They follow a prearranged pattern through the streets. Each is lit up with lanterns and the effect is spectacular.

There were huge crowds milling about, looking at the floats. There came a point when we needed to go underground to cross the street (Onoda-san, Mrs. Asano, Keiko, and me). There were hundreds of people coming out of the narrow underground walkway and hundreds wanting to go in. Instead of one lot giving way to the other, each group milled closely together and slowly pushed forward inch by inch. This was done calmly and patiently and was reminiscent of the troupe last night, when the point was to push a group of bodies very closely together and to move together. It was also reminiscent of the kite war—the force of one kite against another with neither willing to give way. If I had not participated in the ceremonies I would have found the milling at the underground tunnel incomprehensible. As it was, I joined in quite happily, waiting to see what happened, and eventually the people coming out got through and we could then move in. A new boundary between self and other to be learned.

Finally I collapsed into bed but did not sleep much as I was anxious about taking off on my own to Nara the next day, leaving the security of this wonderful hospitable family and the generous support of Mrs. Asano. Keiko and Masako's mother and father took me to the station to see me off. Onoda-san taught me to ask where things are in case I got lost and wrote the question in Japanese on a card so I could show it if I needed help and couldn't say the right words. He also bought me some lunch to have on the train. He showed me how to find the platform and carefully counted the stops so I would know that Kyoto was the sixth stop. He then made me rehearse the words for changing train lines to Nara so I would be able to make my way competently to my next destination. I felt very sad to wave goodbye to them and be off on my own solitary search for the experience of *wabi* and *sabi*.

Nara

From the train window I saw beautiful hills covered in forests but with huge powerlines criss-crossing them. If the Japanese have a love affair with technology, perhaps the powerlines are not a defiling of the countryside as Alex Kerr (1996) suggests but a sign that electric power can be taken everywhere. There were many towns, always uniformly the soft grey-brown colors of natural wood, and there were small farms—vegetable gardens and rice paddies interspersed with houses. The boundaries between city and countryside, between farm and countryside, between house and farm, were, to my eyes, haphazard and chaotic. The boundaries I expected to be able to identify, to make the landscape describable, were not there. This seemed in strange contrast to the tight boundary between the inside and the outside of each individual house marked by the ritual taking off and putting on of shoes.

My first experience of Nara was to get lost looking for the hotel. The map I had from Masako seemed completely wrong and the map I got from the information desk at the train station unclear. I headed off in the wrong direction, dragging my heavy luggage, crammed full of books, behind me. Finally, with some help from a young woman, I got back on track, arrived at the hotel, hot and flushed, only to be told I couldn't check in until one o'clock. But the bus tour on which Masako's mother had booked me left from the train station at 1:05. I was running out of time to catch the bus even without this delay, but the woman at the desk couldn't understand me. A porter discreetly handed me a cloth to wipe my sweating hands and face and explained he would look after my luggage. I rushed off to find the bus station.

More difficulties. I couldn't find the bus station. Nor had I been able to find a toilet in the train station that did not have a queue outside it. Eventually I found the bus station with only minutes to spare. I asked in my best Japanese where the toilet was, but no one seemed to understand me. The bus was due to go. I was in a panic. I found a toilet and rushed in. I rushed back out only to find I'd now lost my ticket. Panic. I had the whole bus station looking for my ticket. They made me another one. A man spoke to me in English and I started to calm down. I had behaved hysterically even by Australian standards. I seemed to myself grossly out of place in this highly controlled landscape.

I sat on the bus amongst all Japanese people and a Japanese tour guide spoke loudly on a microphone in Japanese the whole trip. My sense of alienation and not belonging grew as I failed to find my way into any sense of embodiment that would enable me to relax and enjoy what was happening. If *wabi* means lonely and without comfort, I was having a *wabi* experience, though at that point I could find no beauty in it. And since I did not feel resigned and tranquil, my experience was very far from *sabi*.

The Japanese tourists seemed to sit happily, receiving the never-ending flow of words from the guide speaking through her microphone. I tried to block out her words, to look out the window and see what was there, but the never-ending stream of sound drowned out any possibility of quiet contemplation. When we stopped at each site, she would gather us together and speak to us again, and then release us to look for ourselves for a short period of time. The Japanese tourists seemed to flow easily in and out of the passive and active mode, as we went from one site to another. They did not seem bothered by the fact that we had no time to settle anywhere, or to discover the particular feeling of each place. Even after we had visited the last site, the endless stream of talk continued, ending only when we finally arrived back at the bus station. My desire that she stop and leave me in peace seemed in marked contrast to the others, who applauded her with enthusiasm at the end of her talk.

I walked back to the hotel, exhausted, and didn't bother about dinner. I had blisters all over my feet, a sure sign that I had been unusually stressed. This had not been a good experience. I had several tickets for tours in Nara and Kyoto but I didn't think I would use them. There was no way I could organize my body to do the quick-regimented inspection of temple after temple that the Japanese tourists seemed to find both normal and enjoyable.

Next day I set out independently. I found the Hannyaji Temple Alex Kerr wrote about with its cosmos and cornflowers and sweet peas growing in wild profusion. It was hard to find, but I saw many interesting things as I walked through the streets searching for it and it was so peaceful to be there on my own, quietly taking it in. Also important to me was having a sense of where it was, because I'd walked there. I felt at home because the flowers were all the flowers I grew up with and had grown in my own gardens when I lived on the tablelands of New South Wales. I lit incense in one of the little shrines in the garden, chimed the bowl, and began to reclaim a sense of equilibrium that I'd lost the day before.

Another note about new boundaries to comprehend: Some of the little stone gods I saw had cloth aprons on. Some of the trees had ropes tied around them, seeming to signify something religious, and many trees had white paper hanging in them. The sacred tree or rock is not separated from that which is manufactured, but combined with it.

On the way back I saw how the wooden houses and old-style roofs are deteriorating and wondered at the cost of maintaining such places. Many houses have been rebuilt, reroofed in the old style but using new materials. Modern housing would be unthinkable here in this ancient and beautiful city. Kerr complains of the wooden houses being pulled down, but my impression was that they were, many of them, sagging and crumbling into the earth with their extreme old age. It is amazing that wooden houses have lasted so long. Apparently they are built from Japanese cypress, which somehow continues to live long after it has been cut down.

The day was incredibly hot and sunny and I did not have any cool clothes. I looked in the store for sandals—no such thing—or something light to wear, but the glittery clothes in the shop windows did not look like anything I could imagine wearing. I felt so conscious of my difference there.

In the evening it cooled down a little and so I went out for a walk. I walked around the lake, which is famous for having no known water that goes into or out of it. It reflects the beautiful golden five-story pagoda in the evening. It has more fire, they say, than water. Some people were feeding the turtles. Lovers strolled around the lake and others just sat and looked at the water, or the heron in the middle of the lake on a rock. I then walked up the long flight of steps to the five-story pagoda, which was lit up and looking more beautiful by night. I had come here on the tour and not really appreciated it at all. Now I heard a gong in the distance, which sounded beautiful, as if tranquil Buddhist priests were at work. After a while I strolled towards the sound. It was a small temple where incense was burning. Very quietly, people would come up to it, put some money in the box, beat the gong, and pray for a minute or so. There was a man, a priest I think, reading in a softly lit room nearby. The place for washing your hands and face had water spouting out of a dragon's mouth and spilling into a stone trough. There were brass ladles for catching the water to wash yourself.

I stood for a long while watching the people coming to pray here. It seemed so simple and so peaceful. I wanted to try it for myself, to see how it felt to wash at the dragon's mouth and to pray at the temple. I was afraid it would feel like a superficial, self-conscious gesture, and that no matter how carefully I had watched I was bound to get it wrong. Eventually I gathered together my courage. With some hesitation, I put some money in the box and carefully rang the gong. It was a very tranquil, gentle sound. I was alone, and yet, in following the ritual, I felt not alone, but imagined myself connected to people carrying out similar acts through the centuries. The cool water from the dragon's mouth, the sound of the gong, the feeling of tranquility as I bowed my head seemed so simple and yet so beautiful.

Alone before the shrine
In the soft evening air
The gong chimes softly. (BD)

Strangely, when I went back next morning to take a photo of it, it was not the same place at all. Even at eight in the morning, noisy tourists (Japanese) were throwing money in and clanging the gong and praying for two seconds. Some businessmen on their way to work did the same thing. It appeared to be an empty ritual—though presumably not to them. What would it be like, I wondered, to pause each morning on the way to work at such a beautiful temple, even if only for a few seconds?

Kyoto

In Kyoto I stayed at the Three Sisters' Inn, a Japanese-style inn catering specifically to Westerners and run by three sisters. I was surrounded by rules and regulations. There were authoritarian notices everywhere about what I could and could not do even in the shower recess. Interestingly, there was no notice about all the rules with shoes—it was assumed the guests knew that. I was forbidden to do washing, though I was allowed to wear my Japanese dressing gown, or *yukata,* to breakfast. I must turn on the taps in the shower exactly as instructed (though neither I nor any of the guests I spoke to could get the showers to work properly). I must not place my bag on the quilt cover; I must not soil the futon or else I will pay half the price of a new one; I must not let children jump on the floor.

When I arrived, hot and sweaty, exhausted as usual by the transfer from one location to another, the sister who greeted me was very disapproving of my plans. She disapproved of the fact that I had made my own plans (well, actually, Masako's mother had made my plans) and especially disapproving of the day's taxi hire with an

English-speaking driver. She gave me a map of the local area and instructed me to go for a walk, showing me which routes to follow. It was 12:30 when I arrived and check-in time was not until three, but miraculously I was allowed in early. So I unpacked and took off on my walk as instructed, abandoning my organized tour. I had been given many maps of Kyoto before arriving. I had studied each carefully but could not make much sense of them. The streets are rarely named and the patterns of streets on each map seem entirely different. The Three Sisters' map of their area was different again. Within minutes of setting out, I found that the map bore no resemblance that I could find to where I was walking. With no street names to guide me, and no recognizable pattern of streets, and no way of telling what counted as a street to be placed on the map, I soon decided I could only cope if I accepted the fact that I was lost and did not worry about it.

I thought of the passage in Kenzaburo Oe's book *A Personal Matter* in which the central characters drive around the city and keep getting lost:

> For a full fifty minutes now they had been making a grand tour around the same hollow. They had driven up and down hills, crossed a winding, muddy river any number of times, blundered down blind alleys, emerged again and again on the wrong side of one of the steep slopes that rose out of the valley to the north and south. . . . [When they descended] into the crowded hollow with its maze of narrow streets . . . it would become impossible to say with any certainty even which direction they were heading. (Oe, 1969, pp. 153–54)

I hadn't understood when I read this why the author had described getting lost in such detail, and I had thought it rather improbable. But as I accepted the inevitability of getting lost I wondered if getting lost is somehow integral to the experience of Japanese body/landscape relations.

The Kyoto streets were also narrow and winding and branched off endlessly. I came, unexpectedly, by the side of one of these roads, to a stone wall in front of which were round stones, each about twelve or fifteen inches high, and each with a red apron tied around it. In front of them was a stone pot, and the roots of an old dead tree with small stones placed on it. It seemed a sad place, somehow neglected. I gazed for a long time trying to comprehend what such a place might be.

Eventually I found myself right at the edge of the city and able to walk, through shrines, into the mountains. The most exciting find was a small forest with pathways of torii gates leading into the hillside. The feeling of the hills was very much like Australian rain forests but there were also maple trees and azaleas and of course many other trees I didn't recognize. It was misty and the ground was a carpet of leaves and the light shone through the canopy of leaves into a cool, tranquil, shady place. There were seats to sit on, so it was possible to rest and contemplate. I found a pond surrounded by trees and with huge carp in it. A spurt of water came from an invisible source in the canopy of leaves and dropped into a hollow bamboo pipe suspended upright above the surface of the pond. The pipe filled up with water, making a long, deep, hollow sound, and then tipped over, pouring the water into the pond with a softer, faster, splashing sound. Once empty, the pipe then tipped back, with a *"chock"* sound of empty bamboo pipe, and, after a brief pause, filled with more water. It was hypnotic watching it and listening to it slowly repeating its rhythm, slow, faster, fast, stop. Time stopped while I sat in this place. Nothing else mattered, except the pleasure of finding somewhere so peaceful, where I could sit with no thought of anything, just aware of the silence, the busy traffic of Kyoto not able to be heard.

Later, when I was writing of this experience, it seemed that the pattern of sound was the same pattern as the movement used in the tea ceremony, *jo, ha, kyu, zanshin*:

> When wiping the tea scoop with the *fukusa* in the tearoom, we were taught to start slowly (*jo*), speed up a bit at the centre of the scoop (*ha*) and finish off at the end quickly (*kyu*). At the instant one draws the *fukusa* off the tip of the scoop, there is the closing *zanshin*, which means "leaving behind the heart." Then one returns to zero, in preparation for the next rhythm of *jo, ha, kyu*. (Kerr, 1996, p. 112)

Kerr says this rhythm lies behind all of Japan's traditional arts. It "is the fundamental rhythm of nature—it defines the destinies of men, the course of eras, even the growth of galaxies and the very ebb and flow of the universe" (1996, p. 112).

So an apparently simple folly in a temple garden contains, potentially, all of this. A bamboo pipe filling, tipping, returning, pausing—and in the pause, a moment of emptiness in which the mind is able to stop still.

By the time I had found this shrine I had already visited several temples, none of which had a name bearing any resemblance to the names of the temples on my map. Of course, all the writing was in Japanese script or in kanji. Even comparing these closely I could find nothing familiar. By one of the pathways in the forest, sitting quietly on a bench, was a Kyoto lady—elegantly dressed and with white gloves on. She resembled the Kyoto princesses Kerr described—quietly elegant and dignified and clearly separate from anything except the most refined society. I cautiously approached her and she graciously glanced in my direction, making it possible for me to speak to her.

"*Sumimasen, kore wa* (pointing at the forest surrounding us), *doko desu ka* (pointing at the map and looking hopeful)."

She studied the map for a while and then pointed to a sign on the map that said Yoshida Shrine and had symbols that might be for torii gates.

"Domo arigato gozaimasu." (I later learned I should have said *o-okini*, which is the correct word for thanks in Kyoto—oh well.)

So now, taking myself to know where I was, I once again attempted to use the map to extricate myself from the maze, but it did not work. So again I abandoned the map and just walked. Eventually I came to a street I had seen before, and by searching out the small details of what I had seen earlier, I eventually made my way back to The Three Sisters Inn. I had been lost in the maze for nearly three hours, but I had seen wonderful houses and streets and gardens and temples and shrines, probably far more interesting than the officially recognized ones for tourists. Alex Kerr writes about the contained order of the shrines in Kyoto and feels that the original spirit of them is lost. But what I had seen were not tourist destinations where you pay to get in. They were just there, and they did not seem "contained," and they were beautiful, simple, and completely unexpected.

At night as I was going to sleep, or not long after I went to sleep, the weirdest thing happened. It was as if a group of very negative but childish spirits burst into my room, and two of them flew screaming around my bed. The high-pitched buzzing sound they made formed a tight circle around my bed. Half asleep, half awake, I was desperate to break the circle and I flung my arm out, feeling as if their metallic presence might hurt my arm but knowing I had to stop their screeching. As soon as I managed to fling my arm out they were gone—out the door and down the stairs. Where had I trespassed during the day, I wondered, to bring this upon myself? Was it the round rocks with the aprons on? Or was I just going a bit crazy?

Next day, I had an English-speaking taxi driver booked for the day. I asked him to take me to the Tenmangu shrine in Kameoka, where Alex Kerr lives. It sounded magic from Kerr's description and he had lamented in his book that no one would take the trouble to visit him there. I had written to him via his publisher, and he had not replied, so it was with some trepidation that I had decided on this excursion, uncertain of his presence or his welcome. But it was not to be. Kameoka is not part of Kyoto and the taxi driver's knowledge was only of Kyoto, he said. Having set my heart on this trip, and having paid such a large amount of money, I felt very frustrated. I wanted to go there. One of the sisters was assisting in the negotiations. She had already told me when I arrived that it made no sense to go to the Tenmangu shrine in Kameoka, especially with the taxi driver: *It is only a small shrine. You can go there by train. My brother lives in Kameoka, he goes there by train. You have a J.R. train pass. Why have you hired the taxi. You should not have done that. It is only a small shrine,* etc. etc. In sharp contrast to the sister's views, it seemed to me that the very fact that it was inconspicuous and overlooked made it all the more likely that it was important to visit. But she and the taxi driver made a collective force of resistance that I did not know how to overcome. I was to behave as tourists are expected to behave and to view the correct places. And, I thought, perhaps I should resign myself to not making contact with Alex Kerr, however important his writing may be to me.

So I chose the next two places on my list, Fushimi-Inari and Byodo-in Temple, where I had planned to go by train the next day. These he would take me to. They are no closer than Kameoka, but they are correct places to visit. The taxi driver wanted to know where else I wanted to go. For me, these were enough for the day, so I said let's visit these first and then see how I feel. He was not happy about this. I tried to explain to him that my preference was to see a little with depth, and not a lot superficially—that I needed time to gain any true understanding of the landscapes I visited. I asked him if he knew what I meant and he said no. And we drove on in awkward silence.

On the way through the streets of Kyoto the taxi driver pointed out to me the place where the Kabuki theater takes place, Gion. A *maiko* girl with a white-painted face and bright red lips, ornate wig, and traditional kimono walked by in her wooden clogs. Kyoto contains this, too. I had read about it and seen pictures, but the image is not quite believable until you see it for yourself.

I knew from Kerr's description of Fushimi-Inari that it was possible to walk through it for hours. I guessed the taxi driver would not be happy about this, and he wasn't. He said we should walk through the first set of torii gates (about 100 meters) and then return. I insisted (quietly and calmly) that I wanted to walk through the rest. It was raining and he had given me an umbrella (which he had got out of the trunk of the taxi, his private space) and walked with me through the first set of gates. Once he accepted my wish he said he would wait in his taxi. He showed me the map, on a board, of the pathways, which again looked infinitely complex. (Even Kerr, lover and long-term resident of Japan, describes getting lost here. He describes the late evening light casting shadows that made him afraid and the statues that seemed to come to life.) I asked the taxi driver if I would get lost and he said no, pointing out the path he thought I should take. He told me it would take one hour. I was gone for more than three hours, and could happily have stayed all day if it weren't for my concern about him waiting for me.

The torii gates form an archway or vermilion tunnel into the forest. Through the spaces between the pillars you can see the forest in all its beauty and power, but you know you are safe, in a charmed space as you walk there. The fact that you need protecting makes the power of the forest much more vivid. It is alive, and far more powerful than you are. In case you might be worried that the spirits of the forest do not like the intrusions of the gates, you can see that the cross beam of the gates is turned upwards to appease the spirits. Kerr quotes the Taoist scholar John Blofeld as saying to him:

> In ancient South-east Asia, the very raising of a building was considered taboo. Sinking pillars into the ground and setting a roof above them was believed to be a sin against Mother Earth. So they took the eaves that pointed and turned them back up towards the heavens. By doing this, they were absolved of having broken the taboo. (1996, p. 195)

And so I walked safely into the forest, experiencing the profound, ancient presence of it and at the same time aware of my protectedness within it. The torii gates divided into two paths at many points, and so before long I again accepted that I could not know the pattern and that I was lost, but safely so. Resignation, or abandonment to the moment, seemed natural in this place. Leading out of the protective tunnel were many paths, which wound through the trees to a shrine. These shrines were magical. There were special places for lighting small candles; beautiful carved calligraphy on the stones; animals such as foxes and horses and lions beautifully carved out of stone; clear, pure water in large stone vessels for washing hands and mouth before approaching each shrine. Luckily, there were also occasional little shops, which blended in with the forest, selling candles and matches, and so I could light my own candles and pray. I had observed the ritual that others followed and was at first hesitant, but I finally tried it, just putting my hands together and bowing my head, and a sense of tranquility washed over me. For a few seconds I experienced the kind of silence that comes with the deepest meditation. But the feeling also reminded me of the time I had listened to an old man singing in the Taj Mahal at dawn, his voice threading up through the curved spaces, lifting my spirit in joyful, unexpected spirals. Yet these shrines had nothing of the opulent magnificence of the Taj Mahal and there was no sound other than the birds and the running water.

Here, it seemed to me, the land was deeply cared for. And deeply sacred. Yet anyone could come here. Though there were very few people here, each one seemed free to come and to bathe themselves in the water, light their small fire at the shrines, and experience the holiness of the place.

I got completely lost, in many senses of the word—lost in the wonder of it, lost in not having any sense of direction or knowledge of how to get out, lost in terms of not knowing what meaning this place had for Japanese people. Later I read Kurosawa's writing about making the film *Rashomon* in a forest near Nara. He praises his cameraman with these words: "The introductory section in particular, which leads the viewer though the light and shadow of the forest into a world where the human heart loses its way, was truly magnificent camera work" (Kurosawa, 1982, p. 185). Instead of the filmmaker's art, I had the pathways, the sheltered cave of the torii gates, and the shrines and animal statues along the way—and my own imagination.

When I finally arrived back where I had begun, the taxi driver expressed great concern that I had taken so long. It is a puzzle to me that this most beautiful place, offering the kinds of experiences the poets describe, should be seen as desirable to so few Japanese people, except as a place to visit briefly in a ritualized encounter. Later the taxi driver took a photo of me at the Byodo-in Temple with its beautiful phoenixes on the roof. It is my favorite photo from the whole trip. I look tranquil and happy standing in the misty rain with the Temple buildings behind me, their lyrical phoenixes looking as if they are about to take flight from the roof.

It was May. Springtime in Japan. I was too late for the cherry blossoms, which come in early April on this island, and the wisteria had just finished. Some of the azaleas were in full bloom, and irises were growing by the ponds and waterlilies blooming in the ponds. The roses were blooming, too. The color of the houses and streets varied in subtle shades of wood and stone. The hillsides were green and yellow. I don't know what the yellow leafed trees were, perhaps maples. In autumn the hillsides would be a blaze of yellow and red.

Wabi-sabi comes in an infinite spectrum of grays: gray-blue brown, silver-red grayish black, indigo yellowish-green. . . . And browns: blackish deep brown-tinged blue, muted greens. . . . And blacks: red black, blue black, brown black, green black. . . . (Koren, 1994, p. 71)

Driving through the winding narrow streets from one place to another, I saw many orderly school children walking in groups, each sheltered under a small umbrella. Two boys, the only exception to this orderliness, were bending over peering with excitement into some grass growing by a fence. At one point the taxi pulled up alongside a small bus for preschool children. They, too, were very orderly. One beautiful child gazed out of the window for a long time at the taxi driver. Then he glanced in my direction and his eyes slid away immediately. He held his head erect and looked straight ahead until the traffic lights changed and he was gone. In contrast, another small boy I encountered at a bus stop gazed directly at me, though at first his mother gently moved his face and eyes to avert his gaze. He continued to stare and so I smiled at him. His gaze remained fixed and unresponsive. The mother's shaping of his "correct bodily attitude" reminded me of the highly visible shaping of trees here. Very often I see beautifully shaped trees, but even the adult tree is sometimes held in shape by supporting poles. In Australia we think nothing of shaping and supporting vines, and we do prune trees but we expect the shape to appear to be "natural." I wonder what we mean by this—able to support itself, perhaps? The same with people I suppose. We prune them as children and expect them to become natural—and self-supporting. In Japan it does not seem to be a problem to leave the supports visibly in place. Perhaps we do the same and I just can't see the detail of it.

The next day I returned to my independent explorations. After a long and horrible misadventure in which I failed to find the bamboo forest I had set out for, I made my way back to the Inn, exhausted and desolate. I decided to go to one of the nearby temples I'd found on the first day. It was late afternoon. From the temple came the most wonderful sound of monks singing. I sank down onto the ancient stone steps and let the sound wash over me. The sound of their singing seemed many centuries old—not unlike some of the music of Hildegarde of Bingen. I listened to them for at least an hour and slowly regathered my sense of equilibrium, alone in the early evening light. Then as the sun sank low on the horizon, the monks threw open the huge wooden doors, and the slanting rays of sunlight entered the gloom of the temple. They stood there, in the light, singing, their robes glowing softly in the interior darkness.

Things wabi-sabi have a vague, blurry, or attenuated quality—as things do as they approach nothingness (or come out of it). Once-hard edges take on a soft pale glow. . . . Once-bright saturated colours fade into muddy earth tones or the smoky hues of dawn and dusk. (Koren, 1994, p. 71)

The sun was sinking into the grey haze over Kyoto. As I walked down the long flight of steps, the sound of their singing grew fainter until it faded into nothingness. . . .

The next day I decided to go to see the Kabuki Theater, which was on in Osaka. The Kabuki players go from one city to another and would not be in Tokyo when I was there, so it was my only chance to see them. As usual I found the whole challenge of public transport quite daunting. After a nightmarish trip, changing train lines three times, and then trying to find the theater with a map I could make no sense of, I finally arrived only a few seconds after the performance started.

There were two warriors (elaborately dressed in kimonos and with swords) who were squatting in the middle of the stage with large straw hats on. They had a long conversation with each other in exaggerated whining voices, making stylized hand and foot movements. At one point they removed the tops of their kimonos to reveal more spectacular dress underneath. The pattern and timing of their words was matched by a plucked stringed instrument. The only other musical sound was a wooden board hit loudly with two wooden sticks at dramatic moments. Very occasionally there was a chorus of voices singing, once on stage and several times offstage, but these were fairly brief and not of any apparent beauty. Some individuals in the audience were part of the performance, calling out at precise predetermined moments that fit with the rhythm of what the players were saying. The audience laughter sounded a little like a gently plucked harp string and seemed to be part of the performance as well. The players entered through the audience on a raised platform. The auditorium was lit so the difference between stage and audience was minimal. The audience, while attentive, also chatted quietly to each other and rustled their bags of food and drink. People came in late.

The emotions displayed on the stage were very different from the absolute restraint outsiders understand as "Japanese." Here on stage were individual personalities expressing excessive emotions, fighting each other with swords (and in one case an umbrella was used to beat someone up), and yet at the same time the performance was utterly predictable and controlled. The characters always remembered to take their sandals off when they entered the door, and on one occasion, when someone had to stand in the entryway in bare feet, he dusted off his feet with a cloth before standing on the tatami mat. Even extreme emotions do not override such rules. The story involved a seemingly ghastly plot in which a woman was locked in a cupboard for a long period of time, but I could make no sense of the meaning of this event. The performance, just like the Japanese train system, was timed to the second. It ended exactly on time and the players had only thirty minutes before the next performance.

I was at a loss to know how to read what I had seen until I read Tobin's fascinating analysis of the ways in which the ideal Japanese adult has learned to integrate "front-door" polite, formal ways of behaving (*omote*) with "back-door" relaxed, spontaneous modes of feeling and interacting (*ura*). He says, "The ideal Japanese child, like the ideal Japanese adult, is not always or even usually under tight self-control" (1992, p. 38). He elaborates this complex observation through his observations of Japanese preschools:

Japanese preschools function to give children a chance to develop the *ura* as well as the *omote* dimensions of the self. A well-balanced Japanese child should be able to move easily back and forth between control and emotionality. In contemporary Japan it is in preschools where Japanese children have a sense of developing and integrating a twofold sense of self, a sense of self capable of fusing *omote* and *ura*. The large class size, the hands-off approach to dealing with children's misbehaviour, the fluctuations between structure and chaos during the school day, the use of language and even the ordering of space and time, each of these features of the Japanese preschool contributes to the creation of an environment structured to help children learn to feel themselves, to be themselves, in front-door, formal contexts as well as in interactions which are back-door, informal and spontaneous. (Tobin, 1992, p. 38)

So it seems I have glimpsed the fusion of *omote* and *ura* in this Kabuki performance. Or perhaps it is more correct to say I have been shown *ura* for the first time, and seen how it coexists with the highly controlled ordering of *omote*. Because we non-Japanese see emotion and control as binary opposites, we fail to see the dependence of our emotions on our capacity for controlling or producing those emotions and the dependence of our self-control on our emotional commitment to it.

This integration between *ura* and *omote* is not always achieved well and can lead to repugnant contrasts. Kurosawa writes about a stepmother brutalizing her stepdaughter. When he tries to save the stepdaughter by untying her in the stepmother's absence, the daughter orders him to tie her back up because she has no way to escape and her stepmother's torture will be all the worse if she is not tied up on her return from shopping. Kurosawa comments on how it amazed and sickened him that the brutal stepmother appeared to be a normal polite Japanese housewife when encountered in the streets. I read in a daily newspaper a report of a young boy's severed head placed at the school gate with messages from the killer placed in his mouth. I am sure the brutality here is no more extreme than elsewhere, but the gulf that can open up between *ura* and *omote* can be startling precisely because *omote* is so very orderly and predictable.

Outside, in the streets of Osaka, was an entirely different world from what I'd seen in the other cities. Young men and women wandered about with exotic, modern styles of dress and hair. Their hair was often dyed and gelled and many wore multiple earrings. There were even older people lying in the street—asleep or drunk, I couldn't tell. There were lights—glitter and noisy pachinko parlors. Here was a new face of Japan, one that breathed an air of freedom and space for the individual, while still being evidently Japan. I did not feel at all out of place here—if anything, I felt conservative in comparison. When I got home to the Inn I rinsed out my underclothes in the shower, celebrating a small moment of rebellion made possible by a glimpse of a facet of Japan that is not only about control and obedience. I dreaded being caught because the sisters go on and on and on if they think you've not done the right thing. But it was such a relief to resolve the problem of unwashed clothes.

That evening I joined two of the other people staying at the Inn who had planned to go out to dine and to a special event at a temple that was to be lit up for the festival season. While the temple was beautiful, the crowds and the ritualized brief glimpses of many things as we walked along at the same pace as everyone else meant that yet again I failed to enter into the spirit of the occasion. I was becoming more and more aware of the embodied sense of space and freedom that comes with living in Australia with so few people occupying so much space. On the way home we noticed another lighted temple and went in. There was a sound of drums quite different from the sounds we had heard before. A group of Kodo drummers were playing their huge drums with the most wonderful rhythm and energy. Both male and female, and dressed in gymnastic-type outfits, they threw their whole bodies into collaboratively creating the wonderful deep, resonating rhythms. There was a sense of energy and freedom here as the drummers moved from one drum to another, but unlike in Osaka the energy and freedom combined to make a highly disciplined, spectacular performance. McQueen also experienced the joy of these drummers. He writes: "Flew home on the drumbeats of the traditional Japanese percussion group, the Kodo drummers, from the island of Sado. Not only was the music exciting, the drummers were thrilling to watch, partly because their musculature moved in rhythm with their drumming, but mostly because they were getting so much pleasure from their hard work, extracting melody and harmonies from rhythm" (1991, pp. 144–45).

The experience of the Kodo drummers made a fitting end to my stay alone in this ancient city. The next part of my trip was on the island of Hokkaido and mostly involved meeting up with the academics and environmentalists I talk about in Chapter 6.

Part 2 Hokkaido

The flight to Hokkaido was uneventful. Takeshi and Michiko, whom I'd met on their visit to Australia, were at the airport at Sapporo to meet me with smiling, friendly, welcoming words. The next morning I paid a "courtesy visit" to the president of the University, President Fujii, and was later taken out to lunch where we talked of the possibilities of student exchanges. After lunch, the others left and Takeshi and I had time to talk. I was able to ask him lots of questions in relation to my travels.

The white paper and rope (made of rice stalks) tied around the trunks of trees is called *shimenawa*. It is placed on the tree to show respect for the god of the tree, by tending to it and by warding off evil forces—negative and dirty things. When I said that in Australia respect for the tree would be the opposite, that we leave it alone, he said, "We like to *do* with nature. You do not like to do, you stay separate." When I explained that our ideal is to be part of nature—but with nature dominant, he looked doubtful. He explained that in Japan there can be a god almost anywhere, even in the toilet. The different shoes worn in that space are so that impure things from outside will not be brought in to offend the god of the toilet.

He confirmed my sense that the forests and mountains are sacred and that is why Nara and Kyoto are built on the plain. Over lunch I had been told that it was at the base of the mountain that two warriors first wrestled before the gods and developed the art of sumo wrestling in which the point is not to kill the opponent but to save him. Later this performance was no longer for the gods but was used to raise money to pay for the building of the Shinto shrine.

Takeshi observed that Japanese like small gardens, with high walls where you can be private. He was very surprised when he first traveled overseas to see the beautiful front gardens full of flowers and with no fences. The ideal in Japan is to have your own private mountain and your own private forest and your own private waterfall, but all in miniature. In such spaces one can achieve tranquility and repose. Particularly, he said, rich people strive to have such spaces of their own.

After pressing him several times about why the stone statues in the forests wear hats, including garishly colored woolen beanies, he said there was a story in his primary school textbook about an *ozizo-san* who had snow falling on his bald head and was very cold. A poor man passing by took pity on him and wrapped his scarf around the *ozizo-san*'s head. The *ozizo-san* was so grateful that he later rewarded the poor man with a life of riches. Since it is difficult to make hair on a stone statue, the *ozizo-sans* are often bald. So people hoping for riches put hats on the statues' heads. Takeshi also pointed out that at the Buddhist temples the stone baths for washing hands and the dragons spouting water were donated by rich people who hope that the spirits of the dead buried there would reward them with riches.

He also explained the bamboo pipe above the pond, suggesting that the purpose of the sound of water falling into the pipe was to *create* a sense of silence. Complete silence does not do so. He told me a story of Basho walking at the foot of the mountain where warriors once fought in noisy battle. The silence Basho hears emerges from the absence of the warriors. And the shrill sound of the cicadas intensifies that silence. We talked about whether the ritual in front of a shrine of bowing slowly twice, then clapping loudly twice, a little faster, then bowing once to pray is the same rhythm: slow, faster, fast, stop. Later, when we went to the shrine, he read to me the instructions for washing hands and mouth before approaching the shrine. First wash the left hand, then the right hand. Then pour water into the left hand, with which to rinse the mouth. The same rhythm, one hand, other hand, mouth, pause. It is very important to be clean when approaching a shrine as there are so many impurities that can gather on you as you walk about. There is also a stick with *shimenawa* paper on it that the priest can dust you down with to rid you of impurities.

Our conversation took place in the University gardens as we sat by an attractive pond surrounded by cherry blossoms. It was bordered by cement and had a filtration system to keep it clean and had seats 'round it, and cherry blossoms. In the pond was a large sign saying (in Japanese) "The pond is muddy and deep in places so do not enter." I asked if there could be a god in the pond. The answer was no, as this is a university and educated people do not believe such things. But what if an uneducated person came here, I asked. He looked carefully and said the cement surrounds, the person lying asleep on the bench, the young couples wandering around, the openness and lightness of the place, and the filtration plant all made it very unlikely that there was a god here. Then he added that if he were alone in a dark enclosed space in a forest, he might feel the presence of a god in a pond.

Later we met up with Michiko and had coffee in the subway. Then we took the subway to the most important Shinto shrine in Hokkaido. It is at the base of a small mountain covered in forest, but it is quite central to the city. The spaces in Hokkaido are much greater than on Honshu, and you can see large mountains capped with snow in the distance. In the shrine there is a large statue of Shima Yashitake, who established the shrine in 1870 at the order of the Emperor. He carried the gods, which were very heavy, on his back, to bring them from the Emperor to Hokkaido. In the 1960s rebellious students burned down the central shrine because of its association with the Emperor and the oppression of the indigenous Ainu people. The design of the shrine is very different from those in Honshu as it does not have uplifted eaves but rather has straight lines and, at the top, poles that look like the spars of a windmill. It did not seem integrated into the forest landscape in the way the Fushimi-Inari shrine had seemed to be. Takeshi was ever mindful of the unacceptable nature of the invasion, and while he engages in some Buddhist practices he expressed some distance from Shinto and the imperialism of the Emperor over this land. Yet, he admitted, he puts *shimenawa* on his front gate on New Year's day to welcome people. At the shrine he commented that he had never washed himself there before, or noticed the instructions. In his home they have a Buddhist shrine to his ancestors where they light incense, chime the bowl, and bow. At the shrine they speak in ordinary ways to the ancestors, perhaps mentioning it is their birthday or some such thing. The shrine to Michiko's ancestors is in her mother's house, where her brother lives. In taking Takeshi's family name when she married him, she has forgone the right to have the shrine of the family name.

There is always much to buy at a Japanese shrine—good luck in years of bad fortune (age thirty-three for women and forty-two for men), or good luck charms, or wishes you can write and hang up. There was even a fortune box where foreigners could find their fortune at a cheaper price than Japanese! So I paid for my fortune and drew a neatly folded piece of paper from the box. I am to have excellent luck, and my ship is running before a fair wind and is approaching the harbor at which it is going to call. I will also get help from my superiors and my misfortune will turn into luck!

Next morning I began my interviews with Professor Tanaka. An American and an English student were there to translate. He expressed the view that Japan cannot go back in time to undo the environmental damage it has done, but it can teach the children to appreciate nature by showing them the little bits that are left. He expressed great concern for and love of nature, but when he asked me where I would like to go on Saturday and I said the lake, he said, "But it's only a lake, there is nothing to see."

After the interview I met up with Professor Gotoh and his wife, Emiko. We exchanged first names and Mamoru suggested I call him Mo. They took me to Otaru, which was originally a fishing village but is now a tourist destination and is joined to Sapporo by a never-ending stream of houses. When we got there we visited a wonderful glass factory full of the most exquisite glassware in a very old and beautiful building. Most of Sapporo is new grey apartment blocks with very little sign of anything older than 1962, when the winter Olympics were held here and much of old Sapporo was torn down.

Otaru still had some old buildings (well, 100 years old) in the same style as old buildings in Nara, only larger. There was a fairground and amusement park and, to my amazement, a revolving tower in which we bought drinks and sat watching the sun set over the Japan sea. There were snow-capped mountains in the far distance. In the foreground a craggy mountainside with jagged rocks was silhouetted against the pale, calm blue sea and the red sky. As the tower turned us around we also saw a hillside covered in cherry blossoms and a myriad of swifts darting through the evening light. Then we went to a sushi bar and ate raw fish and octopus and crab and prawns and sea urchins and shellfish, and drank sake and soup and ate a strange egg custard. Mo and Emiko made incredible efforts to communicate in English, and for the most part we succeeded. They loved my Hamamatsu story of going to the kite festival, which Mo had already heard once but wanted to hear again in more detail. He enjoyed my observations about Japan, especially my observation that the division between East and West must be a modern fiction. He joked that in some ways I am more Japanese than he is, since I have participated in the Hamamatsu festival as an insider. He said he would love to be able to do that, but at the same time he believed that there is more freedom in Hokkaido and in Okinawa than in the rest of Japan and he valued that freedom. I did not feel nearly so strange here as I did in Kyoto. The children here did not gaze at me and find me strange. There seemed to be much more openness and diversity in the faces of the people. This was even noticeable when I was waiting to get the plane to Hokkaido.

Mamoru, Emiko, and their friend Katsumi also took me to Shiraoi, an Ainu village. On the way we drove through many devastated landscapes. The freeways and the electricity lines cut through the mountains, sometimes (often) in the form of tunnels, but the sides of mountains were being shaved off all over the place to make way for more roads. Katsumi explained that there were six golf courses in the area and that the fertilizer used for the greens had poisoned the underground water supply and killed the fish. The people in the area are protesting and do not want any more golf courses. Interestingly, later over dinner Mamoru said that Japanese want to feel nature, while Westerners want to understand nature. I said that while this might be the Japanese *ideal,* many Japanese seemed to me to have lost their ability to feel nature. Mamoru said very sadly that he thought this might be true. They cannot feel nature if they are not doing in nature, such as playing golf, and the doing seems to take over as an activity in and for itself.

The Ainu village, to my way of seeing, had interesting similarities to Maori culture and also the Inuit culture, in terms of clothing, hunting implements, and to some extent the buildings. The map in the museum that showed the spread of related cultural groups reached north into the Arctic circle but did not reach as far south as New Zealand, which seemed surprising to me. The modern-day Japanese, it is believed, were from Korea. In the 1600s only the south-west coast of Hokkaido was occupied by the Japanese, with the Ainu inhabiting the major part of the island. Periodically, when there was a perceived threat from Russia the whole of Hokkaido was placed under shogunal rule. In 1871 the Emperor set up the prefectural system, occupying Hokkaido and virtually destroying the Ainu culture.

After this visit, and over dinner, Mamoru said he thought it was the economy, in turn, that was destroying Japanese culture. It is easy for the government to do what it has done, because the Japanese people have been convinced that the economy is all powerful. The practice of endless negotiation is probably the one that is of most use in stopping development, since nothing proceeds while the negotiations continue. As well, the multifaceted nature of the culture means that the old discourses of being one with nature are alive and well, despite the massive takeover by consumerism. It is easy to revive such discourses in opposition to the destruction of the developers. Later he added that Japanese people don't notice the destruction of the mountains. They don't feel it is bad to destroy the mountains. The change that needs to take place, he said, is that each person must come to understand that it is his or her task to be concerned about the environment. This is a task for education. The task is fundamentally about developing a moral framework. Each student needs to develop a moral framework for thinking through environmental issues. In the past "right thinking" was passed from grandfather to his children and then on to their children. The old cannot teach the young now, as too much has changed.

I am reminded of Kurosawa writing about change. He says he did not oppose Japanese militarism during the war—he simply survived it. But he adds:

The freedom and democracy of the post-war era were not things I had fought for and won; they were granted to me by powers beyond my own. As a result, I felt it was all the more essential for me to approach them with an earnest and humble desire to learn, and to make them my own. But most Japanese in those post-war years simply swallowed the concepts of democracy and freedom whole, waving slogans around without really knowing what they meant. (Kurosawa, 1982, p. 145)

Dean Abe, a philosopher, also generously gave me his time in Sapporo and in Iwamizawa. He explained to me how, in the area of Sapporo, the river was originally winding and crooked and how the developers made it straight. As a result, when there are heavy rains the river cannot contain all the water and the low-lying areas get flooded. There is a proposal to make a canal that would carry the water south through the estuary and out to sea. However, this would spoil the estuary by allowing salt water farther inland and by draining the wetlands. The birds who use the estuary as a significant stopping place would no longer be able to do so. We visited the estuary and the swans there were amazingly tame—people were feeding them and stroking them.

The most fundamental principle in Japan, he said, is not to meddle with nature. I commented that Japan meddles more with nature than any other country that I have seen. He appeared not to believe this. So I returned to the example of straightening the river. What happens, he said, when you have meddled, is that you need another principle to guide you. Then we fight. The fight over the canal has been going on for fifteen years. He pointed out that another fundamental principle is usefulness. He had shown me the wetlands and said with some disgust that most Japanese think the wetlands are useless (meaning bad); they do not see their usefulness for birds and animals. He then elaborated the principle of usefulness as a good one.

His example was the chopsticks we were using to eat lunch with. He said the tree had originally been chopped down and the chopsticks were a new form that took shape out of the tree. The chopsticks are formed so that they have to be pulled apart, broken apart, by the person who is to use them. It is important to respect the spirit and form of the chopsticks by breaking them open yourself and using them to eat with. I was puzzled, as the chopsticks are then thrown away, which did not seem to me to be respectful of the form of the chopsticks and of the original tree. Later, at the pioneer village. he explained that the carpenters chose the wood carefully for the houses. Old wood lasts longer, and costs more. Strong wood should be used for the supporting pillars. No material should be used that cannot eventually return to the earth. It is also important that what is made is beautiful. The concept of beauty of the houses is carried over into such things as sumo wrestling. You must defeat your opponent *beautifully*.

Over dinner in Iwamizawa Dean Abe talked about the difference between Japanese bowls and Chinese bowls. He said the Chinese bowl is perfectly round and patterned and predictable. The Japanese bowl is rough and has unexpected complications because it is not perfectly round. He compared this to the unexpected patterns of Japanese streets and the way in which Japanese train stations are designed to get lost in. Abe and Sato-sensei talked about how they like the complexity of the unpredictable and the indirect approach. Westerners, Abe said, like symmetry. Japanese do not.

Koren (1994) says that *wabi sabi* is a reaction against the Chinese style of overdecoration and perfection. It is the opposite of the Western idea of the modern. It is ephemeral, imperfect, connected to nature. It is simple, and small. It is connected to shadow rather than light. It is always simple and never elaborate. The tea ceremony combines collective ritual practice with moments of contemplation in which the heart (or mind) stops its busyness. As well, the asymmetrical shape and pattern of each bowl may create such a moment, in an unexpected way, as one stops to comment on one's own and the other's bowl. It seems that the precision and ritual of Japanese life, like the tea ceremony, provides security and mystery at the same time—the highly formalized repetition holds the certainty and the mystery together.

After my trip to Iwamizawa campus, where I gave a lecture on Australian and Japanese body/landscape relations and became quite agitated (in a way that seemed to me inappropriate in this landscape) about the colonialist views of a visiting American professor, I returned briefly to Sapporo. The person looking after me at this point was Professor Tanaka. We went again to Otaru, this time to see the magnificent house built around the turn of the century by a wealthy herring fisherman. Victoria, a student, came with us as translator. I saw peonies for the first time, flowering in the garden of the fisherman's house.[1] The cherry blossoms had fallen like snow and covered the ground.

In the house there were paintings of some of the ancient poets who, 1,000 ago, sat around composing and reciting poetry. Professor Tanaka recited one of the poems and Victoria translated it. One hundred of these poems are collected in a famous anthology, which all Japanese children learn. In Professor Tanaka's childhood there was a card game that families played which involved knowing these poems so well that they could be recognized at a glance on seeing only a

---

1. In the following year, in Copenhagen, I found some peonies in the flower market. I placed them in a drinking glass beside my computer, and as I watched the buds open and the petals spread over the next few days, I realized that that first sighting in Japan was not the first. I have gazed at still-life paintings in which images of peonies are caught in perfect detail, and that detail returned, almost photographically, to my mind's eye as I gazed at the flowers on my desk. So this was not the first time I had seen them; it was, rather, the first linking of the name peony with the image I had already gazed at and made into my own—in the sense that I found it later, vividly present in my imagination. Later, in Copenhagen, I realized that when I had originally seen the paintings, the most important gap in my knowledge was probably not the name, but the powerful scent that almost overwhelms the senses, and which makes me sneeze and my eyes itch.

written fragment of them. In these poems, he explained, the connection between the poet and the landscape is fundamental to the meaning of each poem. I became quite excited about these poems and their relevance to my search. Professor Tanaka undertook to find some translations of them for me, as he did not think his English good enough to know whether Victoria's translations were giving me the subtle and complex meanings of the poems.

The next morning Professor Tanaka picked me up from the hotel and took me to a beautiful coffeehouse that epitomized the spirit of *furyu,* or refined and sophisticated artistic style. From the outside there was nothing to draw you in, to tell you such elegance and artistry existed behind the curtain in the doorway. But inside there were vases of fresh flowers, the lighting was dim, the music soft and tranquil— Chopin, I think—and, to enable us to read and write, a small lamp was switched on, creating a small circle of light around us. The food we ate was exquisite—a sweet bean soup with sweet rice cakes (the sort usually eaten at New Year) and a tiny sour green fruit on a tiny plate on the side. This was accompanied by red tea, each item in a handmade bowl. On my tray was a single flower and on Professor Tanaka's tray was an origami of a stork in flight. I admired his bird and he insisted that I have it.

After he had dropped me off the previous evening, he had gone to a meeting until ten P.M. After that he had gone to three different bookshops looking for English translations of the ancient poetry I had said I wanted. He could not locate what he wanted so he found a Japanese version at home and photocopied it and then translated a dozen poems, which he chose for their evocation of *wabi* and *sabi.* He was worried that the translations were not good, so in this idyllic place we immersed ourselves in the poems and the task of translation, he explaining to me the meaning of the words (most of which are no longer used in Japan today) and drawing pictures to help me understand the visual image the poet had in mind. It is possible in the seventeen syllables of (the more modern) haiku poem to say everything, always including reference to the four seasons. Because precise meanings and the associated knowledge and images are shared amongst Japanese people to the extent they are, it is possible to tell a universe of meaning in few words. The small gardens can do the same. Because the love of nature is universally understood, the brief small statement of it can represent, beautifully, the whole universe.

The syllabic structure of the ancient poems is 5, 7, 5, 7, 7, and each poem contains a repeated image: a reference to the long autumn night may be connected to the length of a pheasant's tail. The repetition of the idea of length ties the two images together, lending meaning from one image in the poem to the next. Further, it is important that much is *not* said in the poem. In the poem that begins with the poet standing on Tagonoura beach, for example, the reader must know that the sea is very blue, the pine trees along the edge of the beach are deep green, the beach is long, and Mt. Fuji is very distant. Without this knowledge the poem cannot be understood. It is precisely the brevity of the poem that makes it so evocative. It does not describe; it evokes meaning from carefully combined images, with which the reader is familiar.

And so we set about our collaborative translation in this exquisite space. We began with the translations he had attempted the night before. He would tell me both the literal meaning and the evoked image, and I would search for ways to say the literal meaning in English so that it might evoke the same image or emotion. When I tried to insert some of the words that were evoked by the poem, he was very definite that this could not be. For example, in poem 79 the autumn moon is referred to. The autumn moon is blue-white, and one must know this to understand the poem, but the poem cannot say blue-white. Over the sixth poem we translated together, he was not quite content with what we arrived at. He asked the woman in the restaurant to help us—a young, very beautiful woman, who laughed at her own incompetence and explained how difficult they were to understand. The poem we were struggling with was this:

48 *Minamoto-no Shigeyuki*
Kaze o itami
iwautsu namino
Onorenomi
kudakete mono o
omoukorokana

We told her what we had arrived at already, and she struggled to explain what else must be added. She said the poet's heart is like a butterfly, but not quite, and that he loves someone who does not love him, yet his mind is filled with the thought of her. We had agreed on the first lines:

The strong wind blows and
the waves break on the hard rock.

The second part, which we were not happy with was:

I long for one who breaks my heart.

After much negotiation between the three of us, this became:

My mind is filled with thoughts of her
and my heart flutters, and breaks.

The task was to ensure that the loved one and the rock are parallel, and the waves and his heart are parallel. So the image of the heart breaking contains the visual image of the wave breaking against the rock, and the woman contains the image of a rock that does not break no matter how much the wave breaks against it.

These poems are called tanka and are 1,000 years old. One hundred of them are especially revered, and each of these is numbered. They are much older than haiku and haikai, which are only 300 and 400 years old. The translations that we completed on that magical morning were as follows:

5 *Sarumaru Dayu*
Okuyamani
momizi fumiwake
nakushika no
koekikutokizo
Aki wa kanashiki

The deer steps on the fading autumn leaves
as it wanders deep into the forest.
I hear its cry; alone in the forest,
the chill wind pierces my heart.

3 *Kakinomoto-no Hitomaro*
Ashibikino
yamadori no ono
Shidario no
naganagashi yo-o
hitori kamonemu

The long autumn night stretches
Like the long tail of the copper pheasant.
I sleep alone and desolate.

Implicit knowledge: We know that this poet writes love songs, so love is not mentioned, but we know that he is waiting for his lover, who does not come.

9 *Ono no Komachi*
Hananoirowa
uturini kerinna
itazurani
wagami yo nifuru
nagame seshimani

The color of the flower fades
and withers in the rain.
I look back at the long rains falling
through the long years of my life.

Implicit knowledge: This poet was a very beautiful woman but she is aging, like the flower. The poem is a lament for her passing youth.

84 *Yamabe-no Akahito*
Tagonoura ni
uchiidete mireba
shirotaeno
Fuji no takene ni
Yuki wa furitsutsu

I stand on Tagonoura beach
and far off fine snow falls on Mt. Fuji.
I can see the white snow falling
on the high mountaintop.

Implicit knowledge: The image of the beach is long, the sea is blue, the pine trees are green, and Mt. Fuji is very far. The name Tagonoura alone evokes this image. We know that the second sentence refers to the poet, and that there is snow falling in his heart.

79 *Sakyo-nodaibu Akisuke*
Aki-kaze ni
tanabiku kumono
taema yoni
moreizuru tukino
kageno sayakesa.

A cloud is carried by the autumn wind.
It breaks off, and
for a brief moment
the moon's light shines clear and cold.

Implicit knowledge: The autumn color of the moon is blue-white, autumn wind is fast, clouds are long—the effect is very *wabi*, the combination of dark and light.

And then it was time to catch the train to Kushiro. Professor Tanaka drove me to the station and Mo and Emiko came as well to say farewell. I was very sad to say goodbye to these exquisitely generous and hospitable people. I had already undertaken several interviews on environmental issues and the week in Kushiro was to be taken up almost entirely with more interviews.

One of the wonderfully generous people in Kushiro who helped with the interviews was Chie. She explained to me that for people in Kushiro the environment is not a friendly place. The winters are so bitterly cold and the job of going out fishing is one that requires the capacity to face the unfriendly elements in ways that require great endurance—an ability to *withstand* the environment. Fishermen are famous for being short-tempered—and are allowed to be so because of their endurance. The land is not only unbearably cold but erupts regularly in earthquakes, and the volcanoes are still active. The land is far from benign. Later I said to her husband, Douglas, that after being in Kyoto and Nara I was horrified when I saw the tunnels through the mountains in Hokkaido and I could not understand how the mountain gods had been appeased. He said, well, they did get their revenge— only recently a tunnel collapsed and killed a busload of people and others who were crushed in the tunnel.

When we visited the forest and climbed the observation tower and asked the forest rangers questions about their forest, Chie and I became progressively more frozen in the chill wind that blew there. I began to understand what she meant when she said she does not regard the land as benign. She grew up in Kushiro, which is built on the marsh. The land is always wet and soggy and there is always a danger that when there is an earthquake the whole town will sink below the sea. The people, she said, are very aware of their vulnerability in the face of natural forces.

When we drove to Shibecha to see the forest and the wetlands, we drove past many hills that have been clear-felled. The erosion is worse than I have ever seen. Half of the hillside in many cases has just fallen away, revealing bare rock. Some hills have collapsed onto roads and completely blocked them. I had been so intent on looking for beauty and discovering Japanese culture that I had not been able to see the extent of the devastation. Chie opened my eyes with her very clear, flat statement that she cannot love this landscape. This thought is so depressing it's almost unbearable.

And so...

Here I am, finally, in Tokyo, almost on my way home. With Keiko and Iguchi-san I made a day trip to Nikko in the mountains. Later, when having dinner in the hotel, as I split my chopsticks open I felt a connection with the spirit of the tree just as Dean Abe had said I was supposed to do. It felt like a blessing. I was very aware of how delicious the food was, eaten from those wooden chopsticks. Smoked salmon and fresh green salad. I felt so calm reading Koren's book and using the chopsticks I felt connected to, that I even discovered I could now cut the food with the chopsticks. It was a small moment of deep contentment, of (be)longing in the Japanese landscape.

Yesterday the hotel building actually trembled quite strongly for about fifteen seconds. Apparently this happens all the time. Last night I read Kurosawa's description of the great quake in Tokyo earlier in the century, when the whole central district was burned down. I had just bought his book during the day at the famous Maruzen bookshop, and his story of the earthquake begins with his own trip to the Maruzen bookshop to browse for a few hours and to buy a book for his sister, only to find the shop closed. Only two hours later, when he would still have been there if it had been open, this bookshop crashed to the ground when the earthquake hit. The subsequent fires and devastation—especially the utter devastation of people's humanity in the face of such catastrophe—was extraordinary to read about while lodged in my trembling hotel. Although the great quake was in 1923, the coincidences made the danger seem very close to me. This land is not benign, Chie said. Land and sea fold and refold themselves, unpredictably and violently. The coexistence of controlled, detailed, repetitive order and strong emotions in the beings who take up their embodiment in this land begin to make sense to me. These ideas are extended and developed in the conversations with the environmentalists in the next chapter.

Here, the cherry blossoms
are throwing away
their platinum lives;
evening twilight deepens

Meiko Matsudaira
(Lowitz, Aoyama, and Tomioka, 1994, p. 91)

~6~ Japanese environmentalists talk about Japanese body/landscape relations

THE CONVERSATIONS ON WHICH THIS CHAPTER IS BASED were all undertaken on the island of Hokkaido. The people I talked to included forest and wetland rangers, a farmer-activist, people working in environmental agencies, volunteers working to conserve the wetlands, women who took me from one place to another and who helped with translation, and academics who are interested in environmental issues. Some of the conversations were in English, and some were in Japanese, with a translator.[1] The picture that emerged in this talk was one of extraordinary complexity. There was an interlaying of modern environmental ideals and practices with traditional Japanese aesthetics. Ancient Japanese oral language and concepts of embodied being in landscape were interlaid with written kanji in which people are no longer represented as continuous with nature. A belief in the inevitability and even desirability of industrialization was talked about as being in tension with a longing for preindustrial Japan. A commitment to traditional practices and beliefs, which are fundamentally collective in nature, was interleaved with an urgent sense of the need to develop individual conscience and responsibility for the land. And perhaps most complex of all, a wish was expressed by some to be rid of the controlling force of the emperor system. This was associated with a rejection of the traditional Shinto connectedness with nature because of the emperor's use of Shintoism to dominate and control the people. And coming from another perspective, the basis of Japanese body/ landscape relations are described as embedded in formal manners and in the festivals, and yet the young are described as not committed to the continuation of these practices. Through the rapid industrialization and subsequent increase in wealth, the children are described as losing their sense of direction and any sense of connection with nature.

---

1. The conversations were recorded and transcribed, with a Japanese transcriber using both the Japanese words and the translator's original interpretation of what they were saying, to make an accurate written translation of what they were saying. I then edited these translations to eliminate incorrect grammar. When I wrote up the original version of this and Chapter 4, based on these conversations and my journals, I returned to Japan, having sent copies of the chapters ahead of me. I then talked again to as many of the people whose words I had used as possible, to ensure that I had found appropriate words in English to represent their ideas. In this second round of conversations I also asked the people with whom I had talked to critique what I had written. When necessary, a translator was present to facilitate this process. These second conversations led to considerable rewriting of both chapters. Those rewritten chapters were then sent again for written comment to several of the key participants.

To enable me to understand this complex picture the interviewees drew my attention to Japanese history and to the extent and complexity of change that has taken place in the last 130 years. One of the threads running through many of the interviews was a nostalgia for the past, for traditional Japan and its ways of being. This nostalgia, in some cases, was for something that was understood to be in the past, but just as often it was incorporated into a statement about what it means to be a Japanese person now. Japan has undergone rapid and complex changes both during and after the Meiji Restoration (1868), during and after World War II, and finally in the last two or three decades of rapid industrialization.

According to Kenzaburo Oe's (1994) analysis, the Meiji Restoration was the process through which the Japanese feudal system was turned into a nation-state. In that same process "foreign culture" no longer meant Chinese culture but came to mean European learning. The intention of the Meiji Restoration was to contribute to the modernization of Japan, and the concept of the Yamato spirit, used to unify cultural consciousness in the interests of creating a modern state.

During the Meiji period (1869–1912) there was a stress on the absolute, unified nature of Japanese culture, with the emperor as central. The Yamato spirit became a slogan for unified imperial Japan. "Japan's modernisation reveals the history of an Asian country that sought to extricate itself from Asia and become a European-style nation" (Oe, 1994, p. 55). At the same time, the absolute rule of the word of the emperor as living deity and absolute ruler could not be questioned. Now, for many people, the emperor system is associated with fanaticism and absolutism (Oe, 1994, p. 20) and with oppression of the Ainu people.

When the emperor ordered that Hokkaido be brought under Japanese control, he ordered that the Shinto gods of the Japanese landscape be carried across the water to Hokkaido and that Shinto shrines be erected there. Professor Shindo describes the Shinto practices of that time as containing more reverence for the land than the postindustrial period:

When the Japanese came to Hokkaido it was originally just a virgin forest. The first thing they did was to put a stake in front of the forest saying that this is a sacred area. Like the torii gates you saw, what is behind them is a sacred forest. So what they first did was put some kind of stake and then maybe a rope and then the torii gate and then build a shrine. This Japanese way of thinking is that by protecting the forest and the gods of the forest you're protecting the water in the forest and the trees. The gods of the trees become the gods of the river and the gods of the river change into the gods of the rice paddies. The traditional way of looking at that relationship between humans and mountain gods and the relationship between the farmer and the river gods is in terms of the cyclical maintaining of the balance between the seasons of spring and summer, autumn and winter. The cyclical balance between the planting and the harvest involves maintaining the relationship with nature. And that has been forgotten by most Japanese people now. After the war it started to change. It is that shift to increased industrialization, more than modernization that's caused the problem.

In contrast, Oe sees the post–World War period, when the emperor no longer declared himself a deity, as one in which freedom of expression was established and a "suppressed literary energy burst forth" (Oe, 1994, p. 47). Like Professor Shindo, however, many of the people I talked to were more inclined to see the post-war period as the beginning of environmental problems in Japan associated with an increase in industrialization.

Yoshinaka-san, for example, who is Head of National Parks and Wildlife in Eastern Hokkaido, talked about the embeddedness of humans in what is understood to be nature in Japan, and his simultaneous concern that Japanese people, generally, have lost their connection with nature, since the long cultural traditions of living in a particular landscape have been disrupted by industrialization:

Japan has a much longer history and cultural base than your country. For tens of thousands of years we have been living on this small island, which we consider to be a "natural environment." We kept a balance between the humans and natural resources. We were not separate, we had a very nice relation between humans and nature. But in the last thirty years or forty years, Japan has changed quite a bit.

But the groundwork was already laid, at the beginning of the Meiji period, for the development of a deeply complex sense of what it means to be an embodied Japanese person inhabiting a Japanese landscape—schooled in the practices of Shintoism and Buddhism and yet developing European practices, while being united under the absolute rule of the emperor. As well, this multilayered complexity has been compounded in the post-war period with the extensive development and industrialization that people like Yoshinaka-san talk about.

Despite so much deliberately orchestrated change, traditional meanings are still present in many people's consciousness, though they may hesitate to explain those meanings. I asked Professors Asayama and Katanuma to explain to me the difference between the two words *hito* and *nin* that Dean Abe had told me were central to understanding Japanese body/landscape relations:

K: Oh, it's very hard. He's a philosopher.

BD: But just from your point of view.

K: Hito *is a Japanese word and* nin *or* jin *is a kanji or Chinese character which is pronounced* jin *in Chinese. Our ancestors used* hito *before the written*

kanji came into our culture. "Hi" means spirit, and "to" means "stop" or
"remain." Hito means the state of the remaining spirit. So it's different from the
meaning of the original Chinese character nin *or* jin.

BD: So nin *means?*

A: Nin *or* jin *means all the human beings, that's all. Originally the kanji*
character represented the person from the side, in profile.

BD: Nin *or* jin *is many people and* hito *is more a person alone in nature or a*
spirit of a person alone in nature?

A: Yes, that's why we didn't have a word "nature" in our ancient times right
up to the Meiji period.

BD: When humans became separate from nature?

A: Yes, that's right. The Japanese people have been influenced by the Chinese
culture so they lost the total idea about human beings and universal matters
that they had had originally.

K: So right now the older generation can understand what Professor Asayama
said and the unconscious way I think they used to do that was through man-
ners, but the younger generation—

BD: —don't think so?

A: Oh, no.

The interlaying of Japanese language and kanji, or Chinese characters, adds a further layer of complexity to understanding the ways in
which Japanese language and culture create a sense of Japanese
embodiment in landscape. Professor Katanuma explains how the underlying concepts have not needed to be attended to consciously or ana-
lyzed, as their meaning has been carried by the formal manners of the
Japanese way of life. But there is a problem with this now, as the children do not place the same value on formal practices—not understanding, perhaps, how much those practices carry the subtle and complex
meanings of the culture.

Professor Shindo explained the ways in which communal use of
and reverence for the landscape in Japan have been intricately connected with festivals such as the kite festival that I had participated in,
in Hamamatsu:

The festivals are very much tied to events that occur in each of the seasons.
Although a lot of people may not know this at this point, the original thinking

*was that when the cherry blossoms bloomed the gods will be calmed down when
we welcome them to a celebration underneath the cherry blossoms. We welcome
the gods to the harvest or to the planting. So although that may be forgotten
now, it's still very much ingrained that the cherry blossoms are communal. The
joy of life was all tied into these events that happened. The moon-viewing party
happened in the fall, the cherry blossom festival happened in the spring. Our big
events were tied to the different seasons and enveloped the whole rice-planting
way of life, the wetland agriculture. But that part of Japanese culture has been
so damaged by progress that it's driven a wedge between the culture and the
seasons, because rice planting has now become a business rather than a way of
life. The culture that surrounded all these events, that surrounded the rice planting and the music and dance, has been destroyed because of the change.*

The traditional body/landscape relations that Professor Shindo
describes are, according to Berque's analysis, similar to those found in
the writing of the Japanese philosopher Watsuji Tetsuro, who wrote in
the 1930s:

Whereas in the modern Western view self and environment are opposing terms, in Japan they are seen as interactive; the self melds with the
environment by identifying with patterns of nature which are, nonetheless, culturally constructed. (Berque, 1992, p. 93)

What Watsuji Tetsuro described as a difference between Japan and
the West thirty years ago has, at the turn of the century, almost
reversed. Western environmentalism has introduced a sense of connection between self and environment, fundamentally shifting traditional
Western concepts of body/landscape relations, while Japanese industrialization has undermined the patterns of practice through which the
connection between self and landscape has traditionally been established and maintained. Of course, the West is full of industrialists and
Japan has deeply committed environmentalists, so a sharp line dividing
Japan from the West cannot be drawn with the kind of certainty that
seemed possible to Watsuji Tetsuro only thirty years ago.

Professor Kanda sees the undermining of body/landscape relations in
Japan as beginning before industrialization, with the Meiji Restoration,
when old Japanese beliefs about landscape were overridden: the power
of landscape was abandoned in favor of the power *over* landscape:

*In the old times, very old times, in Japan, nature was so big and secret. Gods
lived in big mountains and in tall trees, they lived in large rocks and in the
lakes. Nature was like a god to the Japanese people. With the building of shrines
or temples they didn't cut out the old growth, just a small area, and they built
temples or shrines and they conserved around that area, around the Shinto
shrine. That's a very traditional thought of the Japanese people. But almost 130
years ago the Japanese social system changed drastically, importing ideas from*

foreign cultures. Then they began to develop nature, and they thought Japanese could control nature. Development was seen as good, as an improvement—in competition with European countries. Especially in Hokkaido—the government came to Hokkaido with the idea of developing it as a food source for the Japanese people. At that time there were no temples and shrines in Hokkaido, there were no rice fields in Hokkaido. They developed a new kind of rice to grow in this climate, so farming was successful here. Where shrines and temples were built, there the land remained untouchable—it was holy. Now many Japanese continue to think they can develop all aspects of nature in Hokkaido. But 200 years ago the Japanese people didn't think that way. They didn't control all of nature because nature was a huge force. In the last 100 years, people think that they are stronger than nature. After World War II Japanese people believed we must develop the land—we must work hard to catch up to Europe and the U.S. We achieved that aim, but after that we realized, some of us, that there are many environmental problems, and in the minds of young Japanese people. Because of the economic wealth children have been over-indulged. They have become unhappy and lost any sense of hope. There are many suicides among young people. We ask, now, "What is a good life?" and we realize it does not equate with economic success as we previously thought.

The rapid industrialization and the sense of competition with the West in terms of industrial development has meant that Japanese children have experienced material wealth and at the same time an intense pressure to do well in school, to learn by heart the vast curriculum that incorporates Japanese culture, Chinese kanji, and Western knowledges. Professor Kanda, like others, expressed strong concern about the current situation of the children.

Combined with the problem of children's attitude to traditional practices was the fact that very few children have access to outside spaces where they can play freely. The freedom that Kenzaburo Oe saw bursting forth in literary circles has not extended, it would seem, to the children. In many people's eyes, they have actually lost freedom. Professor Kasama says he recognized this for the first time, with a shock, when he was traveling in Mexico:

When I went to Mexico I was very surprised. I was not used to seeing all the children outside, playing. I asked why don't these children go to school? My friend told me it was because the schools don't have good conditions. At first I thought the children were sad and very sorry. But in two weeks my idea changed. Children cried very rarely, they looked very interested in what they were doing, and they were very happy playing "hiding the pig" and swimming in the river, and beside them women washing clothing and singing. So they are poor but they are very good-natured and they have a very good environment and they enjoy themselves.

Some children came to our coach to sell us orange cookies and fresh fruit juice. I particularly remember an eight-year-old girl. She looked at me and she

said, "Please sir, oranges, very good oranges." Her eyes were very lively. I
thought, Japanese children are always very tired. Japanese children don't have
eyes like that girl's sparkling eyes, and also Japanese children don't play in a
good environment. The Mexican children are poor, so that's very bad, but they
had good conditions, much better than Japanese children in Tokyo.

But when I visited some day-care centers in Sapporo (for children
aged two to four years old), I did not gain the same negative impression. It is true that I was amazed to see such small children acting in
perfect concert with each other and with the teacher. In a cooking lesson, for example, thirty or more children sat at desks, scarves tied
around each one's head, each with a ball of dough in his or her
hands, watching and listening to the teacher, who, head tied with
identical scarf, showed what to do with the ball of dough. Each one
followed her movements precisely, and at the same time, each one
seemed completely secure and at ease about their place in the world.
Outside, where there was deep snow lying on the ground, one group
of children shoveled snow, and another group of children played at
throwing snowballs with their teacher. She showed them how to enjoy
the snowball fight, how to fall and roll over in the snow when hit by
a snowball. Her activity with the children seemed fun and instructional
at the same time. In each case the children appeared to be completely
absorbed in the task of shaping their bodies and their practices so
they could coordinate them with everyone else.

I was actually envious of how secure these children seemed. In
watching the children I became intensely aware of the contrasting
experience of loneliness and uncertainty so evident in the Australian
experience of early childhood settings, such as the story told by Helen
of being left in a child-care center in Chapter 2, and also in my own
research in preschools (Davies, 1989). The collective, synchronized
practices these children were engaged in—in song, in dance, in cooking lessons, in play—were both interesting and challenging and
seemed to be an important part of the process whereby these children
were learning to be members of their extraordinarily complex culture.

At the same time, the desire for freedom, for individuality, and the
related development of individual conscience and responsibility is not
ruled out by collective practices, as became clear in the Japanese students' stories in Chapter 4. I experienced a moment of *ura,* of relaxed,
spontaneous expression of feeling, when one of the small boys ran up
to me, threw his arms around my legs, and said that he loved me. He
did this when none of his peers was watching, but in view of other
adults. Later, in his classroom with his peers, he appeared to show no
expression of feeling or any wish to be singled out or to behave differently from the collective. Professor Kasama writes about the way
"freedom" was incorporated into the Japanese National Instruction for
Day Care Nurseries in 1990. In this environment it was believed that

"children could be more spontaneous and free in their growth" (Kasama, 1992, pp. 125–26). Such practices of freedom, he writes, have been difficult to establish and have run into the same kinds of difficulties as the "open schooling" movement in Australia in the late seventies (Davies, 1982). In some day-care centers, for example, where "freedom" has been introduced, the children have run wild and local people have complained about having to warn them not to play on the road or on the railway lines. Tightly controlled collective practices that teach children how to behave appropriately cannot be abandoned without guidance over what takes their place.

In one of the centers I observed, the Nishioka Day Care Center, the policy of the director, Tada Shunida, was to take the children camping in the mountains and the forest where they could be free of the restrictions of everyday life. He showed me a video of one of the camping trips on which children played in the river and walked on trails through the forest and picked potatoes out of the freshly ploughed earth. Here the children did not seem quite so much at ease. It was, as Professor Kasama observed, very unusual for Japanese children to find themselves free to play in the river and in the forest. Their movements were careful and a little hesitant as they discovered how to move and act in ways they had not practiced before. There was a look of shock on one child's face when he slipped and fell on the forest trail and no one rushed to pick him up, and also a look of uncertainty on the face of a girl whose foot slipped on the smooth surface of the rocks in the mountain stream. But each one recovered quickly and continued in their exploration of themselves as embodied beings in this mountain landscape. The director told me that he wished the children to know and experience the happiness of lying on the ground and gazing at the sky. He believed it important for them to camp out there in the forest, to experience themselves without restriction, and to discover the landscapes of mountain forests and streams.

Even though the issues of individual freedom and individual conscience are seen by some to be of pressing importance, the placing of greater weight on being part of the collective has a profound effect on Japanese consciousness and conscience. The following interview with Hariu-san brings out the interesting point that responsible forms of environmentalism in Japan are thought in group terms rather than in individual terms. This was puzzling to me at the time. I thought at first he was halfhearted, not really committed, because I could not see that his self was deeply and morally located in the collective ethos of his workplace. My repeated questioning reveals, however, a strong and continuing commitment arising in the first instance from his group membership:

H: Japan thinks, economic activity first, but there are other people who are aware of and care about the environment.

BD: How did you become such a person?

H: I myself am a secretary of Kushiro Nature Conservation Society of which there are sixty members. This was established for the purpose of making the wetlands a national park—and this was when the Ramsar convention was accepted in Japan. In that organization my activities, for example, research or making claims for conservation, had an effect.

BD: Is your involvement because of work or caring already about the environment?

H: It's because I work for the museum and the main theme of the museum is the wetland and the people around the wetland. If I worked for another place, I'm not sure that I would have been interested.

BD: Is it from the heart, now, or for work?

H: Half and half. Because I worked for an environment agency for two years I was sent to the Ramsar convention, and so we had a lot of opportunity to get information from all over the world. The reason why I am secretary of the society is half obligation and half responsibility.

BD: What do you mean by responsibility?

H: I feel that in order to conserve the global environment we must start locally.

BD: If you retired would you keep working?

H: Yes.

BD: If you were of an age to retire now, would you keep doing this work after you retired?

H: Yes.

My difficulty in understanding the locatedness of self in group responsibilities was sometimes met by an equal difficulty on the part of my Japanese hosts in understanding that my body/landscape relations were, in my understanding of them, primarily individual. I wanted to walk in the forests on Hokkaido as I had on Honshu, so I could feel and imagine and experience, in an embodied way, the Japanese landscapes about which we talked. I explained this failure of communication to Yuko when she was taking me to interview Sato-san at the On-en-ai Center. What happened as a result of this conversation opened a new vista on Japanese body/landscape relations. Later, I wrote in my journal:

The On-en-ai Centre is in the middle of the wetlands. Since I had talked at length to Yuko about my difficulty with Japanese tours and my puzzlement at the way Japanese people do not seem to want to walk quietly in the forest or the wetlands but always have to be entertained, or lectured to, she asked me did I want to walk in the wetlands or interview Sato-san. I said both were important for my research so it was impossible to choose. So we went for a walk in the icy wind and talked as we went.

The On-en-nai Centre was a high-ceilinged, spacious wooden building with views out over the wetland and a wood-fired stove. It had feeders for small birds and also for mice. Inside there were two tall trees with very impressive birds' nests in them and a wooden carved and painted bird flying down to the nest. There are very large fabricated nests for owls available here which are being placed in appropriate places for the owls. The park ranger we had arranged to meet was Mitsunori Sato. The Centre is part of the Kushiro Shitugen National Park.

We put our coats on and went out to walk on the boardwalk. The ice-cold wind swept across the vast undulating expanse of straw-coloured grasses and reeds. I had no idea how to see or hear what was there, almost overwhelmed by the icy elements against which I felt I had little protection. But Sato-san and Yuko quietly drew my attention both to the minute detail of the flowers amongst the tall grasses, to the sounds of the birds, and to the geographical features of this vast space. We paused in our walk at a sinkhole where the water is many metres deep. Apparently cows and horses got bogged in these sinkholes and drowned when the farmers used the wetlands for farming. For the first time in Japan I saw and heard many birds. Yuko knew each one by its call and by the look of it. As we set off, a Japanese bush warbler or nightingale began to sing and sang for an unusually long time. Yuko drew my attention to the birdsongs as we walked along the boardwalk through the ice-cold wind, making them bearable to me by singing them to me.

Because summer is so very short here, the flowering season is quite brief. Although we are well into spring now, it being the end of May, the plums were only just starting to bloom. One of the water weeds we observed has a little net with which it catches plankton to feed on. We also saw an uprooted plant that the tika deer likes to feed on.

Many thousands of years ago this area was five metres under sea. It is possible to dig up fossils of oyster shells in some areas. Later there was a river that brought down soil from higher up. Sato-san showed me how to see the pattern of alder tree growth which follows the ancient path of the river. He also showed me how to see that the marsh is divided in half by the man-made levee bank, which is there to control flooding. He said it is not yet clear what effect the levee bank has on the wetland. There were quite a few broken trees and branches, which had been caused by an unusually heavy snowfall last winter. This area, they told me, is popular for cross-country skiing in winter.

By the time we got back to the Centre my toes were completely numb and I couldn't feel my fingers either. Yuko and Sato-san were cold, too, but they didn't seem to mind, as their pleasure in nature overrides the concern about being cold. And of course I now have the thin blood that comes from living in the tropics for four years. Sato-san made us coffee to warm ourselves and we stood and gazed out at the wetland and talked, warming our fingers with the hot mugs. Sato-san feels it has had a profound effect on him living and working out here. He feels deeply connected to the land. As I listened to him talking to Yuko, I was suddenly struck by the fact that the music of the Japanese language is very similar to many of the warbling bird sounds we had heard. The staccato pattern of syllables is like the staccato sound of the bush warbler. Both of them have soft gentle voices, so the similarity was quite striking. I said I thought English language was more like water flowing, whereas Japanese was more like the birds. Take the words "heart" and "kokoro" for example. When I told them what I heard, they laughed, and when we thought about it we could not tell whether the way they spoke had been influenced so much by their lives spent with birds, and so the similarity only existed in their way of speaking, or whether it could be generalized to all Japanese speakers.

Professor Asayama described such connectedness to nature as having deep roots in Japanese culture. The connectedness sought by the Australian environmentalists, which they construed as outside culture, in Japan lies at the heart of the culture:

Some Japanese people are aware of the inner part of the world. They are in harmony with and continuous with the world. These people's consciousness, their feeling, their will, and their judgment, the inner being of these people is continuous with the mountains and the forests. Taoism and Shintoism had the same meaning—nature is not around you. In Buddhism, nature is Buddha-hood. The mountains, the river, the grasses are of Buddha's spirit, and humans are included in this. If the human heart is defiled or invaded, then the same might happen to the mountains. There is an expression in Japan, "Jigo jitoku," meaning there are natural consequences for one's (mis)deeds. But you know some Japanese people are getting away from this way of being. The inner god, inner mind, might be invaded by something.

We talked, then, with Professor Katanuma, about the way the commitment to environmental issues and the connection of these to the traditional understanding of humans being at one with nature are still profoundly meaningful to some people, while for others, whose interest is in development and industrialization, they mean nothing.

BD: There seems to me, as an outsider, a lot of destruction of the environment, mountains being cut in half and forests being cut down, and it seems that Japanese people's love of nature or being at one with nature is clashing with the developers' destruction of the environment.

A: I think Japan has two kinds of character, generally. One is very traditional and one is very modern. Japan has been industrialized in many ways. It was thought that nature should be used for industrialization. But right now Japanese people are becoming aware that that kind of trend should be changed. Should be stopped.

BD: So you think most Japanese people are worried?

K: Uh huh, worried, yes.

BD: So what do you each think the ideal Japan is in environmental terms?

A: It's my personal opinion, but I strongly believe that a lot of the Japanese people are now thinking of the possibility of living together, human beings and nature, and therefore that human beings should not destroy nature. That is the kind of ideal picture the Japanese people are painting.

K: My opinion is that Japanese people can't move back to the pure traditional way. They want to live in a better community, in a better house so some part of forest or plain should be developed. That's a reality. But you know I think there should be two kinds of groups in Japan. One group is, okay, we don't care about nature at all, we just live in the condominium-type of housing that we call mansions, no garden, not even a small portion of soil around it, just a concrete wall, but they don't feel frustrated about it. Another group are thinking that we should stop that kind of very rapid industrialization and think of ourselves and go back a little bit and study how our ancestors might have had the ideal life. So in this part I agree with Professor Asayama.

As this conversation continued I tried to find the similarities between my experience of body/landscape relations and the ways in which Japanese people who care about environmental issues experience themselves in relation to their landscapes. As Tada Shunida, the preschool director, said, the roots of East and West are very different, but when they climb the mountain, they see the same moon. I explored this idea with Professors Katanuma and Asayama, using David Suzuki's *Declaration of Interdependence*:

BD: There is a statement by David Suzuki, the Japanese-American environmentalist, his Declaration of Interdependence, *which is his ideal statement about the way we should be. He says "we are the earth through the plants and the animals that nourish us and we are the rains and the oceans that flow through our veins and we are the breath of the forests of the land and the plants of the sea." He is making an idealistic statement about the relationship between the person and the environment that will help people to think how they should behave in relation to the environment, and it seems to me that this is a very Japanese kind of a belief from ancient times about the nature of the relationship between the person and the environment. Would you agree with that or how would you see that kind of statement?*

A: I would agree. That has real meaning for me. This is very understandable for me, very understandable. Buddhists, both Chinese and the Japanese, believe that everything is changeable and relative. Even when their philosophy is not articulated, a person, through repeated practice, can bring their spirit up to the level of Buddha, then come back to this world again. A person reaches that level through recognition of the truth. So from that point of view, Suzuki's statement would be considered as a pure thought, not mingled with social and political thought. But it should be interpreted in such a way that people can comprehend it and their practice be informed by it.

Professor Katanuma, in contrast, interprets Suzuki's statement in terms of Shintoism, and he finds it not an acceptable inspirational basis for action:

K: My observation is different. Sometimes tradition coincides with progress. Tradition is very beautiful, but on the other hand there was much misery and trouble. That kind of thing is very beautiful, I think, the sentences are very beautiful, the feeling is very idealistic. But you know, I recognize that this kind of animism was not necessarily the thing which brought the Japanese people happiness.

BD: So you feel a little bit wary about a statement that seems too close to the animism of Shinto religion?

K: Yes, yes. That's my honest opinion.

BD: And in what way did it not bring happiness?

K: Ahh, for example, the kind of thought that the emperor should be top among our society you know, because the emperor, as you know, is god in Japan.

While Professor Katanuma rejects Shintoism as a basis for modern-day principles, for others acceptance of those same traditional aesthetic principles may actually occlude some central aspects of their newly adopted environmental discourse. I was startled, for example, at the negative attitude some people expressed towards the almost extinct bears and the extinct wolves. Yoshinaka-san explained that animals such as bears played no part in the traditional discourses:

Generally the idea of the national parks in Japan has been to conserve the natural beauty of the scenery, and we have not been concerned about ecosystems or animals at all. But that attitude has been changing a little bit, and now many people have begun to think about ecosystems, and about how to conserve not only the scenery but also the ecosystems. The bears are now endangered, too, so the attitude towards the bears has changed quite a bit in the last five or ten years. Some restrictions on hunting have been put in place, but unfortunately in those two or three years there are too many conflicts between the bears and human citizens in the national parks, and also outside the national parks between the bears and the farmers.

As one of the volunteers working to conserve the wetland said:

Human beings and animals who live together have a lot of trouble. Because the forests are decreasing now, deer or the bear come to our villages. Crops have been eaten by animals, and farmers suffer a lot of damage. It is significant trouble. What do we do? I can't answer, but I had a small farm until the past year. I grew corn but the deer ate it. Sometimes bears came through the village and killed in a savage way.

I raised this particular problem with the forest rangers in Shibecha. They had taken us into a restricted access area of the forest, where we climbed a very tall observation tower from which it is possible to see the 80,000 hectare forest. They told us how the old-growth forest had burned down because of fishermen and farmers fishing there and lighting fires or smoking cigarettes and throwing away the burning butts. It took them ten years to plant the area with one carefully chosen species of pine that is now thirty to forty years old. They are now planting other kinds of trees in the shelter of these pines to create a forest similar to the original forest. Some birds and small animals are returning to the forest, but there is not yet enough variety of trees to attract very many. They showed us some of the cranes through a telescope in the tower. The crane is the particular bird they are protecting. When I asked about the wolves and the bears, they said if they see bears they tell the hunters and the hunters find their nests, and if the bears are in places too close to people, they move them. Bears and wolves are not liked because they harm people and farms, and they have no protection. They were a bit worried that I thought they were not friendly to the bears. In fact, they said, the habitat is not yet suitable for the bears. Although the mountain streams do have fish, the restoring of the forest probably needs to go further before animals such as bears and wolves can live here without territorial disputes with humans.

Interestingly, the rangers observed that the replanting of the trees has improved the quality of the water going into the wetlands, and in turn the water where the oyster farming takes place is now more suitable for the oysters. The water is a higher temperature, which is good for the oysters. These rangers were the first people I talked to who made a connection between good environmental practices such as restoring forests and the effect of that on the health of wetlands and sea. More usually, people talked only about their area of expertise and claimed no knowledge of related fields.

Although the rangers were aware of the connections between the forest and the wetland, suggesting an integrating holistic approach, their suggestion that their particular responsibility was for the crane was rather puzzling to me, as I could not understand the focus on one and not on the whole. Berque's analysis provides a useful insight:

> As is well known, Japanese culture has paid scrupulous attention to its natural environment, but this was not environment in general: it was a selection of some places (*meisho*), some plants (e.g., *momiji*), some moments of the year (e.g., *jugoya*), etc., all entangled into certain sets of regular associations. Elements of the objective environment not included into these representational sets might not be considered at all. The white birch (*shirakaba*), for instance, was not appreciated until Meiji. Ordinary coppice (*zokibayashi*) did not aesthetically exist until Kunikida Doppo discovered its charm in Musashino. Environmental disruption (*kogai*) was neglected until it became an international concern, and so on. (Berque, 1992, pp. 97–98)

Related to my puzzlement about the attitude to the bears was my puzzlement about the Japanese propensity for tours in which there was no time to stop and contemplate. I had also been puzzled at the lack of interest in walking through forests or near lakes unless there was a specifically designed activity there or, as Takeshi had explained to me, something to create the silence for you, since silence in itself is nothing. The long cultural history with the intricate interlaying of humans with/in landscape means that those landscapes that are valued are the ones most clearly inscribed with recognizable cultural patterns: a shrine, a temple, a tourist village, a place about which a poem has been written. The idea of the place outside culture that the group of Australian environmentalists sought seems rather strange in this context. As Professor Shindo explained when we discussed the meaning of *wabi sabi*:

S: Wabi sabi *is not nature as it is, nature in its natural state; it's nature as presented by humans.*

BD: *So it's more to do with the act of the imagination?*

S: *I am making nature, this is nature. The kind of water fountains where you wash your hands in the garden and maybe a tea room, set off to the side and opening into the garden.* Wabi sabi *is definitely not to be experienced in a natural place.*

BD: *So is there a Japanese word that would capture the equivalent feeling of tranquillity in nature as opposed to tranquillity in man-made surrounds?*

S: *Are there any natural spaces where humans haven't meddled?*

BD: *And yet Dean Abe says that the most fundamental principle in Japan is that one should not meddle with nature.*

S: *There is also the principle of usefulness. Cutting the tree is to kill the tree and using the chopsticks is to reconcile cutting the tree. The notion of* wabi sabi *is very much part of the traditional way. It is to do with sensing in both active and passive ways at the same time.*

This capacity to hold apparently contradictory ideals and values in place at the same time can lead to strange decisions in the courts where action is both seen to be incorrect (according to one set of values) and yet allowed to proceed (in terms of another set of values). The women who worked as volunteers in conserving the wetlands in Kushiro expressed their frustration with the determination of government and those with power to continue development even when it is recognized to be wrong:

V: *Once the governmental agency determines to build up some project—*

BD: *It's very hard to stop them?*

V: *Yeah. The people can't change it.*

BD: *Oh, they can—in Sapporo they have been fighting for fifteen years.*

V: *It is very rare.*

BD: *Yeah.*

V: *Many people notice this environment is in danger.*

BD: *Mm.*

V: *But the government is not conscious of the environment.*

BD: *Mmm. I wonder if you think that it's possible for ordinary people to change the thinking of the government?*

V: *I guess this might be possible, but in Japan I guess there is no resolution of the citizens, they are very used to giving up.*

V: *In Hidaka, in the center of Hokkaido, there was a case against the building of the dam on the sacred land of the Ainu people. There was a very big movement—*

V: *And they won the case—*

BD: *They won, the judge said that the Ainu people were right that the land should not be built into a dam, but the dam should go ahead.*

V: Yes.

BD: It's crazy.

V: That kind of craziness is, I think, very typical. There are many initiatives in Japan to destroy the environment. The government wants to continue building things.

I will end this chapter with Sakakibara-san, an activist farmer, who told Japanese environmental history in terms of his own story of one growing up on a farm and becoming a farmer. Sakakibara-san gives a strong sense of one who is able to think as an individual and at the same time act strongly: he has already called a halt to some aspects of industrialization on his farm and he has very clear plans for bringing about a better future. His insights, like Professor Kasama's and my own, come in part from observing the children. Sakakibara-san inherited his farm from his father when he was quite young. His farm is now a holiday farm for children and young people to learn about nature, as well as a farm that demonstrates progressive, environment-sustaining techniques. The Ramsar convention was a crucial turning point for him. He found people he could talk to about the problems created by the government paying subsidies to dairy farmers to extend their farms into the wetlands. The next important connection for him was the Association of National Trust in Japan, which has helped him convert his farm into a place of learning. Twenty-five years ago, when he was twenty-two or twenty-three, his father died, leaving him the farm. About four years after he took over the farm, he had the mind of a landowner, but he was also aware of the fields of flowers blooming on the seashore:

S: I didn't think the flowers were of much importance, or needing protection. There was not much invasion of cars at that time. But in 1970 to '75 gravel brokers came and started taking the sea sand for construction use. They took the sand from the beach right on the edge of my land and caused erosion on my land. The erosion was very bad. Eventually the Hokkaido government started to talk about erosion and so made it more difficult to get a licence to remove the sand. The town didn't mind about the erosion, but eventually people began to see the erosion, as it was so bad on the seashore. There was much criticism of the Hokkaido government. It took three years in my case to stop the mining of the sea sand.

BD: That battle made you see and feel differently about your land?

S: I could see the contrast between now and when I was young. When I was young there was virgin forest and fields of flowers. In 1960 we coexisted with nature. Immediately after World War II we did not have much big equipment. In

1965 to 1970 we got big machinery on farms and in the forests. Before that we had a blacksmith in the village for making horseshoes. In the sixties we started to buy machinery. The mechanization of farms and forests took place in 1965. It started in 1960 but then we didn't see much effect. Horses disappeared. In 1955 there was no motorized equipment. In 1965 loans were made available. I got a tractor in 1960—that was very early—in 1957 the Hokkaido government made tractors available. At that time my father began exploiting the marsh.

BD: How did he do that?

S: He could see that the dairy farm would grow big, and that if he didn't expand the farm, he couldn't manage it. He needed to cultivate the wetland. The government subsidized the movement into the marshes and into the forest. The farm became an exhibition farm for wetland cultivation.

BD: So both he and you were forward-thinking people?

S: Yes. At first I didn't care about nature conservation. But when I was a child I liked to go to the mountains to pick wild strawberries and small kiwi fruit. I went to the mountains with my friends to pick fruit, and to the river and the forest. We climbed trees and broke the birds' nests and learned about nature's ecosystems. Year by year, as I've grown older my thinking has changed. I don't have children of my own, but I watched the young people who came to my farm each year. An important thought came to my mind. Children can play in nature without restrictions. But whenever they play in man-made spaces, there are restrictions. I noticed that the children were changing from year to year. I also thought it was important for the next gener- ation to have access to true nature. Because I saw different young people each year, rather than watching my own children grow up, I could see the change. Each year ten to fifteen young people of high school and college age would come to work on the farm, from Kushiro and other places. I became very wor- ried about contemporary families, worried about what they think about nature, even around their own homes. I want people to do conservation, even in their own back yard. Families don't involve the children in work around the home any more. When I was a child we were poor and we had to haul water from the river and chop firewood and help with the farming. That farm work and home work has disappeared. I don't think the computer is everything. We have a very big responsibility for the next generation. The government encourages us to expand and compete with Australia. Farmers don't care about conservation, they just want to expand and get more subsidies. In 1963 to '64 the govern- ment encouraged expansion and subsidized expansion in numbers of cattle. Farming used to be much more diverse, we grew vegetables and such things, but because of the subsidies the forests were cut down. First the forests are cut for logging, then cleared for dairy farms, and the rivers were wrecked. There is no assessment of the environmental impact before a forest is designated for clearance. They just draw a line on the map and cut that forest down. It is only after that destruction that they sometimes begin the reforestation programs.

BD: What makes you so different from other Japanese people?

S: I guess I am a cranky man. I saw my farm being eroded. My anger made me ask questions and become an activist. Farmers and villagers are generally not aware and think I am crazy. My new idea of having people come to stay on my farm to learn about nature has not yet taken off. Parents have not yet realized what their children have lost.

At the same time as he is capable of standing apart and being profoundly different, one of the ways in which Sakakibara-san plans to establish a different future is to set up a foundation. The text of his proposal for the foundation taps deeply into the group ethos, the sense of collective responsibility of Japanese people. He writes:

We are about to lose the charmed feeling that nature gives us. Around us, trees and streams are disappearing, shores are "reclaimed" and green is replaced by concrete and asphalt. The nature around us supports our healthy life, and it has no exception even in the valley far from the city. In mountain villages, so different from the city, the countryside culture has coexisted with nature. But recently the demand for new buildings is threatening the existence of the countryside culture. Considering our own needs and the balancing of the ecological system, we must rethink what nature is and how we treat it. It is our responsibility to ensure that the next generation inherits a living earth. This is our responsibility because we live on this planet. We must learn more about the earth and begin the process of reform. Our only possibility of life is to live in the closed air on the surface of this planet. It is too thin, a helpless space floating in the black universe. It is not for humans to live selfishly. From ancient times, nature is keeping humans alive and allowing us to evolve. Now that very evolution has become a burden. We are the zenith of living things on the planet, and only we can stop the destruction of the environment. We live on this earth. We should take responsibility, and ensure the life of this precious place for the next generation. This is our duty.

And so...

Different political histories, different alignments, make possible different take-ups (or refusals) of new discursive folds in the landscape. The male environmentalists in the Australian political and discursive landscapes described in Chapter 3 take up environmental discourse as an embodied, individual experience outside of culture and in partial opposition to traditional forms of masculinity. Environmentalists in the Japanese discursive and political landscape may also constitute aspects of traditional culture as incommensurable with environmentalism, or, like the environmentalists in Australia, they may intricately interlay aspects of the new discourse into the old. Because of the deep commensurability of some aspects of deeply valued aesthetic/cultural tradition with aspects of environmentalism, it is predictable, in the Japanese landscape, that environmentalism would primarily be understood as a collective/responsible practice, not least because industrialization can be seen to obliterate those landscapes valued by artists and poets.

While it is possible to make up a story of difference between, say, East and West out of the stories told in this chapter and Chapter 3, it is just as easy to disrupt such essentializing. I could write here, for example, that modern Japanese environmentalism as it is practiced and spoken about by the people I talked to in Japan is subtly different from Western environmentalism as it is understood and practiced in Australia. Japanese environmentalism can draw on the long cultural history of Japan, with its highly developed sense of visual aesthetics, and at the same time, the politics of that history, associated as it is with control by the emperor and the oppression of indigenous people, may weigh against an easy acceptance of environmental principles if environmentalism and the ancient traditions are seen as continuous with each other. As well, the weight of traditional aesthetic principles may occlude some central aspects of the newly adopted environmental discourse. The ways in which knowledge is taken to derive from authoritative sources in Japan, I could go on, tends to place discourse and its correctness and usability at one remove from those who use it. The understanding is inherent in the fine detail of traditional practices and only poets and philosophers can authoritatively produce the words to express it. In contrast, in Australia, the long cultural history and meaning-making of body/landscape connections is not available to the environmentalists. Such knowledge belongs to the indigenous people and is revered, but it cannot be appropriated. Within the brief history of Western presence in Australia, poets and philosophers have not produced words through which we might all know the detail of our bodies with/in Australian landscapes. This, along with the Australian *attitude* towards knowledge as personal discovery, enables the Australian environmentalists to actively seek their own embodied experience of the discourse of environmentalism in appropriate(d) landscapes. Further, the practices of spending childhoods in "nature" gives Australian environmentalists a sense of power in their bodies that makes possible the strong enmeshment, or inlaying of self, in such appropriate(d) landscapes. Such work towards achieving those strong bodies, I could argue, is shown in my own stories of my childhood and also in the Australian collective biography stories. The sense of oneself as appropriately strong is told in stories of water. The Japanese body/landscape memories do not include such experiences. They take place in stories of learning correct attitudes (going fishing) and correct practices (writing), or of attentiveness to the sounds and sights of the seasons (the clock ticking, the taste of mulberries), or of enmeshment in collective practices with others (the *Matsuri* festival, or playing with friends on the way home from school).

But I would prefer to point out that these are not *essential* differences. I would prefer to draw your attention to Seiji, who, as an environmentalist and as Japanese and as a traveler, actively rejects those aspects of Japanese traditions that he, personally, finds oppressive. He seeks out and finds experiences more akin to his Australian friends. The Australian collective biography stories reveal that the children in that landscape worked just as hard to become appropriately embodied as did the Japanese students. It is what they call it that differs: the Australians find in their appropriate(d) bodies the signs of their difference from each other; the Japanese students find the signs of their sameness. The Australian environmentalists seek experiences in which they shed culture, yet they do so in ways that are directly informed by the language of environmentalism (that is, by culture) and that link them with ancient Australian indigenous images. The Japanese environmentalists (like the Japanese students) are schooled in seeing the links between culture and individual practice and so make them readily visible. The difference is primarily a matter of emphasis, though it is also a matter of the collective building of perspectives and sets of practices.

An eyebrow raised
slightly;
sound of bird

Koko Kato
(Lowitz, Aoyama, and Tomioka, 1994, p. 66)

Part 3 ~ Subjection and the eclipsing of the constitutive power of discourse through fictional texts

THE EXPERIENCE OF READING THIS BOOK, until now, is one in which I have invited you to immerse yourself in the experience of reading, of coming to know differently, through your own remembered past and the past of others, and through imagining other worlds, other folds in the landscape that you had not known before—and so to experience body/landscape from multiple vantage points, or "perspectives," in the landscape. I have invited you to interact with the texts of this book, not solely at the level of *logos*, or intellect, but as embodied readers, with feelings, with imagination, with the capacity to know differently, with the capacity to read from the body. I have adopted a style of writing that is poetic, an invitation rather than an instruction, to know bodies, and to know them with/in multiple folds in physical, political, and discursive landscapes. What I have invited you to "know" as a result of this reading is as much in the manner of what I have written as it is in the content. It is in the manner of writing that I have attempted to give meaning differently, to open a space for other possibilities of understanding embodiment. It is in this opening up of imagined possibilities that the writing I have undertaken is similar to the writing of fiction writers.

The four writers, Yasunari Kawabata, Sam Watson, Rodney Hall, and Janette Turner Hospital, whose work I have chosen to explore in the third part of this book all write in ways that make visible the movement of characters through different folds in the landscapes in and through which they take up their being. They take us back into the past and forwards into the future of what is possible: they provide the possibility of both historical critique and critique that is projected forwards through their mode of representation of body/landscape relations. As I said in Chapter 1, this book is not just about finding keys to unlock cultural meanings of bodies and landscapes in order to make them visible. It is also about transgression, about finding other ways to speak and write with the grain of bodies and landscapes. It is an exploration of the power of language, not only as it seeps into bodies and shapes the very grain of them, but also as a powerful force that individuals and collectives can use to retell lives against the grain of what Morrison (1994) calls "dead language." Through dead language, Cixous suggests, we become ignorant of ourselves and have no agency. We are like corks, bobbing about on the sea of discourse:

The most incredible is to notice to what extent we are all ignorant of ourselves. To what extent we are 'stupid', that is to say without imagination. To what extent we are sort of corks without poetry, tossing about on oceans. . . . Yet I am convinced that we all desire not to be corks tossing on an ocean; we desire to be poetic bodies, capable of having a point of view on our own destinies; on . . . humanity. On what makes humanity, its pains and its joys. Which is not the point of view of a cork . . . we no longer even know how to let ourselves feel, how to allow ourselves to feel as we feel. Nor how to accompany this feeling with the song that echoes it and restores it to us. (Cixous, in Cixous and Calle-Gruber, 1997, p. 12)

The direction of this book so far has been towards recovering a sense of permission to use what Cixous calls the poetic body, and away from abstract, disembodied discourses. In the next four chapters I use my readings of the texts of four fiction writers, and my conversations with three of them, to unfold what it might mean to talk of recovering language that enables us to recognize our feeling, poetic body, and accompanies it "with the song that echoes it and restores it to us."

Embodied reading and embodied writing are intimately implicated in the recovery of the song. We are used to thinking of reading and writing as being processed by one part of our bodies, that part which we tend to split off as "mind"—the brain. In Chapter 2, on collective biography, I described embodied writing as the writing that comes from close attention to the remembered embodied self and learns to avoid clichés and explanations. The participants in the collective biography workshop were learning to read their own bodies in an embodied way, and to write from their bodies. They learned to listen in embodied ways to each others' stories and to extend their own remembered knowledge of their bodies through doing so. The body that they read, and that they read with and wrote with, was not a headless body but one that had learned to disrupt the idea that mind rests in only one part of the body, or that mind operates independently of the body. And their use of language and of well-practiced discursive strategies was as much what they learned to observe and to question as the knowledge resting in their bodies.

These concepts of poetic/embodied reading and embodied writing raise interesting questions in relation to the concept of subjection. What I am *not* wanting to suggest here is that we can find a way of reading and writing that escapes subjection. Bodies are subjected. Bodies learn to recognize themselves through clichés. Bodies learn to separate mind from body. Yet bodies can also learn to use the very powers they gain through being subjected to turn their reflexive gaze on the discursive practices and the habituated ways of being those practices make possible, making them both visible and revisable, and opening up the possibility of developing new ways of knowing. We take up language as our own in multiple ways, not in any simple linear or monolithic way. We have many modes of speaking and writing, many possible ways of knowing. It is amongst and within this complex web that one form of knowing can be used to trouble another. Deleuze's concepts of nomadological or rhizomatic texts is useful here:

> Instead of a Derridean model of the text as textile, as interweaving—which produces a close, striated space of intense overcodings, a fully semiotized model of textuality . . . texts could, more in keeping with Deleuze, be read, used, as modes of effectivity and action which, at their best, scatter thoughts and images into different linkages or new alignments without necessarily destroying their materiality. . . . Instead of the eternal status of truth, or the more provisional status of knowledge, texts have short-term effects, though they may continue to be read for generations. They only remain effective and alive if they have effects, produce realignments, shake things up. In Deleuzian terms, such a text, such thought, could be described as fundamentally moving, "nomadological" or "rhizomatic." (Grosz, 1995, pp. 126–27)

We are subjected through discourses and within relations of power, and there is no clear boundary between what we are or are in process of becoming and those discourses through which we are subjected. But, as Deleuze points out, discourses/texts/thought are not static, any more than subjects are. In the very processes of becoming speaking, knowing subjects, we become subjects in transition, subjects who can use the powers that their subjection by and through discourse gives them, to trouble, to transform, to realign the very forces that shape us:

> Power acts on the subject in at least two ways: first, as what makes the subject possible, the condition of its possibility and its formative occasion, and second, as what is taken up and reiterated in the subject's own acting. As a subject *of* power (where "of" connotes both "belonging to" and "wielding"), the subject eclipses the conditions of its own emergence; it eclipses power with power. . . . [T]he subject emerges both as the *effect* of a prior power and as the *condition of possibility* for a radically conditioned form of agency. (Butler, 1997, p. 14)

To *eclipse*: to cast a shadow, to overshadow or surpass in importance: the subjected being, in its trajectory, overshadows, surpasses in importance, the discourse through which it takes up its being. Fiction writers such as Kawabata, Watson, Hall, and Turner Hospital enable us to see, in their writing, just what such trajectories might be. That play and opening up of possibilities in fictional texts does not entail "escape" from being constituted through discourse. To think of it as escape would be to place it in some binary relation to subjection.

Rather, we are subjected, we become human, and in that becoming can search out the possibilities for creative movement beyond the apparent fixity in the terms of our subjection. Poetic/embodied writing, Cixous says, makes possible the unleashing of that creative potential and in so doing enables us to "become more human":

> We live, but why do we live? I think: to become more human: more capable of reading the world, more capable of playing it in all ways. This does not mean nicer or more humanistic. I would say: more faithful to what we are made from and to what we can create. (Cixous, in Cixous and Calle-Gruber, 1997, p. 30)

Within poststructuralist theory, language is understood as the most powerful constitutive force shaping what we understand as possible, and what we desire within those possibilities. Cixous suggests that we embrace the intoxicating power of language, using it to move into the not-yet-known:

> To think that we have at our disposal the biggest thing in the universe, and that it is language. What one can do with language is . . . infinite. What one can do with the smallest sign! . . . This may be why so many people do not write: because it's terrifying. And conversely, it is what makes certain people write: because it's intoxicating. Language is all powerful. You can say everything, do everything, that has not yet been said, not yet been done. (Cixous, in Cixous and Calle-Gruber, 1997, p. 12)

In the chapters that follow I want to look more closely at the ways in which four very different writers produce writing that invites the possibility of an imaginative take-up beyond what is already known. In entering into the writing or reading of a novel, we are also, to a large extent, entering the "already-known" and experiencing it afresh, perhaps finding how the already-known can be spoken for the first time. We find certainty there in that already-known. But we may also find the unexpected, the thrilling, the element that unsettles, that makes undecidable that which we understand as the controlled, the rational, the already-decided. The openness to undecidability, to movement, is what many have an ambivalent relation to: the power that subjection brings with it often resists the questioning of the terms of subjection, since such questioning might undermine the power already grasped. Yet taking risks, going beyond, also seems to be what being human leads us to. Cixous sees that openness to risk, to movement, as *indissociable* from human life:

> [O]rdinary human beings do not like mystery since you cannot put a bridle on it, and therefore, in general they exclude it, they repress it, they eliminate it—and it's *settled*. But if on the contrary one remains open

and susceptible to all the phenomena of overflowing, beginning with natural phenomena, one discovers the immense landscape of the *trans-*, of the passage. Which does not mean that everything will be adrift: our thinking, our choices etc. But it means that the factor of instability, the factor of uncertainty, or what Derrida calls the undecidable, is indissociable from human life. (Cixous, in Cixous and Calle-Gruber, 1997, p. 52)

So now I am asking you to turn your conscious attention to writing: to enter the folds of the body/landscape opened up in the texts of these four writers and to be conscious at the same time of the strategies they use, and the effects of those strategies, in terms of the possibilities of body/landscapes that they open up. The first chapter examines a Japanese novel by Yasunari Kawabata. I wrote to his publisher seeking an interview with him, but I received no reply. The strategy I adopted, then, was to open a discussion about the novel with Takeshi Osanai, Dean of the Kushiro campus of Hokkaido University of Education—and that discussion became the chapter that follows.

~7~ An exploration of body/landscape relations in Kawabata's *Yama no Oto*

THE EXCHANGE WITH TAKESHI OSANAI on which this chapter is based took place after my first trip to Japan and while I was searching for ways of understanding and writing about what I had experienced there. This chapter is made up out of the emails, letters, and faxes we sent back and forth during the months after my trip. We both became immersed in this exchange about embodiment in Japanese landscapes as it emerged in our unfolding of Yasunari Kawabata's *Yama no Oto* (*The Sound of the Mountain*). Our discussions about the novel are interspersed with comments about our embodied selves as we write to each other about the overly busy lives in which our work is embedded, and about the student exchange program between our universities. We have edited much of this discussion out, leaving enough to create the sense of ourselves as embodied writers.

I began the correspondence by asking Takeshi whether he thought the central character in *Yama no Oto*, Shingo, should be read as typical of Japanese men of the time in which the novel is set (the late 1940s), or whether he reads him as surprisingly different from what one might expect. I had found when I arrived at the end of the novel that I could not tell which of these ways of reading might be appropriate. Had Kawabata thought of Shingo as a character intricately and appropriately interlaid in Japanese cultural landscapes, or was he creating someone who could be read as out of his place and out of his time? Takeshi's first reply to my emailed question was as follows:

Dear Bronwyn,

I reread *Yama no Oto* last Sunday. As you of course know, the author Kawabata won the Nobel Prize for Literature in 1968 and four years later, in 1972, committed suicide. I remember hearing that news with surprise. It was then that I read this story first, but I did not find it very interesting; maybe I was too young. It is a long time ago. How time flies! While reading it again, I was surprised to see how much I have forgotten in detail of the story.

Shingo's wife Yasuko is sixty-three years old, a year older than he. She is plain-looking. He does not love her; he actually wanted to have married her elder sister, who was beautiful. Still, he lives with her in the same house in peace, with their son, Shuichi, and his wife, Kikuko. Yasuko knows her husband loves Kikuko. Kikuko is beautiful and always reminds Shingo of his wife's sister, whom he could not marry. Kikuko likes or rather loves Shingo; she does not seem to love her husband Shuichi. Shuichi has a mistress outside. In the story, it is hinted that he made his mistress pregnant. However, the mistress, Eiko, insists to Shingo that the child is not his son's, saying that she has no intention to make Kikuko worry about her pregnancy. Shingo is struck with her pluck. (I feel this part reflects a sign of the times in the postwar period when Japanese women became stronger than before and started to regard themselves no longer as men's sexual subordinate.)

All those subtle deceits and distorted love are described against some typical Japanese settings, such as the rustling of autumnal winds, traditional ways of celebrating a new year, a shower cloud of the blue summer sky, etc. Strangely enough, it is not clear what kind of job Shingo is involved in, except that he runs a small company. He seems to be rich but you cannot tell how rich he is. Everything is so vague. As the two generations live in the same house, it may be a big house, naturally, but you cannot tell how big it is, either.

Conversations between the characters are all polite forms of standard colloquial Japanese. Yasuko, Shingo's wife, and Kikuko talk of daily topics casually but expressively. Shingo likes Kikuko's way of talking especially. He is afraid he may not be able to live long. Again and again, he regrets that he did not marry Yasuko's sister. Every time he feels sorry about that, he feels more tenderly toward Kikuko. On one occasion, Shuichi suggests to his father that Kikuko is an "independent woman," meaning he does not mind him doing anything with her. Of course, Shingo does nothing of the sort.

Shingo represents the older generation; he strictly keeps his old moral code; he cannot forgive his own son his immorality but is always conscious that he himself may be immoral at the deeper level of the heart. I presume that Shingo is described as the character representing the older generation and in that sense he is a typical member of the upper-middle class of that time. He is critical of his son, but not bold enough to make his presence as a moralist; he is timid, after all. This timidity may have been repaid by nothing but the ugly daughter Fusako, who comes back home betrayed by her husband, and the shameless son Shuichi. However, the autumnal winds coming through bamboo bushes, for instance, soothe his tormented conscience. I think Kawabata is describing Shingo as a typical Japanese ageing man of that time, deeply lamenting, however, because he thinks that men of that type are quickly disappearing.

I am not quite sure whether I have answered your question clearly, but the above is what I figured out. I am curious to know why you wanted to read this story and your feedback to my comment.

. . .

I hope you have recovered your energy. I would love to hear from you.
Best wishes and sincerely,
Takeshi

Dear Takeshi,

It has taken me a long time to continue the conversation about *Yama no Oto*. I have been under too much pressure at work and simply could not find any time to devote to the questions I had raised. But this morning I find I have woken very early (like Shingo himself) and so I will take the time in this space before the sun comes up to think about what I want to say. . . .

Your email tells me exactly what I need to know. Shingo represents the older generation's morality and is typical of the upper middle class of his time. The novel is a lament that men like Shingo are disappearing. Yet it still seems to me that it is an unusual novel, in that it sets the main male character in a completely domestic setting and tells about those forgettable small details of everyday life that men (particularly men these days) do not usually bother about.

What I would like to do next is to take some of the passages about Shingo that I found interesting, and tell you my reading of them, to see whether I am reading them in ways that make sense to you as a Japanese person.

Early in the novel Shingo wakes during the night because of his wife's snoring. He is saddened by his negative reaction to his wife's ageing body. He opens the window and looks out:

> One of his daughter-in-law's dresses was hanging outside, unpleasantly gray. Perhaps she had forgotten to take in her laundry, or perhaps she had left a sweat-soaked garment to take the dew of night.
>
> A screeching of insects came from the garden. There were locusts on the trunk of the cherry tree to the left. He had not known that locusts could make such a rasping sound; but locusts indeed they were.
>
> He wondered if locusts might sometimes be troubled with nightmares.
>
> A locust flew in and lit on the skirt of the mosquito net. It made no sound as he picked it up . . .
>
> There was a vast depth to the moonlit night, stretching far on either side . . .
>
> He thought he could detect a dripping of dew from leaf to leaf.
>
> Then he heard the sound of the Mountain. (Kawabata, 1970, pp. 7–8)

Here we see Shingo alone at night. He is aware of nature in its tiniest detail. I have been reading again about *wabi sabi* in a book I bought in Tokyo in the last days of my visit. The author writes, "Truth comes from the observation of nature" (Koren, 1994, p. 46), and that in the context of *wabi sabi* "nature" refers to:

> the dimensions of physical reality untouched by humans: things in their pure original state. In this sense nature means things of the earth like plants, animals, mountains, rivers, and the forces—sometimes benign, sometimes violent—of wind, rain, fire and so on. But nature in the context of *wabi sabi* also encompasses the human mind and all its artificial or 'unnatural' thoughts and creations. In this sense nature implies 'all that exists,' including the underlying principles of existence. (endnote 20)

This passage about Shingo in the night captures, for me, Shingo's experience of truth as it is defined here in this description of *wabi sabi*. Shingo is aware of his own thoughts, of "nature," and of the simple human acts such as putting a dress out to catch the dew.

In the second passage I would like to discuss, the family is sitting down at breakfast and Kikuko observes that the gingko is sending out shoots again. Shingo is bothered because he has been noticing the shoots for some time, and is surprised that she has only just noticed. She points out that he sits facing the tree at breakfast time.

> Yet Shingo was troubled: that she had not noticed unseasonal buds on the great tree suggested a certain emptiness.
>
> "But you ought to notice when you open the shutters or go out to clean the verandah," he said.

"I suppose that's true."

"Of course it is. And you're facing it when you come in the gate. You have to look at it whether you want to or not. Do you have so much on your mind that you come in looking at the ground?"

"This will never do." Kikuko gave her shoulders that slight, beautiful shrug. "I'll be very careful from now on to notice everything you do and imitate it."

For Shingo, there was a touch of sadness in the remark. "This won't do either."

In all his life no woman had so loved him as to want him to notice everything she did.

Kikuko continued to gaze in the direction of the gingko. "And some of the trees up the mountain are putting out new leaves." (Kawabata, 1970, pp. 53–54)

This is very hard for me to interpret. If I were to read from my perspective now it could not make sense. I would find it difficult to understand why Shingo thought he had the right to tell Kikuko what she should see, why Kikuko thought it was good to imitate Shingo. Nor could I understand why Shingo thought the offer to imitate him should be read as love. If this were in a modern, Western novel I would have assumed Kikuko was being sarcastic and that Shingo was overbearing. But I don't think that is what is happening. I read it as a very subtle scene of love in which Shingo's affinity with nature (his capacity to experience *wabi sabi*) is something he wants to share with Kikuko. He wants her to experience *wabi sabi* as he does because in that shared spiritual knowledge they can love each other. Her willingness to enter into this shared knowledge is a sign of love.

The third thing I found surprising at first was the degree of responsibility that Shingo took in relation to the interpersonal relationships in the family. It is his responsibility to talk to Shuichi's mistress, it is his responsibility to talk to Shuichi about Kikuko's abortion, and so on. In my own experience these things are women's responsibilities and men who can talk about them and take responsibility for them are admired and very rare. So I didn't know whether to see Shingo as one of those rare men, or whether all Japanese men at that time would be expected to act as he did. Then I read a short story called "Nightingale" (*"Uguisu"*) by Ito Einosuké, which is probably set in Hokkaido and which may be just before the war rather than after, but around the same time. In this story, which is set in a police station, the policemen take a detailed interest in and responsibility for the details of the lives of the peasants in ways that are really surprising to me and yet not unlike the kind of responsibility Shingo takes in his family. This made me think that in Japanese society (as compared to Australian society) the individual is much more subject to the ruling of the society, and so men such as Shingo, and the policemen, have important work to do that revolves around regulating the lives of those around them such that they conform to an agreed understanding of correct forms of being. So I conclude that I should read Shingo's involvement with the family as the responsible and regulating actions of the father.

But this brings me to a fourth point. There are quite a few clues in the novel that Shingo is depressed, or rather that the author is depressed. When you said you were surprised that Kawabata committed suicide not long after this novel won its prize, I thought that it did not surprise me somehow, and so looked for clues on my second reading. The difficulty Shingo has in loving and controlling the lives of his two children, Shuichi and Fusako, seems to me to make him feel quite depressed. The world is changing in ways that mean he cannot any longer control those things for which he is responsible. His children are behaving in ways he does not understand. Only Kikuko can share with him the things that seem to matter. In some ways he too is changing. He thinks Yasuko should have a mind of her own and, for example, should want to leave her own suicide note if they were to commit suicide together, rather than rely on him, as she suggests she would, to write such a note for both of them. He is uncomfortable to think that this old woman has no identity apart from him. He is caught in a rapidly moving point in history that is very painful for him. Even the landscape is not the same as it was any more after he finds out that Kikuko has had an abortion because of Shuichi's attitude to her:

> The pines were no longer just pines. They were entangled with the abortion. Perhaps he would always be reminded of it when he passed them to and from work.
> This morning, of course, it had been so again.
> On the morning of Shuichi's admission, the pines had melted back into the grove, dim in the wind and rain. This morning, standing apart, associated in his mind with Kikuko's abortion, they somehow looked dirty . . . (p. 185)

There is another terrible passage associated with the abortion. Shingo has come home from work early and Kikuko is minding Fusako's baby on the verandah. Some American military planes fly overhead.

> Shingo was touched by the gleam of surprise in the innocent eyes.
> "She doesn't know about air raids. There are all sorts of babies who don't know about war." He looked down at the baby. The gleam had already faded. "I wish I had a picture of her eyes just now. With the shadow of the airplanes in it. And the next picture . . ."
> Of a dead baby, shot from an airplane, he was about to say; but he held himself back, remembering that Kikuko had the day before had an abortion. (p. 171)

This passage suggests to me that the abortion and the war are overlaid on each other as terrible losses of a destructive kind that he is barely in control of. This is a small sign in an otherwise tightly controlled novel, that there is something terrible and almost out of control that the author is not telling us about. His horror of old age and the death of his friends and the fascination with suicide are probably the other clues that something is wrong, but this image of the dead baby shot from the airplane is much more telling.

So—there are my thoughts. The sun is long since up and it is time to have some breakfast. I am looking forward to hearing your reactions to these thoughts of mine. Does my reading of these passages make sense to you?

My reason for choosing this novel when I went to the Maruzen bookshop was that it looked as if it might give me some clues about the body-landscape relations I am trying to understand in both Australia and Japan. But in Japan, unlike in Australia, it seems that any of the stories I read that are very recent make no reference to this relationship at all, so I keep going back to older books such as this one. It seems I am looking at something that is almost lost, and I don't know what to find in its place. Perhaps I am reading the wrong things.

. . .

I look forward to hearing from you
Bronwyn

Dear Bronwyn,

It was very nice to hear from you again. Your comments on *Yama no Oto* were interesting. They were good hints for me to scrutinize this delicately bizarre story.

The first part you quoted I found worthy of further discussion between you and me. As for the second and third parts, I would like to tell you my interpretation on another occasion.

The point I would emphasize here for you is that the translation you read may have taken you towards the biased impression that this story is an embodiment of Japanese *wabi sabi* view of nature. I have no intention to contradict your perspective on how *wabi sabi* "nature" should be interpreted. Especially the part you illustrated with a quotation from Leonard Koren was thought provocative to me: *wabi sabi* surely is the matter of physical as well as metaphysical nature. However, my impression of that particular passage is that it is about more than *wabi sabi*: in short, the author Kawabata attempted to describe Shingo's "melancholy" towards ageing, making full use of subtle changes and movements in the natural world.

The idea of *wabi sabi* is quite often related, in my understanding, to a simple, quiet life, standing aloof from the mundane. A person who leads such a life, it is thought, could feel him/herself as part of nature and inter-communicate in sympathetic ways with nature. Matsuo Basho, often ranked at the top of Japanese *wabi sabi* haiku poets, was typical of such an artist.

It seems to me that the translator of the version of *Yama no Oto* that you read put a one-sided emphasis on the description of nature from the *wabi sabi* perspective, unduly neglecting to convey to the reader Shingo's turbulent deep psychology, mixed with the fear of death and the irresistible but weak flame of sex.

The following is my awkward but very direct translation of the same part that you quoted. I hope that it might give you some of the idea I put above.

Yasuko sleeps well. He supposes it is due to her good health. Sometimes Shingo awakes from sleep at midnight to think that it was because of her snoring. Yasuko had got the habit of snoring at the age of 15 or 16. He had been told by her parents that they had made efforts to cure her of the habit, only to fail. The habit, however, ceased when she got married to Shingo. It started again when she became over fifty.

When Yasuko begins to snore, Shingo holds her nose and sort of shakes it. If that act does not stop it, he shakes her by the throat, which he does when he is in good humour; if he is in ill humour, he feels the ugliness of ageing in his wife's body that has long been his companion.

Tonight he is in ill humour. He switched on the light and kept staring sidewise at her face. He held her throat and shook it. It was slightly sweaty. Shingo thought to himself that maybe it was only when he stops her snoring that he touched her body by stretching his arm in a decisive way. Then, he somehow felt a deep sorrow in himself as if the bottom of sadness had gone. He picked up the magazine at the side of his pillow but, as it was stiflingly hot, he got up and opened one of the sliding wooden doors. He squatted there.

It was a moonlit night. Kikuko's one-piece dress, hanging outside, came in Shingo's sight. Its colour was unpleasantly whitish, loose and slovenly. Perhaps she had forgotten to take in her laundry, he thought; but, on second thoughts, he guessed it might be left there to take the dew of night, for it was sweat-soaked.

There was a short, shrill sound like "Gyah-gyah" heard. It was from a cicada on the trunk of the cherry tree to the left. Shingo doubted that a cicada could give such an ominous screech, but a cicada indeed it was. He wondered if a cicada might become frightened by nightmares. The cicada, he guessed so, flew in and lit on the skirt of the mosquito net. Shingo seized it, but this time it did not give any sound. It was a different one from the one screeching on the cherry tree. He threw it away with his full force toward the higher place of the same cherry tree, so that it might not wrongly fly in again, directed by the light. There was no responsive sign.

Shingo was looking toward the cherry tree, holding the sliding door he had opened. He had no idea whether or not the cicada he threw away reached the cherry tree.

There was a depth to the moonlit night, stretching far on either side. Though it was before August 10, insects on the grass were already chirping. He thought he could detect a dripping of dew from leaf to leaf. Then he heard the sound of the mountain. . . . The sound was like distant winds, but it had a deep sufficient bottom, like an underground rumbling. He felt as if the sound was being produced in his own head; he shook it, thinking it might be a ringing in his ears. The sound stopped. Perhaps it was the sound of the winds, or the sea, he thought. He was sure he had given careful and calm thoughts to the sound, but he hit upon another possibility that such a sound did not exist; still the sound was heard.

It was the sound as if a devil had passed by and made the whole mountain rumble.

From my translation, though it is blunt and far from an embellished literary style, you may have noticed several expressions symbolic of Shingo's mental condition. For example:

1. "Kikuko's one-piece dress, hanging outside, came in Shingo's sight. Its colour was unpleasantly whitish, loose and slovenly." (This sentence conveys just the opposite image to Kikuko, whose movements are brisk and dignified.)

2. A dumb cicada which seemed to lack in substance when Shingo threw it towards the cherry tree. (This description is associated with Shingo's declining mental power ascribable to ageing.)

3. "There was a depth to the moonlit night, stretching far on either side." (When we say the night is deep, it is almost equivalent to "the night is hollow and blank." We feel so especially when we seem to have been trapped in an aimless life.)

4. "Yama no Oto." (The phrase may seem just a literary description of powerful nature. Truth is, however, that it is such a kind of sound that gives a shudder of fear to the person who hears it.)

That is all for today. Sleep well, Bronwyn; otherwise you will be knocked out from the pressure of work.

* * *

I have just been to Sapporo on business. In the train, I reread your letter and the second part of *Yama no Oto* you quoted. I want to convey to you what I thought on that part before it erodes. As for that passage, you said, "This is very hard for me to interpret. If I were to read it from my perspective now it could make no sense. I would find it difficult to understand why Shingo thought he had the right to tell Kikuko what she should see, why Kikuko thought it was good to imitate Shingo. Nor could I understand why Shingo thought the offer to imitate him should be read as love."

First of all, please remember that there is a small mountain behind Shingo's house and that a shrine stands at the edge of the mountain, where the ground has been turned flat so that it could be used as the precinct for a shrine. The gingko tree in their conversation grows there. Seen from the dining room of Shingo's house, it looks as if the gingko was growing in the mountain. The season is autumn, and recently a typhoon has hit the area and caused the gingko tree to lose all the leaves. Naturally, gingko trees send out shoots in spring. However, this particular gingko has started to come into leaf again though it is autumn. It is quite unusual.

I would say there are two important points to be read carefully to attain the correct interpretation of the part you quoted. One is this sentence you mentioned: "Yet Shingo was troubled: that she had not noticed unseasonal buds on the great tree suggested a certain emptiness." I cannot be sure at all what "a certain emptiness" means: where is it? whose "emptiness"? "Emptiness" of what? etc.

The reason I felt that way may be because the translation is too broad. If you were to read the original sentence carefully, you would find the following closer to the original, though my translation is far from refined and literary:

> Admitting the truth of what Kikuko said, Shingo suspected that her mind was vacant for some reason and this mental condition might have caused her to pass the days without noticing the unseasonable buds of such a big tree.

The other sentence I would draw your attention to is: "In all his life no woman had so loved him as to want him to notice everything she did." This is the translation to put things upside down. Probably the following is closer to the original, I believe.

> To wish your partner to notice everything you do and see—you might have such a passion toward a woman you love, if you really loved her; truth is, however, that Shingo had never loved a woman in that way.

If those two arguments I raised above regarding the translation have a reasonable ground, your feeling of difficulty in interpreting the whole passage will melt away. I should think that it is far removed from the original in meaning to envisage that Shingo thinks he has the right to tell Kikuko what she should see, much less that Kikuko thinks it is good to imitate him. Kikuko's words "I'll be very careful from now on to notice everything you do and imitate it" seems to have a note of joking sarcasm.

Let me stop here tonight. I need some sleep. Do you sleep well? You should. Honestly I enjoyed the conversation with you on *Yama no Oto* very much. Recently I feel I am a bit tired with keeping myself mentally alert all the time. Maybe I need a loose life.
Best regards
Takeshi

Dear Takeshi,

Thank you for your fax, which I received on Friday. . . .

Kaori is doing well. I met with her in my Japanese students' collective biography session last week and her English has improved dramatically. She seems to be growing quite confident. She has joined the collective biography group this semester since Seiji, who was part of the group in first semester, has dropped out, having finished his thesis.

She said she had had an email from you suggesting you meet up with her on your visit to Australia next month . . .

Now—to our interesting conversation about *Yama no Oto*.

I was very interested to see your translation of the first passage I quoted. It is different in subtle ways from the translation I have. The lines that I had typed out were not the complete passage, but the ones that seemed to give me a sense of a man attuned to *wabi sabi*. When you bring in the extra lines, the emphasis is clear—that it is a story about Shingo's melancholy about ageing and death and his sexual fascination with Kikuko. My emphasis was wrong. I was aware of the aspects you emphasize (the translation I have does not ignore them), but I was not focusing on them for the moment, because I was trying to get some insight into what I did not understand, rather than what I felt I could understand. In other words, I think the fear of ageing and death, and sexual attraction to a beautiful young woman, are probably common to both cultures. The way in which the body is experienced in relation to the landscape, I think is not common. I am so fascinated by the Japanese sense of body/landscape relations and the concept of *wabi sabi* that I have given them an emphasis that distorts what is there. You are quite right that the translation can lead me astray. It has done so in more ways than one. I was very startled when I read your translation to discover I had imagined the scene of Shingo awake during the night so wrongly. My translation described him as opening the window and sitting by the window. Your translation of the original tells me he slid open wooden doors and squatted. I see immediately that I was imagining him in a more Western setting and so bringing a whole lot of inappropriate Western imagery to the passage. Given my interest in body/landscape relations it is not a minor error, to have imagined him embodied so inappropriately. I feel betrayed by the translator on this point.

I suppose my question about whether Shingo should be read as typical or not was in part needing to know whether what I was struggling to understand was a commonly shared aspect of Japanese culture, or an unusual aspect of Japanese culture. To the extent that the part I have to struggle to understand seems to coincide with the principles of *wabi sabi*, then it seems the answer is that what I am trying to understand is something very deep about Japanese culture—although according to my Japanese students in the collective biography group, this may be an aspect of Japanese culture which is in process of being lost, as young people do not appreciate such things, being too much influenced by American television.

In the book by Koren that I quoted before, he also says that there are three lessons learned from millennia of contact with nature which are incorporated into the wisdom of *wabi sabi*. These are:

1. *All things are impermanent.* The inclination toward nothingness is unrelenting and universal. Even things that have all the earmarks of substance—things that are hard, inert, solid—conventionally not beautiful—present nothing more than the *illusion* of permanence. . . .

2. *All things are imperfect.* Nothing that exists is without imperfections. When we look really closely at things we see the flaws. The sharp edge of a razor blade, when magnified, reveals microscopic pits, chips, and variegations. . . . And as things begin to break down and approach the primordial state, they become even less perfect, more irregular.

3. *All things are incomplete.* All things, including the universe itself, are in a constant, never ending state of becoming or dissolving. Often we arbitrarily designate moments, points along the way, as "finished" or "complete." But when does something's destiny finally come to fruition? Is the plant complete when it flowers? When it goes to seed? When the seeds sprout? When everything turns into compost? The notion of completion has no basis in *wabi sabi.*

"Greatness" exists in the inconspicuous and overlooked details. *Wabi-sabi* represents the exact opposite of the Western ideal of great beauty as something monumental, spectacular, and enduring. *Wabi-sabi* is not found in nature at moments of bloom and lushness, but at moments of inception or subsiding. *Wabi-sabi* is not about gorgeous flowers, majestic trees, or bold landscapes. Wabi-sabi is about the minor and the hidden, the tentative and the ephemeral: things so subtle and evanescent they are invisible to vulgar eyes. (Koren, 1994, pp. 46–50)

Now it seems to me that Shingo's emotional state exactly replicates these three lessons. His life is impermanent, he and the members of his family are imperfect, and his failure to experience love as he partially imagines it with Kikuko shows life's incompleteness.

I was fascinated to know that "the night is deep" means the night is hollow and blank. "Deep" in English usually means filled with significance and meaning. This sense of hollow blankness that Shingo feels is something I understand too well of late. I wish I didn't. I am so tired and overwhelmed by the changes at work and I am close to despair much of the time. The new dominant discourse in university decision making is economic rationalism. That discourse belittles values, making them out to be totally irrelevant in the larger scheme of profit and loss. This is deeply incompatible with my idea of what a university is. I try to fight off my sense of "deep night," but it is hard to fight things when you are exhausted. (I thank you for your words about sleeping well and being careful not to be knocked out by the pressure from work. I wish I could find a way to manage it better!)

I was also delighted to read your translation of the passage on the gingko tree and I can now see that my reading was inadequate. As it happens, I had my collective biography group read that passage last week, and we talked about the way the new leaves were unseasonal, because the typhoon had blown the summer leaves away. Hiroko commented that the old tree might stand for Shingo and the new leaves were like the love in his heart for Kikuko, weak little buds of love that should not really be there in an old man, but which are there, and are beautiful, and must be noticed. I was very moved by this linkage, and it seemed very right to me. It also explained why he might (unreasonably) demand that she notice them. Just as he can dream of other young women who are not really Kikuko, so he can querulously demand that she notice the new leaves, without realizing the symbolic meaning the leaves actually carry. Your translation does not contradict this interpretation, in fact, I think it supports it and adds subtle detail to it. If he is to be read as behaving as a slightly unreasonable and querulous old man, and if we acknowledge that Kikuko loves him in her own way, then her response is indulgent and, as you say, jokingly sarcastic. This is a rich and complex interaction which lends much more depth to the characters than they had for me before.

I understand what you mean about tiredness coming from having to be mentally alert all the time. . . . I like your concept of a "loose life." There is a term in Australia which young people use: to "hang loose," which means to be at ease and let the day unfold as it will. That is a skill I have forgotten. I used to gain peacefulness through meditation and then I got too busy to have time to meditate. Yesterday I decided to start meditating again.

The students said an interesting thing in one of the collective biography sessions the week before last. I asked them what they had learned in the discussions we had had in first semester, as a way of letting Kaori know what we had been doing. I had been encouraging the students to write stories about their memories as these came up in our discussions, but they found this very difficult to do. I was puzzled as to why, in contrast to Australian students, they found this so hard. Masako said she had begun, through our discussions, to get a sense of herself as an individual that she had not had before. This really surprised me as I take a sense of one's own individuality absolutely for granted. In theory, I know that I should not take it for granted, yet when confronted by the discovery that the workshops were being experienced in terms of identity construction, I was surprised. For Australian students, the collective biography process works to reveal the commonality of experience, which the students are not aware of (being focussed primarily on their own separate and distinct identities). For the Japanese students, the experience goes in the opposite direction, towards recognising difference. Of course, this leads me to a major revelation—my original question about Shingo did not make sense. If what I am coming to understand is correct, then of course he is to be read as Japanese, rather than as an individual who runs against the grain of Japanese culture. At the same time, he is Japanese as that is understood in that particular landscape and at that particular time. There are apparent universals in Japanese body/landscape relations, but on closer examination, there are also major regional and historical differences—the commonality comes through the shared literature that everyone knows and through which the landscape is told. The differences are an inevitable concomitant of the sensitive and detailed imbrication of specific selves with/in the actual landscapes and times in which the self is embedded.
* * *

Later—Monday morning

After I had written that, I was puzzling over the words you wrote about the sound of the mountain. I realized I could not understand them. I wondered, thinking about the volatile nature of the Japanese landscape, whether it was anything to do with volcanic activity, or a fear of it. Then, I was reading another novel, *Snow Country*, or *Yukiguni*, also by Kawabata, and I came across the following passage describing Shimamura's experience of the sound of the mountain:

> In this snow country, cold, cloudy days succeed one another as the leaves fall and the winds grow chilly. Snow is in the air. The high mountains near and far become white in what the people of the country call "the round peaks." Along the coast the sea roars, and the inland mountains roar—"the roaring at the centre," like a distant clap of thunder. The round of the peaks and the roaring at the centre announce that the snows are not far away. This too Shimamura had read in his old book. (Kawabata, 1957, pp. 158–59)

Shimamura is a very empty (deep?), well-to-do man who has a relationship with a geisha who fascinates him, but whom he is totally incapable of loving. It is one of the saddest stories I have ever read. He knows and experiences very little first-hand. He only knows about the roaring of the mountain because he read about it. Shingo, in contrast, is alive to such detail—so much so that he is not even sure whether the roaring might not be inside his own head. But what caught my attention was the idea that the roaring signals winter. If the roaring Shingo heard signaled the winter of his own life, then the story is, for me, all the more poignant. I think I am beginning to understand how to read Shingo and his embeddedness in the landscape of Japan.

What do you think?

Bronwyn

Dear Bronwyn,

I am sorry that I have not written for a long time. How are you? Are you going well? Busy as usual? Maree has made a perfect itinerary for me. I am looking forward to visiting Townsville.

I am now rereading your last email. I was fascinated by your very interesting insights here and there in your comments on *Yama no Oto*. I have found that this is really a new way of undertaking discourse analysis. I mean that through the exchange of views between a foreign reader and a native reader on a single piece of literary work, we can deepen our interpretation far more effectively than otherwise. I would like to tell you what I have felt about your comments on *Yama no Oto* and the difference between Japanese students and Australian students when I see you.

. . .

I have just finished a meeting and there is one hour left before the next job starts. When I tried to put my tired self together, I hit upon the idea to reread your email and it was very nice to see there your calm and self-assured image. Now I think I am getting to know what you mean by *wabi sabi*. It is interesting to see that your way of understanding this word is more flexible and less stereotypic than mine. Well, take good care and sleep well. I look forward to seeing you soon.

Best wishes,

Takeshi

Dear Takeshi,

It was wonderful to see you and to find time to talk to you at such length. I am sending some photos of you out at the Reef, and on my verandah, which I thought you might enjoy. . . .

What I will try to do in this letter is to pull together some of the many threads of our talk and our earlier correspondence about *Yama no Oto* and Japanese body/landscape relations. Since we have decided to put our thoughts together as a chapter for this book, I am now writing more self-consciously with that chapter in mind. I have gathered together our various emails and faxes and put them into order and edited them a little. I wonder what you will think when you see them in this context. A little startled, perhaps, at the radical departure from traditional forms of academic writing?

Our trip to the Reef was probably the highlight of your visit. If it had not been for my visit to Japan, during which I sought every opportunity to experience the Japanese landscape as if I were Japanese, I would not have been so bold as to suggest that you find the reciprocal pleasure of experiencing an Australian landscape in an Australian way. I think it was on the jet boat trip back from the Reef that we had our most significant conversation about embodiment in these two very different landscapes. Your experience of the Australian landscape is that it is so vast that it cannot possibly be controlled, nor the meaning of it captured in words that might shape the experience of it for all members of the culture. It thus holds more of its own life force, and each individual must find their own way to interact with it, without the guiding, controlling force of language. This is even more so in the far north of Australia, where it is so hot that the skin is in immediate contact with air and sun and water all the time. In Japan, in contrast, the land is known to be dangerous with frequent earthquakes and tsunami. It is far less benign than the Australian landscape. Even the fauna, such as the bears, are more dangerous, and people are glad they are no longer roaming about. So there is a cultural obsession with control: rivers are straightened and lined with concrete, mountains are flattened, or the sides coated with cement, and roads tunnel through them rather than running round them. The poets have described in careful detail each moment of Japanese nature so that it is chronicled and the words learned "off by heart" by each child. And in that chronicling, the human heart is simultaneously chronicled, imbricated in the landscape so it does not and cannot be experienced as separate from it. There is very little room in such a scheme of things for any individual person to imagine that they can experience the landscape in a new way, against the grain of traditional discourses and practices.

One of the moments of insight into the relationship between language and body/landscape relations in Japan came when I was working with Professor Tanaka on the translation of the 1,000-year-old poems. When we translated poem 84 by Yamabe-no Akahito, for example, Professor Tanaka explained to me that in order to translate correctly there were many things I needed to know about Tagonoura Beach but which must remain background knowledge and not appear in the words of the poem.

The Australian experience is, for me, so different from this. When we visit a beach we have not been to before, there is no poem telling us how to see and feel about this particular beach, and if there is, we probably have not read it, nor are we likely to think it would be important to do so. We draw instead on cultural knowledge about surfing, about sharks, about rips and tides, and about "swimming between the flags." But since I have begun this study I have had a different experience of the Australian landscape. I was visiting Rodney Hall to talk to him about his novels, which are set in the area in which he lives. While eating fish and chips in a local restaurant and gazing out to sea, I noticed that the shape of a distant mountain was similar to that described in one of his novels. Mt. Dromedary, shaped like a camel lying on its side, emerged from the landscape in an exhilarating moment of poetic recognition: no longer a vague shape on the horizon, it was the place I knew within a powerful storyline, invested with emotion and quite specific knowledge. I realized that the connection to the landscape through such imaginary storytelling is a profound one that I barely know how to articulate. In Japan such investments of the landscape may be completely taken for granted, or they may even be experienced as claustrophobic and controlling, robbing the individual of the possibility of seeing the landscape in an immediate way. What you may have come to take for granted (and in part no longer fully appreciate) is the richness of experience that comes from living in a landscape so invested with story and images. What you have, it seems, is similar in some ways to what Aboriginal people in Australia have: a way of telling the landscape that enables each person to experience the power and majesty of the landscape as well as the intimate and intricate detail of being embodied in it. The Aboriginal people cannot take it for granted in the ways they might if they had not experienced being robbed of it. In contrast, we invaders have brought a foreign language and foreign stories to the land that do not resonate with the land. We are, some of us, intensely aware of ourselves as inarticulate in the land, not knowing how to read or listen to it or to tell its power.

Thus in moving from Japan to Australia, from the written to the unwritten, you find a bounty in the freedom that you experience in a largely uncontrolled landscape. You can begin to discover for yourself what it is to be in that landscape in ways not open to you in Japan. I, in contrast, envy the richness of experience the written landscape of Japan offers: it teaches me to see and to be in ways I could not have imagined for myself. I am impatient to know Australia in the same way, to seek out the writers who can listen to the Australian landscape and find its stories in the way the Japanese writers have done. My work with Australian writers who are finding words with which to write the Australian landscape is taking me down this path.

In our reading of *Yama no Oto* I have learned to experience, at least in some small part, the Japanese landscape as it is written by Kawabata, and to gain some elementary knowledge of what it might mean to grow up into a world in which oneself is taken for granted as intricately imbricated in landscapes in ways that are written by the poets and practiced through the rituals of the culture. I can imagine, again in an elementary fashion, what it might mean to live in such a volatile landscape and to experience myself as safe in the achieved orderliness of it, knowing it/myself intimately through words written over many centuries. I understand for the first time the enormous value of learning the words of the poets off by heart. In counterpoint to that, I understand, in a new way, the sheer disruptiveness of the Second World War and the cultural and personal implications of the loss of certainty that was entailed. Shingo's story is a very moving one for me now, particularly in light of Kawabata's suicide.

For your part, in accepting my broader definition of *wabi sabi*, it seems you may have opened up the possibility of your own individual telling of the landscape, and yourself in relation to it, that was not so vividly possible before. Our work has not been static, as we have both moved in understanding as we engaged in it, such that the clear differences that I am trying to write about here are already blurred, and boundaries between one way of knowing and another already interestingly traversed.

And so...
I leave the last words to Takeshi:

Dear Bronwyn,

Thank you very much for the draft of the chapter. I wanted to have sent this reply to you before you started for Norway, but I had to spend most of my time making every possible effort to let the University cut its way through the recent evil omen of the Japanese economy. Honestly, that is not what I feel myself good at, but I am trying my best simply because I do not like to escape in the face of difficulty.

The concluding part of your draft reminded me of the visit to the Reef with you. Although I have visited Australia several times, I had never been to the Reef before. Certainly, it was the occasion of "experiencing Australian landscape in an Australian way." I put on a wet suit and a snorkel, floated myself on the waves, and saw a lot of corals. I did not know that corals are so colourful. I saw a dazzling variety of tropical fish among those corals. From time to time, I came across huge sea slugs lying on the bottom of the sea. Everything was richly and clearly coloured in the sea. Also, everything seemed surprisingly big. The colouring and size of those sea things were so different from what I liked to see in the sea of western Hokkaido when I was a school kid. At the Reef, I enjoyed snorkeling, finding my own way to "interact" with them, "without the guiding, controlling force of language" as you correctly pointed out. It was certain that I became temporarily Australian on that occasion and I enjoyed being so.

However, I agree with you when you say: "The poets have described in careful detail each moment of Japanese nature and the words learned 'off by heart' by each child. And in that chronicling, the human heart is simultaneously chronicled, imbricated in the landscape so it does not and cannot be experienced as separate from it. There is very little room in such a scheme of things for any individual person to imagine that they can experience the landscape in a new way, against the grain of traditional discourses and practices." Through the discussions over *Yama no Oto* with you, which I enjoyed more than I could describe in words, I found how much of my experience with nature had been formed by the power of Japanese language. I would presume that Kawabata is a real artist of Japanese language. He described every tiny change of the landscape with his very sensitive and finely tuned linguistic skills. His style is full of melancholy and transparent aimlessness.

I can definitely say that since I have begun this study of *Yama no Oto* with you, I have become more careful in trying to see the body and landscape relations. Of course, I must confess that I am still confined in the limited boundary of my native language Japanese in terms of the experiences with landscape. For instance, now is the season of cherry blossoms in northern Japan, where I live, and there are two Japanese tanka poems I always recollect to myself at this time of year. They go as follows:

> The spring has come, and once again
> The sun shines in the sky;
> So gently smile the heavens, that
> It almost makes me cry,
> When blossoms droop and die.

> In lonely solitude I dwell,
> No human face I see;
> And so we two must sympathize,
> Oh mountain cherry tree;
> I have no friend but thee.

Naturally, it is hard for me to leave behind the Japanese perspective about cherry blossoms; we tend to see a connection between cherry blossoms and human lives. A Buddhist priest in the eighth century, Kobodaishi, once said that the current of life is ever onward and that death comes to us all. Just like him, I believe that through the disintegration of the old the re-creation of the new becomes possible. Whenever I see cherry blossoms, I say to myself that Change is the only Eternal. Strangely enough, the feeling I experienced when I was snorkeling at the Reef was very different from such a sentiment; what I felt there was that nature is powerful and you can never control or regulate it. At that time I firmly believed that I would never succeed in describing what the coral reef looked like in the Japanese language, however hard I might have tried. This language does not seem adequate to describe the glaring and stalwart nature of northern Australia.

I hope that your opinion will not be very different from mine when I say the collaborative way we have organized to interpret *Yama no Oto* is a truly fruitful one. It was a compilation of cross-cultural perspectives based on our personal experiences with body and landscape. I have approached this famous post-war literary work of Japan mainly from checking its English translation. Your method of collective biography has certainly shed a new light onto the interpretation of the story; I can definitely say that your *wabi sabi* perspective on *Yama no Oto* has made my understanding of it go far deeper than before. Some day, in the near future, we can come back to this joint venture, choosing another Japanese or Australian literary work, which you might call a "two-in-one" approach to discourse analysis and interpretation.

Good-bye and best wishes,

Sincerely,

Takeshi

Against the *shoji* screen—
the muse's
shadow

Teiko Inahata
(Lowitz, Aoyama, and Tomioka, 1994, p. 56)

~ 8~ Reading and writing *The Kadaitcha Sung*: A novel by Sam Watson

In this chapter I am co-author with Sam Watson, indigenous writer and activist and author of The Kadaitcha Sung. *The choice of joint authorship comes at least in part out of the parlous nature of relations between indigenous and nonindigenous Australians at this point in time. The history of some nonindigenous researchers using indigenous knowledge for their own purposes looms large between white researchers and indigenous people. As well, the danger for white researchers is that they might adopt the stance of the objective all-seeing I/eye who takes all responsibility for/control of what can be written, even when it is not their intention to do so. The joint writing here, then, is an attempt to avoid those pitfalls. It is also an attempt to find ways of negotiating some folds in the landscape on which we can stand together.*

OUR PURPOSE HERE IS TO REVEAL some of the struggles for meaning engaged in by Sam as indigenous writer and by Bronwyn as nonindigenous reader of his novel. *The Kadaitcha Sung* re-views the history of Australia through the eyes of its original inhabitants. Our readings of it sometimes coincide and sometimes diverge. We discuss both the coincidences and the divergence in terms of our different lived histories of being in the world and our different experiences as white and black.

Toni Morrison (1993), in accepting her Nobel prize, spoke of the writer's struggle and the sweaty fight for meaning and for "response-ability." Each writer inevitably *responds to* and *is responsible towards* the multiple social and political contexts in which they find themselves:

B: *What response-ability do you have other than to yourself?*

S: *To do it. To write. I think that's the crux, the kernel of the responsibility is to write.*

B: *Why is that?*

S: *Because we all have missions in life, and the old people reach down and touch you in a particular way. . . . An old uncle of mine said to me a long long time ago that, uh, other people need a tribe, but he said in many ways you're a tribe unto yourself. And he says, you've got a long road in front of you and at many times it's going to be lonely but you've got to walk that by yourself. No one can walk that for you. And I feel totally comfortable in that because that reflects the great loneliness of the long-distance writer, I suppose. It is a long, lonely journey and because you have everything, your book is living within you, hidden, within your spirit.*

B: *So that's why it's not a political novel? That's why it is a novel of the imagination?*

S: *. . . I think what happens with, particularly Murri writers, is that they're living time capsules, because the act of passing on information and knowledge is very much a verbal dynamic within the Murri experience. So Murri people, until quite recently, have never really stopped passing down all the knowledge and wisdom that one generation needs to impart to the next one. We've never stopped doing that through verbal dynamics, through talking, through dance, through song, through experience, through interaction between young people and old people. So, I think what I create in my books is just an echo of things stored within my own psyche, and the points of reference on my individual dreaming path, because every Murri person has a special dreaming path that was mapped out for that person at the point of creation, and has been prepared for me by every single generation since then. I'm walking that dreaming path now, and it's very easy for me to be able to put down on paper situations and events and then put in those situations and events, characters. And I can see them, what they are doing. I really think that everything in my writing has actually happened, or is going to happen. So boundaries don't really restrict the Murri writer because Murri writers don't respect boundaries. We don't allow ourselves to be intimidated by boundaries. I, as a Murri writer, make it my practice to at least step over or just go through boundaries. So, I don't allow myself to be restricted by time, by place or political correctness. I write what I want to write one time and that's my only prerequisite, then at the end of the day I'm happy with the page. I don't aim to please, I don't try to fit in with other people's expectations or hopes. I've got a very easy and very positive relationship with my publisher, so my publisher allows me that license.*

B: *One of the things that I notice over and over again in situations with Murri people is a silence that's to do with political correctness. Like "I can't speak" is a phrase I hear more often than anything else, "I can't speak about that," umm, "that's not mine to speak about."*

S: *Within Murri people, Murri people talking about business within the Murri community?*

B: *Mmm.*

S: *Yeah. I'm talking about the genre of fiction.*

B: *So in that you are free.*

*S: That's right. There's a lot of things within the Murri community that need
to stay within the Murri community.*

B: Mmm.

*S   Kadaitcha Sung never ever traded, never ever used real business, or real
special ceremony. That's all out of the top of my head. Because I wouldn't use
that as a trade good. I wouldn't use that as a convenient currency to advance
my own interest.*

*B: But your own dreaming is very real and it's your own dreaming you write in
your book.*

*S: That's right, that's right. And that's mine and it's between me and my pre-
decessors. So that's my business, it's not community business.*

B: So it's between you and your predecessors and the spirit world in some sense?

S: Yeah.

Virginia Woolf says "fiction is like a spider's web, attached, ever so
slightly perhaps, but still attached to life at all four corners." The point
of reality from which *The Kadaitcha Sung* hangs is, in the first
instance, the knowledge that has been passed down to Sam and that
informs his own dreaming. There is a difference between this knowledge and the knowledge that is "correct" community-based knowledge.
There is a license in fiction. It does not draw on Murri political business and is free of some of its constraints. As a novel of the imagination, *The Kadaitcha Sung* can say what might be unsayable if it were
styled as a political novel.

Toni Morrison (1994, p. 4) says "imagining is not merely looking or
looking at; nor is it taking oneself intact into the other. It is, for the
purposes of the work, *becoming*." The imaginary act of readers in
reading a novel is one in which they can and often do *become* the
characters in the novel. For the duration of the reading they live the
imaginary possibility of being otherwise, of being in ways they might
not have imagined possible until they experienced that way of being
in the novel. This is not simply an intellectual/rational act, but something that is lived bodily in the act of reading.

While it is thus a novel coming from Sam's own knowledge
passed down from generation to generation, it is also a profoundly
revolutionary novel in its possible effects on the reader. It opens up
for white readers the possibility of seeing differently, of regarding
Murri people with a different kind of respect and even awe. It opens
up, through a reconnection with the spirit world and through a confrontation with violence and death, the imaginary possibility for Murri

readers of being in control of their lives, of having choice, of being powerful.

In *The Kadaitcha Sung* the invasion of Australia was initiated by a Kadaitcha man who lifted the veils of mist that had protected Australia from invasion by those from the outside, the Migloo. The more usual reading of Murri people as victims of white invasion is erased in this retelling: the invasion came about through conflict in the spirit world.

The god of the South Land, Biamee, ascended to his camp in the stars, leaving Kobbina, chief of the ancient clan of sorcerers, the Kadaitcha, to take up earthly form and live among humankind and ensure that the gods were worshipped and that the natural order of the land was kept. On departing, Biamee covered the land in mist to protect it from outsiders. The Kadaitcha man, Kobbina, had two sons, and when it came to his own time to return to the spirit world, he had to choose one of his sons to be the Turrwan, or high man. Of his sons, "Koobara was tall and fair, and even though he was only a novice his wisdom was great and his patience legend. On the other hand Booka was squat and ugly, possessed of a violence that was fearful to behold" (Watson, 1990, p. 2). When Kobinna chose Koobara to take his place, "Booka's rage exploded into a terrible blood letting. He smote his father and killed him." To protect himself from Biamee's wrath, Booka needed to block Biamee's point of entry into the mortal plane. He entered the red rock where the Rings of Bora formed Biamee's point of entry and stole the key to the circle, the egg-shaped Kundri stone, the heart of the Rainbow serpent. "The mortal plane was now isolated and godless" (p. 3). Because of this, Koobara's power was limited, but he did manage, with Biamee's help, to confine Booka to Brisbane while he regathered the tribes. But Booka nonetheless managed to kill Koobara and so become the only Kadaitcha man on earth as long as he held the Kundri stone.

But what Booka did not know was that already "Koobara's son had been born of a white woman, and Biamee promised his people that the Kadaitcha child would deliver them" (p. 4).

Koobara's son, Tommy, the hero of the novel, is both an ordinary Aboriginal bloke, born of his white mother, Fleur, and a powerful spiritual being born of a Kadaitcha father. As Tommy grows up, Koobara is pleased with him: "With a glint of his eyes, he watched Tommy walk into the Rings of Bora, far below, he noted the lad's grace and beauty. Tommy was tall for a Birri Gubba, his hair brown and straight. He did not have a ready resemblance to his adopted brothers, but his spirit was deep and strong. The lad was a rich brown, similar to the ochres of his chosen tribal land. His totem was Tapu the snake, and Tommy carried the mark in his eyes, which were green" (p. 28).

Tommy's destiny is to save the land from evil. As Kadaitcha man he is capable of changing history, of seizing the Kundri stone and so enabling the spirit world to regain access to the land.

The novel thus opens the imaginary possibility of being both Aboriginal and powerful. It locates Tommy in direct connection with the spirit ancestors, and as having a responsibility to them to act to change the world. He is not a victim of white supremacy, but rather one who takes up his destiny to fight on the side of good against overwhelming evil, that struggle being one that has been there since the beginning of time and always will be there:

S: *One of the great problems is the Murri people believe and accept they're living within a Hades that was created for them by the Migloo. That is wrong. I mean, we're living in a world that was essentially created by ourselves, and we need to accept that, because the doorway out of that world can only be opened by us.*

B: *To me that's the most powerful thing about this novel, that it was the evil Kadaitcha man who started the whole thing, who lifted the veils and allowed the mongrel tribes in.*

S: *Yes.*

B: *I find that so powerful, but I imagine that a lot of Murri people don't want to hear that.*

S: *What I wanted to do with that was, I wanted to go from point A to point Z and have every point in the journey being an event that occurred because of something that Murri people consciously did. So it's a broad trip of Murri empowerment. At no point in that book is there a Murri victim that isn't a self-made victim.*

Tommy's character is a central feature of *The Kadaitcha Sung* through which the victim image is deconstructed:

B: *I'm interested in the introduction of Tommy as one who was riding on Purnung's back, the most feared hunter of all of the spirit world, with Tommy being introduced as both able to settle him and as his co-hunter. That's a fairly dramatic and powerful image to begin with.*

S: *Even as a novice he was a very fierce and able warrior. I wanted Tommy to be able to dominate every setting that I put him into. He had to be a dominant figure. It's only by his own choice that he's placed in particular areas where he acts the victim, but that again is only to further the greater end, only to advance his own struggle. But he's in control at all times.*

B: *This is the undoing of the victim image, this is the creating of a very powerful image.*

S: That's right, yep. At every stage of his journey he has the key to be able to advance or stop.

But it is not just the handing of agency to Tommy that lies at the heart of the imaginary shift that the novel opens up. It is not a mere swapping of roles between usual victim and usual victor. Tommy is handed a responsibility for action and for connection with his spiritual ancestors, for taking back responsible guardianship of the land. There can be no room for him as victim, as one who cannot act, even if that means violent action:

B: There's a bit at the beginning here where you talk about the creation of the world and you say that the world was created and men and women would have dominion over all, but must ensure that the natural order of all things are kept. There's another way of thinking and talking that is starting to be more common, that says, no, you don't have dominion, you're just simply part of what's there. Where do you stand in relation to this?

S: I feel much happier with the concept that we have the old people creating the earth and the natural things and then putting the birds in the air and fish in the sea, etc., then there's the necessary step that we're going to have to place stewards in charge of the natural process so that the species won't overpopulate, etc., or dominate lesser species. Into that picture came humanity. Because I really believe also that the natural environment is perfect in itself and into the Garden of Eden had come sin and that came in through man and women, through the human species. That was going to be the great battleground of the spirit world. Because I believe in warring, in a constant eternal war between the force of good and the force of evil and the natural world is where it's going to happen. So, as men and women populate the earth and as they multiply and go forward, then there has to be connections between them and their roots, which is the spirit world, and I'm suggesting that the pathway of the reconnection is through their relationship, the human beings' relationships with the natural things of the world so that they can reconnect with the spirit, the gods of the natural universe, through their treatment of plants and animals and the natural environment. It's only by being responsible guardians of the natural world that we can then reconnect with those who create us.

The act of reading *The Kadaitcha Sung* can be akin to the experience of *syncope*, a term Catherine Clément uses to describe those moments when we step outside of everyday life through fainting or swooning or ecstasy. She says, "When one returns from syncope it is the real world that suddenly looks strange" (Clément, 1994, p. 1). Syncope involves stepping outside time as we know it: "Physical time never stops. That may be, but syncope manages to achieve a miraculous suspension. Dance, music, and poetry traffic in time, manipulate it, and even the body manages to do that by an extraordinary short circuit" (p. 5). Syncope is compared to a divine jolt, a movement from anguish to ecstasy, apparent death, a disruption, a collision, a space from which one returns and is unable to see the world in the same way again. The biggest jolt for me came in the conversation with Sam. We were discussing the fact that *The Kadaitcha Sung* does not set Aboriginal knowledge up in opposition to the history and mythologies of the rest of the world; rather it is placed at its center. This is a profound move, taking a people and their knowledge—which has been marginalized in the colonizing process—and placing them at the very center, not only of mythology, but of all time:

B: *One of the things that's really vivid is the sense that the mythological base doesn't really just belong to Australia, or it doesn't just belong to Murri history. It seems global to me.*

S: *That's right.*

B: *It's drawing on the Homeric legends and drawing on some aspects of Christian legends, it's drawing on American Indian ways of making connection with the land and the spirit of the land and that's very powerful.*

S: *That's absolutely deliberate. Because what I try to suggest to my white readership is that if they could only close their minds and journey back within their own minds, within their own spirits they will also find their own spiritual roots. The great majority of white Australians are descended from the Aryan tribes of northern Europe, and they're land-/earth-based cultures. And I find that really interesting because those cultures, even the Celtic cultures on the rim of Europe, several points along Wales, Scotland and Ireland, are cultures that express their ceremonies and their songs and dances through standing stones, and that's why I think there's enormous parallels between our different spiritual paths. And unfortunately that journey of white Australians and their spiritual progress was impacted upon by the advent of the Industrial Revolution and the advent of the invasion of Ireland, the invasion of Scotland, etc., the subjugation of those native peoples, subjugation of native cultures, so their spiritual dreaming's been interrupted profoundly by this history. But here in Australia if they could just open their minds and reach out and embrace who they are and where they came from, they would find it very, very easy to connect with Murri people because we're still at one particular stage of development and we need to understand that all of us are descended from earth-based cultures. There's a universality about spiritual journeys and dream paths.*

B: *Although, interestingly, when I went back to Wales for the first time, my father's people having come from Wales several generations back, it wasn't nearly as spiritually profound as when I went to the Centre of Australia. My education led me to believe that my spiritual roots were in Wales. But when I visited the Centre I shifted to being absolutely centred in a spiritual connection to this place. And my kids have the same thing as well, this incredibly deep connection with the land, and it's a very strange and disturbing thing to be told no you don't belong here, or your roots are elsewhere, you don't belong here, because we have very deep roots here; somehow, however, that has happened. It's a very fractured thing to know in one way that you have no rights and you have no long history here, but you've made a connection that is profoundly significant; and it's passed on from me to my kids and presumably to their kids.*

S: Yeah, that probably occurs with a great number of legends that have come out of the Aboriginal tribes right across the nation, that Uluru is the centre of every single dreaming path in the world. And, and on the Biblical parallel I suppose you would refer to Uluru as the Garden of Eden and people went forth from there, outwards. Because on all the paintings, all the dances, all the songs that I've studied over the last ten to fifteen years, there is that one beginning point of the Centre, Uluru, and the tribes just went forth from there, scattered to the four winds and then traveled right throughout Europe, Africa, and those sort of places. So, that well could be.

B: It was just like, this is where I belong, this is the beginning.

S: This is where I return. The circle is now complete. I've come back to where the first woman, the first man, set foot and breathed.

A connection to the land that was politically suspect, blocked by a sense of shame and a dislocated history, is set free. The meaning of being white Australian, descended from the invading hordes, is momentarily undone. The connection between white and black is remade in a way that takes the breath away.

At the same time, *The Kadaitcha Sung* is also a novel of extraordinary violence and hatred towards the Migloo, the invading mongrel hordes, of which I must take myself to be one. The violence works on at least two levels. The first is a factual historical level and involves a telling of what has actually been done by whites to blacks from the time of invasion to the present day. By telling that violence in detail, the reader is drawn into a sense of outrage that then goes some way to positioning the reader as one who shares the desire for revenge. The second is more akin to the shock or jolt of syncope. Entering into the moment of extreme pain invoked by the telling lifts the reader out of the everyday world in a painful way—so painful that on return the world does not seem to be the place you left. The pain of entering that moment of syncope can be enough to prevent some readers from actually continuing to read. It is a jolt they cannot tolerate. The violence done by white policemen to the young woman, Worrimi, at the beginning of the novel, was almost impossible for me to read:

B: When I first read the novel I hated the first part because the men were just so violent, I just thought, I can't back this violence.

S: Yeah, that was written about a period when, in the later sixties/early seventies when I first started knocking around the streets. It was actually common for drunken police to rip young black women off the pubs and the nightclubs, take them to places like Mt. Cootha and have huge parties and multiple rape these women and then just drop them on Brisbane streets.

B: I didn't doubt that it was true, it was just hard to swallow right at the beginning.

S: Yeah, that was exactly a reflection of that and while it's happening, white Australia gets on with their business of watching television, having fish and chips and that sort of gear.

B: But on the second reading I really liked Worrimi and I'm sorry I didn't know her more. In the second reading I got beyond the violence and revulsion and she seemed important to me.

S: That does happen to a lot of people who suddenly are shown a window into the Murri experience. It does overwhelm them initially. You know, people study the holocaust and the horror of Auschwitz and Dachau and Treblinka and then cannot accommodate just what happened on Australian soil. It's quite easy to accept the testimony at Nuremburg but they're unable to accept the fact that every single square metre of Australian soil has a particular story of its own, in terms of tragedy and bloodletting. And yet a death in custody doesn't even make page one anymore. Death in custody is going back to basics and that in itself is one of the most terrifying legacies of the colonial period.

The corners of the world to which the web of the novel is attached include the violence in the streets of Brisbane in the sixties and seventies, the streets of Brisbane themselves, and the pubs Sam drank in, the comparability of Nazi atrocities to Australian atrocities, the blood-soaked Australian soil, white families eating their fish and chips in front of the television, ignoring it all. The novel reveals in stark detail the violence of whites towards blacks, and particularly towards black women. It is a telling that is almost unreadable. It is a graphic depiction both of the violence at the time of white invasion and of present time—it exists now, vividly, in Sam's memory, on the pages of the novel, and thus in the memories of the readers.

One of the illusions created in the living of everyday life is that if it is filled with enough trivial detail, death will be held at bay—death need not be confronted. The fear of death lurks behind the surface of the trivia and the endless activity. Death and violence are dealt with through fantasy rather than in actuality. *The Kadaitcha Sung* insists on bringing the reader face to face with violence and death in a way that lifts the reader out of the trivial surface of the everyday but does not remove that death and violence to a safe and remote and fantastic place that has no immediate bearing on the conscience of the reader. Another one of the corners of reality to which the novel is attached is Sam's own close confrontation with death:

S: So in Kadaitcha Sung *I do confront, I write from the vantage point of someone who's been very close to death. In 1971 I was almost killed in this car accident and I was very close to death. I was absolutely drenched in petrol because our car was collected by a petrol tanker and I couldn't—they had to get me out of the wreckage before the petrol ignited. I was with them, I was totally conscious during that entire time and it was a huge panic because they couldn't use anything, they couldn't use any machinery or anything that would cause a spark, and the engine, you could hear the sizzle of the petrol hitting the hot engine. I can still hear it to this day, even though it's years ago. Everyone was just hoping and praying that it wouldn't ignite. It probably only took about ten or fifteen minutes but to me it was an absolute eternity. So for someone who's been there, it really is true that you don't fear death anymore. I would miss a lot of people and a lot of things that are very close, very important to me. But it's no great mystery to me and once you reach that point you do have a lot, a great deal of personal power. Because at the end of the day, the most sacred coin that we all carry is our own life, and that's where I particularly explore issues of death in custody, through my writing and through my films. At the end of the day, when you reach that point where you can kill yourself, where you've given yourself the right to die by your own hands, that is the most empowering moment in anyone's life. That you can actually snuff out your life and you can deny the hated enemy the right to torment you or abuse you or defile you anymore, by removing yourself from the playing field, by stepping out into the dreaming. You can actually close that door.*

Once the mystery of death is unveiled, and the fear of death is overcome, a powerful sense of choice is opened up—one can choose to die without fear—which also means that one can choose life. Choosing life is quite different from being *subjected* to it. In Sam's film *Black Man Down* (1996) the central character is in prison and in a state of torment. He is visited by a woman from the spirit world who hands him the means to kill himself. He begins to do so, confronting his own fear and overcoming it, and then chooses life instead. In *The Kadaitcha Sung* there is a similar scene:

B: *So the spirit who handed Bully Macow the means with which to kill himself was handing him a powerful thing that he could—*

S: *Giving him the opportunity to make the decision.*

B: *To be able to make the choice?*

S: *And the means to then carry it through.*

B: *So it wasn't inviting him into another world that he would exist in after life?*

S: *No he's just giving him the means to make the decision. Because a lot of Murris, they're in situations where they have to make a decision, but they don't have the power to embrace all the options. And that's what it comes down to.*

B: *The power comes out of choice.*

S: *Choice.*

B: *Without choice you can just get so depressed.*

S: *That's right, I can choose to do this, but I'm not going to do it just because I have to do it. Which is what life is all about. Murris, you've got ten thousand Murris working the system today in order to earn a quid and feed themselves. They don't have any other options. Or they fool themselves to the point where they don't believe they have any other options and that's what political empowerment is about. Giving them the right to express those options.*

The moment of confronting death is another moment of syncope through which the apparent seamlessness of oppression is ruptured and the sense of oneself as powerful is achieved.

The novel does not fall into some of the most likely traps of Western thought patterns with its linear logics and binary modes of categorization. There is no simple binary reversal here in which all blacks are good and all whites are evil. Evil is balanced against good in every sphere—it is the inevitable playing out of the human condition. It occurs within individuals, within groups of individuals and between groups. Evil is recognized as a significant force that must be dealt with. While Tommy is the virtuous hero, he is also violent:

B: *So why was Tommy so violent?*

S: *That reflects the environment in which he grew up because of his childhood, the era of colonial contact, he's a child of the era that saw the hunts and the massacres and the butchery and the like and he is just reflecting it.*

B: *But, he's almost like Christ in terms of coming to save the land.*

S: *At least this Christ is going to kick back. He's not going to turn the other cheek. Murri people have never been taught to turn the other cheek, it's just that previously we've never had the means to kick back. We couldn't fight Martini*

Henry rifles with wooden spears, but in this day and age we can, and that's the next step in my writing.

B: But for Tommy, apart from dealing with the Migloo, Booka was his central target in terms of ridding the land of Aboriginal evil?

S: Yeah. Which is his own alter ego. So in many ways, Tommy and Booka were different facets of the one character. The darker side as it were. So you have a single Kadaitcha core and because they're existing in the same plane at the same time, what I'm suggesting is that they are two shades, two reflections of the one single core character.

B: Oh right. Which is why Tommy's mother could relate to both Koobara and Booka, which was kind of inconceivable to me.

S: Yep.

B: Not that she liked Booka but—

S: Yeah, yin and yang.

B: But she would somehow accommodate him to the extent that he resembled Koobara.

S: Which is the only way Murris can survive in this society, though, by making that constant accommodation. Even though it's evil, even though she uses her body to accommodate Booka, in many ways she's the eternal mother of the indigenous people and she is allowing the act of rape in order to save her child.

So Tommy is Christ but he also kicks back. He is Aboriginal and therefore has not learned to kick back but he does. He is the hero, but he is also Booka: the evil resides outside himself and inside himself. The white woman, a hated Migloo, loved by Koobara, loved and hated by Tommy, is raped by Booka as part of the spirit world's strategy to save Tommy. She is a white woman and yet represents eternal motherhood of indigenous people. Not bound by linear logics and a requirement that he rid himself of deeply contradictory elements of his being, Tommy adores his mother and at the same time abhors the Migloo and the fact that he too is a mongrel.

B: This is really interesting. Where Tommy says something angry about white people, about Migloo, he says "I just cannot love them. They are a mongrel-bred race." Although he's called himself a mongrel as well. He says, "and the land could only survive if every one of that seed were dead!" and Ningi says, "But you've been deliberately placed with certain of the Migloo, and you will do your utmost to learn from their minds. Is that understood?" And I thought that was another one of your boundary crossings where you've said, no, you can't just dismiss the possibilities.

S: *That's right. Because you can't reverse the colonial process, so they're here and you've got to learn to live with them, number one and number two, there's a lot of things you can learn from Migloo.*

B: *Mmm. Because they're not just those evil mongrels.*

S: *That's right.*

B: *They are also the people connected up with the Celtic myths and all the other things that . . .*

S: *. . . they can take strengths from. Which is one reason why the Murri tribal cultures survive. Because they all just borrow from their neighbours, take from their neighbours. So there was an enormous degree of trade and exchange between these different tribal groups.*

This unresolved and unresolvable combination of hatred and valuing of the Migloo is fundamental to the novel and to its revolutionary possibilities. As Sam said earlier, "Boundaries don't really restrict the Murri writer because Murri writers don't respect boundaries. We don't allow ourselves to be intimidated by boundaries. I, as a Murri writer, make it my practice to at least step over or just go through boundaries." *The Kadaitcha Sung* deconstructs the binaries of good and evil. Good and evil are not an exclusive pair with good always opposite to and in the ascendant over evil. By locating evil within the Murri psyche as well as outside, the binary categories of good/evil, black/white are troubled; the qualities that seemed to inhere in people as a result of their category membership are no longer so self-evident; the category boundaries are less clear. One can move across boundaries. Crossing the boundaries between white and black is not simply a crossing in which the white/black binary is deconstructed, where any Aboriginal person of mixed blood becomes both *and* neither. Rather, a heavy emphasis is placed on the "and" of "both and neither," with all the complexity of the simultaneous movement beyond the binary and the maintenance of the binary that that entails.

A tendency in white poststructuralist writing is to work towards disrupting the binaries. A fault line in the deconstructive work appears when the assumption is made that the deconstructive work will erase the categories such that they can no longer do the work that they were doing. At most, deconstruction can only trouble categories—they still exist and still hold power, albeit a power that is shifted. This conceptual error comes about through the difficulty for Western thinkers of holding opposites in mind without at the same time succumbing to the desire to abandon one of them. How can anyone be both of any binary pair, and neither; both good and evil *and* neither? But in *The Kadaitcha Sung* this is made possible and comprehensible.

A different set of metaphors for understanding the conceptual shifts made possible in the novel can be drawn from the Australian Aranda modes of dance and song in which *incorporation* and *folding* are central. If we think of the image of the hunter moving through the folded landscape (folded differently over different geological ages, and folded differently in his viewing of it as he moves over hills and valleys in pursuit of his prey) then we can imagine many ways of seeing, each way necessitated by the particular fold in the landscape one is caught in at any one point in time. As he moves, and the land unfolds differently to his eye, the other ways of seeing, from within each different fold, are not erased—they were there before and will be there again. The Aranda words of the songs and the movements of the dancer's body incorporate the folding and unfolding of the landscape that is moved through, and merge the body, the land, the hunter, and the hunted.

Carter (1996, p. 61) refers to the "flexibly incorporative, or folded nature of Aranda song." The singer of the song and the dancer of the dance fold and unfold in a "reverent mime of the land" (p. 92). The elastic hunter/singer dispatches "on its shallowly-curving arc" the spear that "is the foot of the hunter elongated. It is the ground puckered up and drawn tight as the throat of a purse. The thin projectile sings and quivers over the glinting space, its tone being its vectorial signature" (p. 88). The Aranda language is "poetically and grammatically 'additive', like undulating or cave-pocked country which bunches up planes, thus incorporating more ground" (p. 60). "[W]hat distinguishes the culture of the Aranda might be its capacity simultaneously to hold in place multiple views and meanings, to think, not in terms of paradoxes and contradictions, but in terms of a lesser or greater folding of the land" (p. 103).

Understood in terms of the metaphors of folding and unfolding and incorporation, it is perhaps easier to understand the fluidity and complexity of *The Kadaitcha Sung*. The following conversation, for example, is quite problematic if read in terms of linear thought and contradictions; if read in terms of movement over the land, of the different ways the land looks when perceived from different points on the landscape, it is less problematic. The conversation begins with the question as to why Fleur, Tommy's mother, is white. Sam explains this in terms of drawing in the white readership, making the novel part of their history in a way they cannot escape so easily. It is simultaneously a strategy to enable Aboriginal readers to incorporate their white ancestry into their Aboriginality:

B: So why is she white?

S: Why? Because I wanted to establish a bridge. I couldn't write, I didn't want Tommy to be totally from the Murri world. I wanted him to have components, something within him that belonged to white Australia. So it wasn't just so white Australian readers just couldn't sit there and say, well, this is just a young black guy going on a journey. I wanted Tommy to try to be able to take some of those white roots with him on a journey. Because it really was a period of journey and discovery for him, and for the white readers hopefully.

B: To me, it's not just white readers because it's also all the Aboriginal or Murri people who've got white mothers or fathers or grandmothers or whatever that they've not known what to do with.

S: Yep.

B: Suddenly they can be reclaimed, and to me as a white person that is very profound to be able to be reclaimed.

S: Yep. You can't, you cannot unmake what you are, so embrace it. I mean my children have been brought up to fully embrace and accept their mother's blood and culture as well as their Murri culture, even though they're profoundly Murri in everything they do. They still never turn their back on the fact that their grandparents are French/German and they're still quite enthusiastic about going to France and Germany and reconnecting with family there. And that needs to be done, you can't turn your back on reality. So if your blood lines, if your dream paths, do come a particular way, recognize that, accept it and embrace it. Don't hide it. Because for too long, many fair-skinned Murris passed themselves off as whites or as Polynesians in order to be able to get jobs, to get houses and live within the community.

This last sentence startled me. I thought the discussion and the text logically led to the idea that Murri people should be free to move across the black-white boundary with more ease, to position themselves as both white and black and neither, in a deconstructive move that takes the force out of the inalienable opposition between black and white. For Sam it is not so simple. While this may well be true, there is an issue of identification that is required of those who must engage further in political struggle. That identification involves a definite taking up of oneself as Murri *and not white* in order to name white oppression and deal with it. We talk past each other here, going in different directions, with different ideals in our minds:

B: I heard an interview with a young Murri woman who was able to pass as white and enjoyed moving across the boundaries and thought it was her right to be positioned in the world in as many ways as she could be positioned: for these purposes, for this situation, and in relation to these people, it's this part of my heritage that's relevant. And her friends used to say to her, you've got to *make up your mind, be one or the other and she said, no, I don't, I don't have to be one or the other because I'm not one or the other, I'm both.*

S: *She can probably, she'll probably be able to do that within, I doubt very much that she will be able to do it successfully for a long, long time. But she may be able to. But it won't be her who will eventually bring that to a close, it will be outside influences.*

B: *It will be novels like this where you've got Tommy who says I'm a mongrel hybrid.*

S: *Yeah.*

B: *And I'm a warrior.*

S: *Yeah.*

B: *That's the powerful opening up of the imaginary possibility in writing like that, that can then move you beyond the discourse that says you've got to be one or the other.*

S: *Yeah.*

B: *Because nobody says to him, you've got to be one or the other.*

S: *Australia is heading towards that point where we've all got to make that decision.*

From one fold in the land, *The Kadaitcha Sung* merely uses Fleur's and Tommy's whiteness to entice the white readers in, to enable them to see that it is relevant to them. In another fold, their whiteness holds the most revolutionary possibilities of the novel. In one fold, it is right and good for one's children to embrace all of who they are, and in another, we are living in times where that may be a luxury denied Murris, since the fighting of oppression may necessitate a political decision to be one or the other. All of these ways of viewing the landscape undo each other in a Western linear model of reading. In the Western model, the author should take us to a clear and singular position from which to view the land. But like the Aranda hunter, *The Kadaitcha Sung* takes us to many places and enables us to see from the multiple folds in the political landscape.

The meaning of the landscape of Brisbane is similarly folded. It is a place in which Sam has hung out and learned his political lessons. It is a place of hope, of survival, and of horror. It is a travesty of virgin land and must be removed. Each of these readings of the landscape of Brisbane exists side by side, negating each other if one insists on imposing linear logic onto the landscape, but able to coexist if the folds in consciousness are understood:

S: *There is a real connection between me and Brisbane and particularly inner-city Brisbane. That's probably because my mother's mob are the Mullenjarli people whose tribal land is south-east of Brisbane but used to come through this area every year for the big ceremony at Bunya Mountains. So the Mullenjarli mob have always had, traditionally, a very close link with the land now called Brisbane and particularly with inner-city Brisbane. But I don't try to rationalize it because Murri people are very mobile people and nowadays I suppose 75 to 80 percent of the Murri people would be living outside those tribal lands. So if you feel comfortable and secure within a particular area you should be entitled to camp in that area. As long as you make your representations to the local mob and they give their permission. That's always got to be done. I've got a very close link with the Jagara people because the Jagara people are the traditional owners of the land now called Brisbane and so there's a very secure spiritual feeling I have with the inner-city Brisbane. I learned my politics on the streets of Brisbane. In the sixties I was out there on the streets, mobilizing people at polling booths with a heap of other people in the lead-up to the 1967 Referendum. I was there in '68, '69, '70 in the anti-Vietnam demonstrations and I went right through to the close of the war in '75. And Brisbane has always been a very special place on the Australian political landscape because of people like Joh Bjelke-Petersen and because of events like the Fitzgerald Inquiry, etc. So I really believe that people who came up through the Brisbane ranks and learned their lessons and went on with their political growth have gone on to become very significant people in modern Australian history. So politically, socially, it's a very dynamic place because here, particularly in West End where we are now, we're at the coal face of the multicultural Australia. We have within West End 240 different ethnic minorities and over 80 major language groups. So as you walk through West End of a day you can hear echoes of cultures from all over the world. And the sights, the sounds, the smells, it's a very exciting, a very dynamic place to be. Economically, I can earn a living here in Brisbane. And particularly inner-city Brisbane, because the major Aboriginal community agencies, they're centred here. So it's quite convenient for me to live here and work here because it's close to everything, and in terms of my writing I feel very comfortable writing about events and things that happen here in inner Brisbane.*

B: *There's one point in the book when you talk about the landscape being devastated by the steel and concrete, the actual buildings on the land. How do you deal with that tension between the original idea of the land and the land as it is now, which is basically steel and concrete?*

S: *Yeah, yeah, it's been devastated but that's only skin deep because the devastation only goes down a few metres. I mean even people with the tallest buildings, they're only excavating through the outer skin of the land. So the spiritual strength of the land is still very evident within the land and very strong. One of the things I personally do is spend a lot of, you know, in my times of greatest need I suppose, just go down to the riverbank and just lie on the land, lie on the earth and just close the eyes and send the mind back, and there's nearly total reconnection there, so the spiritual vibration of the land is still very, very strong and still there for people to connect with. Journalists in the modern era go through war zones and look at burned-out bombed buildings and craters and rubble everywhere and say, "This is a wasteland." I walk through the middle of Brisbane one time and see the city skyline, the skyscrapers, and the people in business suits and I say, "This is a wasteland" one time, because it's an absolute prostitution of virgin land that was never created to be used in this way.*

B: Mmm. So you could never be attached to the buildings?

S: No, they are nothing.

B: Never see them as having value at all?

S: They're transient structures that will fall as will the Australian economy because they're all constructed to pursue a god that lives only within their own minds.

The term that Sam uses to encapsulate the meaning of time in "living memory" with past and present being all together in the present moment is "one time." The desolation he sees in Brisbane is "one time" and so, too, from another fold is the undesolated land that existed before and will exist again. The undesolated landscape is there now when we look from Sam's living-room window over the Brisbane River and when he goes down to the River and lies on the banks and dreams. It is there beneath the desolation. This is similar again to the Aranda religion, which brings into dialogue the eternal and the temporal: " 'During the performance of totemic ritual, transient Time and timeless Eternity become completely fused into a single Reality in the minds of all participants' " (Carter, 1996, p. 79, quoting Strehlow). The novel plays with time, telescoping it and expanding it, the way the view of the land expands and contracts as you walk through it:

S: Well, yeah. I've played with the time line, so it could occur anywhere from, you know, the first thirty or forty years of white settlement to the modern day. That reflects the fact that Murri people have no real sense of time, that we live in geological time. So, 1788 to 1996 is just [snaps his fingers] a blink of an eye. And everything we've learned, we learned from old uncles, old aunties, who would tell us these things as though everything happened to them. So they are telling us about the first hunts, the first time the Migloo walked into Moreton Bay region, the first time they killed anybody, the first time they hung people from the tower mill. This is a living memory, because it's living memory to them so it comes on to us as living memory and when we tell our children, it's living memory, so there's no past, there's no future. Only an ever dynamic present that we can shape and determine ourselves. . . .

This play on time is in stark contrast to traditional Western conceptions of time that are "incarnated in Aristotelian metaphysics and physics. The linear conception of history it generates," Carter points out, "is similarly artificial. It is not only water that is parcelled into canals: our Western engineers of the intellect have similarly locked and weired the fluid of time" (Carter, 1996, p. 54).

Linear logic may be a luxury of those powerful enough to be in control of their land and of the people around them. It is an imposition that satisfies and controls. For those who are not so powerfully placed, accommodation and change, multiple ways of coming at the world, must be incorporated. Being a Murri writer, like being a Murri person in the everyday world, involves both the ordinariness and (sometimes) degradation of everyday life and profound spiritual connection. The character of Tommy holds all of the multiplicity of Aboriginal experience as he moves through the landscape and sets himself on the trajectory of weighing good against evil. After a heavy night of drinking and fighting and only three hours' sleep, Tommy can rise from his bed and transform himself into Kadaitcha man where he is at one with the elements and in command of the most powerful spiritual forces in the land:

The light inside the room increased as the sun dragged its fiery bulk higher.

Tommy pulled a new pair of shorts out of the low dresser and slipped them on. Then, on silent feet, he made his way out of the house and slipped quietly down the stairs. The mission was just beginning to come to life. Doors and windows were pushed open, dogs were sounding off and dunny lids were slammed down.

Tommy looked up into the sky. There was not a cloud to be seen and the air already had a heavy, clinging feel to it. It was going to be very warm during the day and Tommy's nose told him of a possible thunderstorm, but not until evening.

The jagged stones bit into his feet as he jogged across to the river bank. He knew that he had been wearing shoes too much, but he forced himself onwards.

It must have been top of the tide. The surging blue flood lapped against the lips of the bank. Out in the middle channel, a wind stirred the heart of the current and tantalised the waters.

There was no one in sight. Tommy took off his shorts and dove cleanly into the deep water off the boat ramp. The crisp coldness hit him like a massive fist and his flesh bellowed out for relief, but he burrowed deeper, ever deeper into the shimmering folds of the river. His nerve endings were singing a pained symphony and his skin felt as though it was paper thin. Still deeper he went, heading out to the middle to seek out the pockets of warmer water. On the way, he closed his lungs down, he did not need them. He could swim with his water brothers for as long as he wanted to.

From the weeds on the bottom, small spirit shapes darted out to greet him. They sang their sacred songs of welcome and wished him well before scuttling back to their secret places.

Tommy smiled and nodded to them, slowing for a moment and looking around. As a massive grey shark cruised past it blinked at the slim shape before it and offered its formal greetings. Tommy nodded and the huge fish accelerated away through the water, with supreme arrogance.

Tommy's body warmed as it adjusted to the foreign environment and he struck out with new vigour. Dituwonga was waiting for him, and the ancient groper was not known for his patience.

In the exact centre of the river, there was a long, flat strip of reddish coral, honeycombed with caves and crevices. This was the camp of the Dituwonga. It had pushed its huge head out of a cave and nodded tiredly as the young Kadaitcha approached.

"I see you, son of Koobara," the old fish whispered. "You are growing up into a fine warrior. Look at you! You are already as big as Koobara."

"How are you, wise Dituwonga? You are spoken of in all the camps of men. They boast of your wisdom and your strength."

"Hmmph! Don't you go trying to flatter me with all your silly words. You are in my keep now."

"Biamee sends his greetings. He says that he will hunt with you very soon," Tommy said carefully.

"Yes, so I hear. I am told that you will go up against the evil Booka soon." Dituwonga shook his head sadly. "I told Biamee in the beginning that the men of the Kadaitcha clan would never be able to settle peacefully in Uluru. They are men of high stature and they are very strong. Isn't that right?"

"Yes, all those lives that were lost. Look at all the land that the Migloo has stolen. What will happen? Will you help the people of the tribes, Tommy? Will you stand with them against the Migloo?"

"Of course. I am now a fully-fledged Kadaitcha man. See my cut!" Tommy pushed his chest out.

"Hmmm." The old fish looked closely at the small scar. "So, you have been raised up and now they will send you against the enemy. Will you best Booka, young Kadaitcha? Will you be strong enough and wise enough to overcome that terrible man? He was one of the finest . . . How good are you, boy?"

"Good enough, Dituwonga," Tommy said without fear. "I will draw him to the killing ground and only I will walk away from that place. But first, my wise elder, I will need your help."

"Hmmph! They all come to me in the end." The old fish chuckled. "When they have nowhere else to go they all come to see old Dituwonga. Yes? What is it you ask? Tell me now. I am getting tired and I may not be in these waters too much longer . . ."

Taking his leave from the revered fish totem, Tommy pushed his way up through the veins of pulsing current and broke the surface in the middle channel.

There were no boats on the water and he was the only swimmer. He trod water and began to breathe air again, coughing intermittently until his lungs were clear. The sun was climbing higher into the eastern quadrant. Languidly, Tommy swam back to the bank.

. . .

Further east, out to sea, Dituwonga trembled mightily as he heard the signal. He turned to his minions and together they began to sing a deadly chant. The waters swirled and danced as the ancient words hurtled through the depths.

A massive body of dark water began to build above Dituwonga's head and he increased the ghostly tempo. Another signal came and the fish totem sent his offering forth, a huge wave that surged across the surface of the bay towards Cribb Island. Dituwonga had kept faith with Tommy. (Watson, 1990, pp. 294–97, 305)

Tommy can transform himself from earth dweller to water dweller by an act of will. He can summon the power of Dituwonga to defeat the evil Booka. At the same time, he is humble in his approach to the ancient grouper; he proudly shows him his initiation scars and accepts the grouper's dismissal of his words as silly flattery. To the ancient grouper totem, Tommy is both a young boy and Kadaitcha with both wisdom and significant power.

S: *Through his meeting with Dituwonga and Dituwonga's role in the eventual downfall of Booka, what I was trying to convey was the closeness of the Aboriginal warrior to all facets of the natural environment in which he lives and works. Tommy has very close bonds with creatures of the air such as Ninji; he uses his magic powers to travel through the air. It was crucial that Tommy had connections with the totemic elders of the water world, as well as the totemic elders of the sky. Brisbane was built around the Brisbane River, which has been a very sacred place to the people of the Jagara nation. In* The Kadaitcha Sung *the Brisbane River does have a significant role; not a large role, but certainly there is a strong undercurrent. Booka was terrified of the Brisbane River, terrified of its malevolence. Bully Macow hears the whisper of the River. The River is a very powerful symbol in Tommy's journey of discovery, that the Aboriginal people are tuned into. The Migloo see it only in terms of—*

B: *its utility and its surface aesthetic qualities, perhaps.*

Sometimes the crossover between one vantage point and another in the complex landscape a Murri person walks across, even in inner-city Brisbane, means an infolding of the landscape where the multiplicities are folded into one moment:

B: *I don't think that any white person reading this novel could ever see a drunk Aboriginal in the street or in a park or even brawling and ever ignore the possibility that this man might also be sacred. You could never adopt a dismissive or superior attitude again, in looking at an Aboriginal man. Not a possibility.*

S: *Thank you. That means with you, the book has worked, it's brought you into my world and it's shown you the way I look at people.*

B: *The thing that I was left with at the end of it was this incredible interlaying of Tommy as this very ordinary bloke who, I didn't count how many drinks he had, but I reckon he'd be dead if he actually had that many drinks by the end of the night.*

S: *Yeah.*

B: *Because he's just very ordinary, speaking in ordinary ways, connecting with the community in ordinary ways and yet he is also at the same time this warrior, this profoundly connected spiritual being, and the two interleave so intricately and they're both so credible that every Aboriginal person on reading it has that now as a possibility of their own being.*

S: *Yeah, I'd just like to make a couple of comments in response to that. Number one: The amount of beers that Tommy drank during the course of one night was important in other ways because it showed that he was never a slave to the grog. So even though he had a drink, and he had a drink because he wouldn't have been allowed into the group, wouldn't be allowed in those places unless he drank, because unfortunately that's one of the rites of passage to adulthood in this day and age, in the urban community, unless you can share a beer and a dirty joke with the mob, then you're a bit of a, you're looked upon as a bit of a wowser and you're not given full entree into the group. It's important that Tommy was one of the mob, he could mix, and he could talk and he could drink. And the other side of the coin is that, even though he did consume an enormous amount of booze, he never lost sight of who he was or what his mission in the book was. Which is important because the booze was just a tool, a key for him to enter.*

B: *This was one of the other questions I was going to ask you. The alcohol wasn't of itself useful in opening the door to the spiritual world? At the beginning of the novel, when Worrimi was chewing the plant to relieve her menstrual cramps, she also became aware of Jonjurri from the spirit world. So I thought there might be something here about drugs opening you up to the spiritual world?*

S: In fact, that goes back to my childhood. Dad used to take me to football games and cricket games, etc., and I would see that the Murri men, and this is particularly true of the men, Murri men who during the week would look so broken down and crushed by the sheer weight of having to work at dreary backbreaking jobs that they hated, in situations and environments that they hated, all for the sake of being able to pay the bills and clothe and house and feed their families. On the Saturday at the cricket, when they could have a few bob in their pocket and have a few drinks with their mates, their faces and their spirits would just cleanse one time. They didn't have a care in the world. They were relaxed people. And they were just so different and I wanted to reflect that.

B: There's actually a line in there where you talk about the drink connecting them to the dreaming so that they can let go of the present and connect to the dreaming.

S: Because it really does. It's a drug, alcohol, and it really does allow people to just step over that boundary, the barriers that have been built up, the barriers in the mind, placed there by the sheer horror of the daily existence of the racism, of having to work within this enormous abattoir that the Migloos created on our land.

B: But it's such a dangerous drug.

S: It is, because it can become an end in itself rather than just the key to the door.

But add to this another fold, walking along a bit, thinking about Booka, the personification of evil.

B: Right. There's a very profound bit here about Booka being the best killer in the land but drifting from, drifting, from misuse of the land, losing his strength.

S: Mmm. So the further he, he's really seduced by the trappings of the Migloo society. So the more he drinks, the more booze that he drinks of theirs, the more food that he eats of theirs, the more women of theirs that he sleeps with, the more trappings of white civilization that he embraces and takes advantage of, the less power he has as Kadaitcha.

B: Right.

S: So the further he's drawn into the web of the Migloo society, the less power he has as Kadaitcha.

The line Tommy treads is doubly dangerous. He cannot be accepted unless he drinks and tells dirty jokes, yet for Booka it is precisely his willingness to participate in these trappings of Migloo culture that weakens him and makes him vulnerable. Tommy's heroism is magnified by the extremity of the risks he is taking in being one of the ordinary people. Yet the booze for the ordinary people is one of the few ways they have of finding themselves "one time" cleansed and free and reconnected.

The folds in this novel are probably infinite. We will end with one last fold, revealing yet again my struggle to unmesh myself from Western thought in order to understand the multiple folds of *The Kadaitcha Sung*. The scene we are talking about is the love scene between Tommy and Jelda: "the most ancient and primitive dance of love. The dwellings, the roads and lights—every facet of the Migloo presence—was pulled in and thrust back into the vast bowels of time. The two blacks were the only beings within their universe. . . . From far off a dingo bellowed a challenge, and the gods laughed once again upon the promised land" (p. 203).

B: *I thought the love scene with Jelda was something else.*

S: *Yeah, well, that was meant to be.*

B: *Very profound. The way they were, it wasn't just the two bodies as it would be in a white sex scene, it was the stars and it was the trees and it was the initiation scar and it was everything, it was all wrapped in together.*

S: *And also because of the setting at the cemetery, in the midst of death.*

B: *And the wiping out of white persons through the profoundness of the act, and the gods laughing [laughs], really something, a spiritual act of the highest order.*
   I got a bit confused about this, though. It seemed like such a profound and spiritual act yet the spirit world didn't like it. They disapproved of him doing that.

S: *Yeah, because she'd been marked for death because she is the Black Possum in the clan. That was his trade-off, by the way, he couldn't see any reason for that. And that's the current generation regarding its links into the past. So, he's going to do a job for them, he's going to wipe out Booka, etc., etc. That's his trade-off, this is my price. You know . . .*

B: *And you won't kill Jelda and her child will be my child.*

S: *That's right, yeah.*

B: *And then the possibility of the Kadaitcha man born through Jelda seemed to me to be so potent.*

S: *Well, Jelda's child is actually the centre of the next book that's on the computer at the moment.*

And so...

What has happened in the writing of this chapter is the creation of unexpected folds and depth/surfaces with/in the landscape of the book. Sam Watson's idea of the Centre of Australia, Uluru, being the origin, the center of overlapping interwoven cultures emanating out from it loops back to my moment in Japan when I heard a startling similarity between the Buddhist priest's chanting and Aboriginal songs in the desert. Inside Sam's storyline, such a connection becomes obvious and predictable. And as I reread now, in the context of this book, the words that Sam and I wrote together, I keep hearing echoes of Buddhist and Shinto landscapes in the images I find there. This chapter also loops back to Robert Dessaix's journey into the Australian desert, and to the male environmentalists' struggles to become one with the Australian landscape. Robert Dessaix experienced the knowledge of belonging in the desert landscape as something that always would be a mystery to him. *The Kadaitcha Sung* is a text that invites him to go beyond the perceived boundary he found in the desert that day. And there is an interesting parallel between the environmentalists' heroic attempts to belong in the sea and Tommy's dive down into the watery depths where he shuts down his lungs and communes with the ancient grouper, Dituwonga. What this chapter suggests is that such belonging is an ongoing struggle and requires work from each one of us, each one deeply affected by history, by the discourses available to us, and by the patterns of power and powerlessness we experience in coming upon the imagined embodiment in landscape that we partially and continually are in process of moving into. Profound historical differences will mean that some others' embodiment in landscape will always remain a mystery to us, while overlapping histories will make possible the discovery of unexpected points of convergence that pay no respect to the discursive boundaries of East and West, indigenous and nonindigenous, white and black, insider and outsider.

The tensions and contradictions between discourses can be read as tensions between different groups, leading, potentially, to violent conflict between those groups. Or we can read them as tensions and contradictions within the discourses through which we each live out our lives. The city of Brisbane, for Sam, is a devastation of the landscape, but the devastation is only skin deep. The land still holds its spiritual strength. At the same time, from within a different fold, he experiences the sights and smells and sounds of this multicultural city as exciting and dynamic. Yet the city itself, he imagines, will fall—like the ancient Albanian city described by Robert Dessaix:

> After an hour or so of bumping and grinding through this wildly beautiful [Albanian] landscape we pulled up at the gates of ancient Butrint (also known as Buthrot and Butrinti), hidden among lush forests where Lake Butrint empties into the sea. We stumbled from our bus into a marshy silence . . . and off we headed up the track toward one of the great lost cities of the ancient world.
>
> At least it feels lost. There has actually been a city here since the early Iron Age, and its massive walls have been here for over 2000 years. There are Roman baths, a theatre hewn out of the side of the acropolis, temples, a gymnasium, a Christian basilica and, up on the acropolis itself, a venetian fort complete with prison tower. As late as the twelfth century the Arab merchant Al-Idriz mentioned it as a vibrant trading centre, with a large agora and many shops.
>
> Yet it feels lost because, except where the archaeologists have been at work, unearthing mosaics, steam-baths and sacred wells, it is almost completely engulfed nowadays by thick, almost impenetrable vegetation, humming with bees. You wend your way these days from baptistry to Roman villa, from city gate to Venetian cannon through a jungle of myrtle, oak, heather and honeysuckle, alive with vipers and butterflies. All those bishops, pashas, governors, sieges, fleets and armies, all those hundreds of thousands of lives lived out here on these streets behind these walls, and now nothing, silence. (Dessaix, 1998, pp. 170–71)

Silence—
and the jeweled wings
of a butterfly

Bronwyn Davies

~9~ *The Second Bridegroom*: A narrative of captivity in Australian landscapes

THIS CHAPTER TAKES UP, AGAIN, the problem of Australian history, this time (re)viewing it through the embodied being of a fictional character in the writing of Rodney Hall. Another fold in the Australian landscape appears in this writing, a fold containing the story of an Australian who is neither indigenous nor invader. I talked with Rodney Hall about his writing and my reading of it in his beautiful home nestled in the Australian coastal bushland of New South Wales, looking out over the sea. We wanted to sit on the verandah looking out over the sea while we talked, but the roar of the waves would have drowned out our voices on the tape recorder, and so we retreated inside to sit at a long wooden table and look through large glass windows at the very sea in which his novels are set. While this is not a joint writing, it is with Rodney Hall's agreement that I proceed with publishing these words from him and about his writing. The words between us and the setting in which they were spoken remains for me an intensely visible, and audible, landscape in which the words that follow are inlaid.

This chapter focuses, in particular, on one novel, *The Second Bridegroom*. That novel, the fourth in a series of seven, tells of the coming into being of "Australia" through the words of a convict who is brought to Australia as indentured labor in the British "settling" of the land. The convict, whose name we are never told, is, at the beginning, an innocent lad. Prior to his conviction, his trade was printing, and his "crime" was to reproduce an ancient text so perfectly that he was taken, at first, to be a thief. In the unfolding of his tale he becomes a murderer, a poet, and a philosopher who struggles to make sense of "the Australian landscape" and of what he becomes in relation to that landscape.

In this chapter I use the detail of the novel to explore some of the meanings to which we, the readers, are captive in our experience of being embodied human beings in the landscapes we think of as "Australia." For several decades now environmentalists have been advising us that we should interact with the Australian landscape differently, that it will not survive our current ways of being. Indigenous people have also been persuading those of us who are descended from the "invading hordes" that we should think differently about our place in the Australian landscape, that we have no automatic right to be here. Often these injunctions to think differently, to *be* different, are located in the future and are filled with moral imperatives about how we *should* be.

But ways of thinking/being differently are not easily achieved by imagining an idealized future, even for those who desire that future. It is quite possible to discursively construct an idealized and highly desirable future but have no way of achieving the individual forms of embodiment nor the collective/communal practices that would make such a future come into being. An interesting strategy is to imagine going back in time, rather than forward, and to reexamine what has already been. If we look with a new, critical set of questions, what we find in the past can sometimes unsettle what we had taken for granted in both the past and the present. Apart from the reconceptualizing of the present that such critical re-viewing makes possible, that which has "already been" cannot so readily be dismissed as mere utopian dreaming (though it is true that romanticized images of the past can be used precisely in that way). Although readings of history are necessarily imaginative acts, in much the same way that utopian dreams are, it is possible to achieve readings of the past that engender a very different sense of what it means to be living right now, in this present moment, in this particular landscape. As Ashcroft and Salter (1997, p. 19) observe of the texts that make up what we think of as Australia, "fictional narratives may be among the most effective ways of understanding (which is the same thing, perhaps, as 're-inscribing') it."

Pleasure and bliss

Hall takes the reader back to 1838, a time in Australia's history when the New South Wales coast was being taken up and "settled" by some of our ancestors, while others of our ancestors watched their familiar landscapes irreversibly "invaded" and destroyed. Through the imaginary world he creates in *The Second Bridegroom* Hall enables us to enter the visual and conceptual landscape of "Australia" again, and to understand differently the competing narratives of "settlement" and "invasion" as they are lived through the embodied consciousness of another of our ancestors: one caught in the middle, a convict, who was not there by choice, and who had no chance of return to his own land.

In a gripping tale of escape and recapture and final escape, Hall opens up, for me, the possibility of living differently in the Australian landscape that is now so familiar. In telling the tale primarily through a letter written by the convict, he invites a self-conscious (re)viewing of the landscape. I can see not just what the convict saw, but, because of the convict's particular awareness of language and of himself in this unfamiliar landscape, I can also see how the very language he uses brings the land to life in particular ways in both his and my imagination. Hall also invites the reader to become immersed in the moral and philosophical critique the convict brings to bear on his own intensely contradictory experiences of entering the Australian landscape.

Hall offers us both the pleasurable experience of being immersed in a gripping narrative and the painful experience of finding our old, comfortable ways of seeing uprooted. A text of pleasure, according to Barthes, is a "text that contents, fills, grants euphoria; the text that comes from culture and does not break with it, it is linked to a comfortable practice of reading" (1989, p. 14). To the extent that *The Second Bridegroom* is a novel written in familiar ways—it is recognizably a novel, a work of fiction intended to engage the reader's imagination—it provides the possibility of that comfortable practice of reading. But it is also, potentially, what Barthes calls a text of bliss:

> [T]he text that imposes a state of loss, the text that discomforts (perhaps to the state of a certain boredom), unsettles the reader's historical, cultural, psychological assumptions, the consistency of his [her] tastes, values, memories, brings to crisis his [her] relation with language. (p. 14)

It may seem like an unacceptable contradiction to say that the text can be both a text of pleasure (confirming the status quo) and a text of bliss (disrupting the status quo). But that which we do not yet comprehend is necessarily constructed out of existing knowledges. Derrida calls this the enigma of invention. Invention, he says:

> [is something] at once requiring and unsettling protocols and rules, at once finding something already implicit in the cultural fabric by means of which to make itself understood and bringing something wholly new into being. Like the signature, the invention is constituted by its originality (a reproduction of a signature is not a signature; a copy can never be an invention) and yet wholly dependent on recognition and legitimation (and therefore subject to codes and laws). (Attridge, 1992, p. 310)

In his conversation with me about his writing, Rodney Hall returned several times to this enigma. He does not believe the author invents out of the unknown but rather invents out of the already known—known to him and to the reader. When I spoke of Virginia Woolf's metaphor of fiction being like a spider's web, attached to life at all four corners, he said that he thought, rather, we were intersection points on a complex tangled web; that as writers we are as much the web as we are the spiders moving along it:

It's more like us being a kind of point at which some incredibly tangled intersection of threads happens to coincide. I think we are moving in a complex continuum and we respond to it at a given moment because at a point in time, that's how it presents itself to us. Not because we are spinning a web ourselves from other things. . . . It's more important to get an idea alive and working than to be able to say this is my idea, I was the first one to do that.

Unlike Woolf, Hall does not find any fixed points in his life to which he might attach a web of fiction. Fiction writing, he says, is more an engagement with the complex tangle of life threads, which intersect in unexpected ways—it is the body of the spider moving in the landscape of the web. As writers we are not, he says, in control of the text in the way a spider might be seen to be in control of its web. Rather, the intersection of familiar threads takes on its own life— sometimes "pleasurable," repeating the status quo, sometimes "blissful" and troubling.

While *The Second Bridegroom* is an historical novel and enables us to re-view "Australia" from a vantage point in the past, it is also an invention, an artful invention. And as Winterson (1995, p. 26) says of art: "Art does not imitate life. Art anticipates life." That anticipation, she says, is of fundamental importance for our survival. Art shifts the palings that guard our hearts and alters what already exists:

> Those Greek myths [of Echo and Narcissus] warn us of the dangers of recognising no reality but our own. Art is a way into other realities, other personalities. When I let myself be affected by a book, I let into myself new customs and new desires. The book does not reproduce me, it re-defines me, pushes at my boundaries, shatters the palings that guard my heart. Strong texts work along the borders of our minds and alter what already exists. (1995, p. 26)

The Second Bridegroom can be a strong text, if you take up its challenge. Or, it offers the potential—for readers who dare—to be traversed by bliss. But bliss is not *in* the text; it is not something that can be pointed to here or there on the page; rather, it is a state of mind that the reader might allow. As Attridge (1992, p. 2) points out, "Literary texts . . . are acts of writing that call forth acts of reading. . . ." Or as Hall said in conversation with me, "What one wants to do is to engage the reader in an act of co-creation in which the reader's part is as near as possible as important as the writer's part. That seems to me to be the definition of literary art." At the same time, what the reader creates from the text may not be at all what the author wanted or expected. It may even be a co-creation the author rejects, as Hall does with some of the interpretations that appear in the reviews of his novels. Finding ways to enter texts that are satisfying to the author can require a specific kind of reading, which the reader cannot routinely be expected to achieve. It was gratifying to us both when, during our conversations, we found mutually satisfying readings of the work. At other times we produced quite different readings and enjoyed exploring how those different readings were arrived at.

The Second Bridegroom

The convict begins his tale with the statement that he wants his reader to know who he is. We find out later that his intended reader is the Mistress, the wife of the man to whom he is indentured. His writing is a set of love letters to the woman who has made him captive for the second time: captive in the sense of being locked in and captive to his desire that she know his embodied being as he experiences it with/in the Australian landscape. In the beginning we can assume, however, that it is each of us, the readers, whom he addresses, whom he wants to make captive—in a third sense—to a particular way of seeing, of being in the landscape of this country. His intention, he writes, is to captivate the reader through his telling of what the land looks like to him now, as a result of his journeying through it during his period of escape. His new ways of reading the land have been made possible by learning from the Aboriginal people with whom he has traveled, and who have captured his imagination and shaped his ways of being. But he is willingly captive to his new ways of reading, and he wants the reader to be similarly captivated. He wants the text to seduce the reader just as he is seduced by his idea of the Mistress knowing him and sharing his way of seeing. He sets out to shift the palings that guard her heart, palings constructed out of her use of the English language and images of the English landscape that she and the Master wish to copy, or reproduce here, profoundly disregarding what is already here in Australia.

The first thing he tells his reader about himself is that he is near-sighted: "I see a blurred world of large simple shapes" (Hall, 1994, p. 3). His failure to see the detail of the wider landscape is compacted by the failure of the English language to tell that new landscape. Of the English language and its clumsiness in the face of the Australian landscape, Hall says:

[As with short sight] everything is in broad, general strokes. Nothing is particular and it's the particular that is the mark of a language that belongs in its land. The local languages are always brilliantly graphic about particulars and in fact the bigger a language grows [geographically], like English, and the more general it grows, the more it sheds, the more it loses. It doesn't get bigger, it gets smaller. The actual useable language gets smaller and smaller. Hence local Aboriginal languages are amongst the largest languages the world's known because they have so many words for what we would use one word for, depending on words that are specific to whether it's morning or afternoon, or whether it's wet or dry, or from what angle you're looking, in what circumstances you are, or which skin group you are from.

Yet to tell the reader what he sees is precisely the enigmatic task the convict undertakes, notwithstanding the blunt tools of his sight and his language. And despite these blunt tools his description of the experience of being in the Master's ship, and first gazing on "New South Wales," makes it possible for the reader to imagine being in the convict's skin, awed by the vividness of what he sees. The "lick of satin" on the surface of the sea is his old life gone, and in its place is an unknown, foreboding present. His description, too, is intimately located in the bodily sensation of riding and subsiding with the movement of the water as the ship sits out at sea, waiting for the Master's instructions to begin unloading. As an Australian reader, it is very easy for me to imagine the sea looking just as he describes it, and to imagine myself standing in his place, feeling the gentle swell of the sea, rising and subsiding:

> But how vivid this ocean is, with a lick of satin parallel to the coast a quarter of a mile out, like a wake and yet too broad to be left by any vessel: it is as if our whole future had already come, swept past, and gone before we even arrived. Meanwhile the past has been scuttled. A slight swell lifts that sleek ribbon and passes beneath without breaking it, like a muscle under skin. A minute later, when the swell reaches us, riding here at anchor, we rise to its gentle authority. We also subside. (Hall, 1994, p. 4)

I rise and subside with the rhythm of the language. I see the satin skin of the water. I stand on the ship, visually and sensually caught in the moment, transported there through language. It is the sea I know, brought to life in language, and I am ecstatic at that loved and largely unwritten place appearing in the text, coming to life in my bodily experience as I read the text. But Hall has also given it new life, life I could not have imagined. Through the metaphor of the muscle under the skin of the surface water, he brings the sea to life, as if it, too, were human, or as if I too were the sea. The binary created in the English language between body and landscape is momentarily dissolved in this metaphor—and I have lived, in the reading of it, the dissolving of that boundary.

This is my first moment of bliss. In the moment of intense pleasure of imaginatively recalling the way the sea looks on this part of the New South Wales coast, I lose my own familiar sense of self, separate from the sea—I experience having no boundaries. Unlike Joseph in Chapter 3, my shift of embodiment does not come after hours of immersion in water, but from an immersion in words—the text is volatile and labile, "a force or energy which creates links between objects, which makes things, forges alliances, produces connections" (Grosz, 1989, p. xvi).

As the convict stands gazing at this "new" land, he assumes his life is literally about to end. During the night, he killed the intolerable brutish bully to whom he was manacled. Relatively weak compared to the handsome monster who had taken it upon himself to degrade him in every imaginable way, the convict has committed the hideous act of smothering him with his own body, taking advantage of the fact that the bully was in a feverish coma during the night. As he thinks about his impending death, he recognizes the inevitability of the judgment of his guilt, since laws were written not for people like him but for those who wrote them and have the power to oppress others. This he knows through the events that led to his conviction:

> Here in a beautiful haven, I thought, my living body is soon to be thrown overboard with his dead one. He will weight me down and drown me. Or if he don't the Master is sure to put a bullet through my skull. That is how it goes with the law. What is the difference between a corpse with a bullet hole and a corpse without? The law is for one part of mankind to explain how its oppression of the other is for the good of all. (Hall, 1994, p. 6)

But the Master decides not to dispose of him. He had, after all, paid good money for his body, his labor. The bully's hand is chopped off in a careless, savage way, and the convict is no longer manacled to the dead body.[1] He recognizes the chance of freedom that this gives him from the brutal regime in which he is no more than an object in someone else's game. The chance of freedom lies between being killed by an outraged Master or being killed by the "natives" whose land he must escape into:

> Was it worth the risk of a spear in the chest or a shot in the back to keep on going, to make a run for it? Most likely I would be hunted down and dragged back by the hair, flogged and starved. (pp. 9–10)

But he runs, plunging among "tall smooth tree trunks and undergrowth." As he runs, he attempts to escape his captors and their cruelty, their failure to recognize who he is, but also to escape his revulsion at the creature he has become while in captivity. But the thick undergrowth and its inhabitants allow him no straight path forward, no path away from fear. "Between death and death, the best I could do was stumble and lurch" (p. 10). Even as he enters the forest, he is aware of the risk he runs of entering a different state of consciousness, of abandoning what he knows along with the rational baggage of the English language:

> Then came the chance to be free of reason itself. In the beauty of the evening, ospreys gliding above, the massed confusion of the unknown taking the form of a forest offered me, on arrival here, a death cleansed of humiliation. The chaos rushed to meet me and dodge me. (p. 11)

---

1. The convict discovers later that the bully was not in fact dead, though he had suffered extreme brain damage. The story of this other convict is not dealt with here, though he too plays an important part in the novel.

Even while he enters the space between those two deaths, he cannot help but misname what he sees as "ospreys." He has, as yet, only the language and images that belong in different landscapes. He experiences this new space as alive, as active rather than passive, rushing to meet him and dodge him. At the same time, he sees this space as offering him a less humiliating death than the one he flees from where he can only be read as "convict." As he stumbles through the bush, he hears the sounds of terrified and terrifying animals thumping away from him, but he does not yet know how to see the Aboriginal people who observe his flight. Their stillness, as they watch him, means that they are, in his perception, merged with the forest he stumbles through:

[T]hose shapes remaining quite still escaped my notice. Some I might have even brushed against without recognising them as human. Slender and dark like young tree trunks, daubed with mud and leaves, as I was later to see, they had painted each other with living earth and the fugitive design of shadows in this place. (p. 11)

Both his nearsightedness and his cultural knowledge, which separates "man" from "nature," occlude his vision—he does not see that the Aboriginal people, standing still in the forest, are actually there. Ironically, his blindness enables him to see the Aboriginal people, not as the savages his Master saw, but more as they saw themselves, as belonging in the landscape. Aboriginal languages do not place them as binary other to the land as English does, but rather in an intricate enfolded connection with the land (Carter, 1996). They are, in the convict's telling, like the trees. They are daubed with living earth in patterns of light and shadow like those cast by the trees. They are still, and they watch, while the convict, seeing and not seeing, blunders through an alarming and alarmed landscape.

With him, I enter again, with my ancestors, seeing (and not seeing) the subtle complexity of what was there. Through this imaginative reentry, the crudity and violence of my own ancestors' perceptions are partially erased—their perceptions no longer serving as the basis for perceptions of the past. The recorded history of my mother's family (Oppenheimer and Mitchell, 1989), which tells of their take-up of the land in "New England," makes no mention of the violence done to the people whose land it was. The violence of their omissions is also partially erased, for me, in this moment of reentry.[2] This is not to say that the violence of those perceptions is not still there, with all its damaging effects. Rather, in imaginatively reentering with other perceptions,

---

2. A second or third cousin of mine, Bruce Blomfield, tried to tell a different story, of slaughter and mistreatment. So outrageous was this act of storying the past to the members of my family that I did not even know of his existence until I heard him give a lecture at the University of New England where he was invited to speak by Aboriginal people.

my ancestors' perceptions lose their sense of inevitability. They lose some of their capacity to shape the present.[3]

This is my second moment of bliss. Ambivalent though my relations with my family history are, I experience a state of loss as I am wrested away from our shared history, and I stand alone, unhistoried. In my mind's eye I have reentered the Australian landscape with the convict. I draw on my own first fearful entry into dense coastal bushland as a child, to reenter, this time without my family having been there before me. It is a fearful experience.

As he writes about his experience of entry, the convict reflects on the stories he has heard that might make this land something he can make sense of, something that correlates with the imagined lands that explorers had dreamed of and discovered. They include ancient stories of heroic exploration, of Sinbad, and cities of gold and fortunes easily made. But Australia, he knows, is no such place:

> Here in New South Wales one thing we do know is that this will be the last foreign shore, the last unknown land, the only adventure to yield none of our desires: no gold, no cities. Even the trees are strange to us and the animals are those useless freaks the whole world hears of, egg laying flying reptiles, fantasies of Nature. Instead of taking us forward, what we see takes us back to the beginning of time. The real and the fabulous have not yet gone their separate ways. (Hall, 1994, p. 17)

But it is not just the stories of his culture that give him no clues as to how to read this landscape. He finds himself bound by the connotations of a language that have nothing to do with the poetry of the landscape he wants to evoke. He speaks of being shackled to the bond of words, "words to be broken out of before the new kingdom could find its airy regions among the clutter of old misfitting uses" (p. 17). Fearful and unnameable as this new land is, he is seduced by its beauty and held in its thrall. When he wakes in the middle of his first night in the bush, he finds an unearthly light has crept into the bush. He searches for words that might begin to evoke what he sees without relying on the specific acts of naming that might misconstruct what he sees:

> Lying there, gazing at the treetops I was astonished to find that what I had taken for a dense umbrella of leaves showed itself as frail lace. Close by my face, where I could focus, starlike growths sprouted

---

3. Other work, such as that of Margaret Somerville (1990), had already mapped the terrain of another story, that told by the Aboriginal people in the New England area, of white "settlement." The knowledge contained in such documents as hers probably also played its part in making it possible to reenter the landscape of my country and to find it differently inscribed.

around me, and glowing fungus. Even the plenteous dead leaves matted on the forest floor each had its own shape when brought up close, its honed edge, pointed and curved. They were like lily leaves afloat on the dark planet. A spider hung silvered in her web. And a radiant veil of harmless insects flew past stretching and retracting. (p. 27)

Later, in the early morning light, the convict is again captivated by what he sees—he marvels at the magnificence. His wish to see the detail prevents him from moving on, even though reason tells him he must continue his flight. Despite the utter strangeness and the danger he is in, he is transfixed by the splendor of the colors in the morning bush:

> I knew I ought to escape, but I could not deny myself the simple marvel of this burst of rosy light as it steadied and strengthened to brilliant gold and the whole top of the tree shone like a hood of jewels. Hints of blue swept through the air above. Even at risk of being noticed I watched until the marvel faded. (p. 27)

I was electrified when I read this description. As the convict described himself being in thrall to this jeweled vision, so like the jeweled visions in the collective memory stories in Chapter 2 (Lekkie in the early morning light at a bush camp, and Rosie gazing up through the trees from her safe place in the sandy creek bed), I remembered a similar moment in my garden in New England when the late afternoon light caught the drops of water on the fresh new leaves of a eucalypt. The grey-green landscape burst into light and I was transfixed. I stood there for a long time, but with no words for what I had seen. The convict's words recall that vivid image. It springs to life in his words, and I am transfixed again, not just because I imagine that he has seen what I have seen, but because it now has a new and different meaning. That image of mine is part of what I draw on to bring this text to life. But more, this literary event marks as significant my own moment in the garden, gifting it with more than beauty. The moment holds, now, a key to my own love affair with the Australian landscape, a key to my capacity to go with the convict and to see it differently, against the grain of the invaders' (my ancestors') perceptions.

Hall says of the convict:

He became for me the personification of courage in that from the beginning of his escape he lets go of wanting to control things. You know, it seems to me that wanting to control things is a failure of courage. Here was someone who found himself in a completely foreign place and was able to say, from the beginning, let it be foreign.

In a sense, then, Hall and the convict share the same willingness to abandon control, Hall of the act of writing, the convict of his language and life. And I, in my reading, traverse the same path, to the extent I am able, living and breathing as the convict lives and breathes, having courage as the convict has it, to shift the palings of my heart.

The convict traverses the landscape with the Aboriginal men (whom he refers to as the Men). They feed and shelter him, and he comes, over time, to know the landscapes they travel through, through the Men's knowledge of them. Yet he cannot become one of them. They do not offer him that possibility. They keep him separate from their community and treat him not as a human, but as one returned from the dead.[4]

When the Men bring him back to the place where they first found him, he can no longer interact with that place as he might have done before he had traveled with them. It has been transformed by the building of roads and fences and houses into an English-style farm. As such, it is, to the convict, excruciatingly familiar, reminding him of the landscapes of his childhood on the Isle of Man, of his life and language, and of the cultural inheritance that he has lost.

But after his long immersion in the bush, he has, without realizing it, learned to see and to exist within the landscape in the way the Men do. When their journeying through the landscape brings them back to the Master's property, he is affronted and repelled by the roads and fences that have been built in his absence. This simultaneous attraction and revulsion is also lived out in his perception of the Master. He describes the Master riding towards him on his horse, not able to see him standing still, with the Men, amongst the trees. He has become invisible, just as the Men are. He stands stock still, staring at the Master, while a snake, also failing to recognize him as anything other than its natural habitat, crawls up his body, as if his body were a tree trunk. Master and convict stare at each other; the Master sees no one, the convict sees the Master and notes the unclear boundary between Master and horse; the Master who imposes his civilization on the landscape is also himself, in part, melded with nature:

> I am expecting the savages, said the Master, we are ready. If that's you up there, you can come for a dose of medicine, you heathens. . . .
> The Master and his servant stared right at me. The snake's head examined my head. A comical thing came to mind, that snakes are famous as being near-sighted.

---

4. As far as the Men are concerned, he is Yuramiru, an ancestor who departed for northern lands in the 1600s and has now returned in spirit form. Hall (1996b) tells the story of Yuramiru in *The Lonely Traveller by Night*.

A shot, fired like a single clap, sounded ridiculous. There was no harm in such a puny thing. I stared at the Master and his levelled weapon, then at his companion. They stared straight back up at me. They were so close I could almost have spat at them and expected to find my mark.

Heathens! the Master sneered. And his trunk sat so firm he seemed part of the horse.

The other's hat nodded.

Only then did I realise an amazing fact. They were looking right at me but I was invisible to them. My snake rippled up over one ear. The rasping scales gave me the shivers. Into my hair the thing went tunnelling. The tail still reached down to my feet. A slender creature this was, filling me with nausea and pride. (Hall, 1994, pp. 52–54)

As the Master departs, the convict is filled with grief at his recognition that he is no longer visible to one who shares his cultural inheritance. He does not want the Master to depart without seeing him, and he attempts to shout out, but he has lost his voice, his capacity to utter words. His desire to be recognized, then, by those with whom he shares his past language, his past knowledge, overrides his desire for survival. His new knowledge has not obliterated the old; the body constructed through landscapes and words now abandoned is still filled with longing. As Lacan (1985, p. 58) says, "the first object of desire is to be recognised by the other." The anguish of his failure to reconnect with the people, the language, and idea of embodied being in landscape that he has left behind is, for me, amongst the most compelling moments in Australian literature. The convict is simultaneously filled with revulsion for the Master and all he has done to the land, with his roads and fences and his cutting down of trees, and a longing to be recognized by him. He holds in this moment so much of the ambiguity and contradiction of life lived in this land we call Australia.

This is the most painful point of bliss, involving the greatest sense of loss, involving the greatest magnitude of refiguring who it is I can be in this landscape. The recognition of the separation between my language and the landscapes in which I have grown is almost intolerable. How can it be that the language that seemed so powerful is in fact not able to accomplish the task I long for it to accomplish—the telling of the landscapes in which I live?

The convict chooses at that point in the story to return to his Aboriginal guardians, to his life lived out differently, to the embodied knowledge he has learned from them.

Much later, he returns again to the settlement, and this time the Men set fire to the Master's dwellings. The dual knowledge of the convict, his embodiment in two cultures, two ways of knowing the landscape, leads to an agonizing combination of joy and grief:

Shouting with joy at the Master's fall, I felt the ground shift under me. Was there ever a time in my childhood before I knew what a house was: the pitched roof, four walls, square windows, smoke which was supposed to spout from the chimney only?

. . . I whooped encouragements . . . [yet the] idea of a house was my inheritance which, however I might be convicted, could not be taken from me. (Hall, 1994, pp. 117–18)

This torn consciousness of the convict echoes the current ruptures in Australian consciousness. We are of this land and shaped by it, we long for it, we belong in it, and at the same time we go on shaping it through contradictory life-forms and languages rooted elsewhere.

During the chaos of the fire, the convict actually sees the Mistress kill the Master. In his confusion he conceives the idea that she killed the Master in order to be free to be with him, to share his newfound knowledge of the land. Instead of leaving the scene, he enters a store room that is not burning and there the Mistress locks him in. It is there he writes his story in the form of love letters to her. He hopes that if he can only tell his story clearly enough she will see him and the country, and come to know it as he does. He wants to transform her, through his words, into one who is capable of seeing what he can now see, but above all he wants her to recognize him as one who sees this way. It is a complex recognition that he wants. His writing is poetic, subtle, and deeply philosophical. He wants her to recognize him as one who is capable of such beautiful writing, and, at the same time, as one who has come to an entirely different knowledge through his contact with the Men. He wants to show her how to distance herself from the extraordinary hubris of European explorers and mapmakers who think that in naming and mapping they know the place they have "found":

[T]here can be no such thing as the discovery of land. Does this surprise you? Granted, we hear tales pitched at having us think there is nothing in the world so interesting, from big discoveries by Marco Polo and James Cook and company, down to little places called Somebody's Folly. But what do discoverers do? They put names to landmarks unknown to them and not named by anybody they ever heard of. But do we imagine the Cape of Good Hope came into being just to be called that name? We might as well talk about the discoverers of ignorance. (pp. 191–92)

But above all he wants her to recognize him outside of the meanings attached to the category of convict or murderer. He will always be marginal to the Aboriginal Men, as they do not regard him as one of them, though they guard him carefully. He is not, and does not want to be, one of the settlers, captive to their assumptions of superiority and their inability to think otherwise than to attempt to dominate and control the landscape, turning it into a replica of the place they have come from. Yet he recognizes with them the shapes and meanings of houses, he shares their language, he understands the pleasures of forgery. Perhaps he can use this shared knowledge to draw another into the space he occupies, which is neither indigenous being nor invading conqueror.

This is a book of moral and philosophical struggle about ownership, about who has what rights in relation to words and ideas—and land. The convict was convicted because he created a fine work of art that was named a forgery. But he refuses to be made captive by the limitations such words put upon who he might be. In his letters, he writes to the Mistress:

> Your husband has had you in bondage to his cause of creating a counterfeit England by cutting down strange trees and digging out plants with no name. He has had you in bondage to the comfort of being able to call this thing a cabbage, this thing a peapod; of fencing animals you can call a cow, a horse, and keeping them fenced in case they recognise freedom with less trouble than civilized man.
> This I can offer you.
> I have already lived a life of knowing about marked limits and being kept in or kept out—of family and foreigner, owner and thief, tax agent and smuggler, artist and forger. But answer one question: Who makes the rule that certain things may be copied and certain things may not? (p. 194)

Throughout all the days in which he writes his letters, he knows he can escape from the storehouse the Mistress has locked him into, but he does not. Only when he has completed his story does he make his escape. In refinding his tongue and his facility with language, he finds the capacity to recognize himself, and thus escape from the illusion that he is dependent on her capacity to recognize him. This, for me, is the most blissful moment of the book. Throughout the letters the convict reveals the extent to which he is caught up in the dominant discourses of the invaders. His desire for the Mistress is symptomatic of his immersion in those discourses. His situation becomes increasingly dangerous, his inability to leave, horrifying. The only possible known endings are that he will die for this woman, or that she will capitulate to his desire. It is obvious, to the reader, that she will not capitulate, and it is intolerable to imagine his life ended. But he writes his way out. He writes a new storyline that enables him to escape the power of those dominant and dominating discourses. He thus enters the Australian landscape as neither Aboriginal person nor one of the invading hordes. He occupies the conceptual space in between, the space that is crucial for the work of troubling the binary that sets up newcomers as absolutely other to the original people.

The Second Bridegroom is a story about language, about being deprived of language, of coming to know the Australian landscape without words—through a language of the body—at the same time as it is a story in which the narrator, a convict, struggles with the words he has available to him to tell us, as readers, what he saw when he took the risk of moving outside familiar linguistic patterns. But this is not a story in which we discover the "real" Australia that has been occluded from our vision through language; rather, it is a novel that enables us to see how the land we take ourselves to know and our relationship to it is multiply inscribed. As Cronen (1996, p. 69) says of the idea that "nature" is something that exists independent of our readings of it:

> Wilderness hides its unnaturalness behind a mask that is all the more beguiling because it seems so natural. As we gaze into the mirror it holds up for us, we too easily imagine that what we behold is Nature when in fact we see the reflection of our own unexamined longings and desires.

The Second Bridegroom is about the power of words to inscribe landscape, but also of the power of the landscape to inscribe its inhabitants, and about the moral questions inherent in that relationship. It is about "ourselves and our perceptions of the land and what we [non-Aboriginal people] have done to it and what we do to each other" (Hall, 1997). It is about the slow process of the land shaping us, if we let it, and of the devastatingly rapid process of us shaping the land.

The Australian landscape is, at the turn of the century, more than at any other time, a *contested terrain* (Cronen, 1996, p. 51). The stories through which we tell what this land is, and what it means, have immediate bearing on the decisions we make about who has what rights to live in the land in what ways. Who we take ourselves to be descended from, whether it be Aboriginal people, or the invaders, or the convicts (or, most likely, some combination of these), is a prominent part of the stories told, of the claims laid. How we understand what land is and what our relations to it are, how we understand what our obligations are to ourselves, to each other, and the land are affected by the narratives through which we understand body/landscape relations, and in this case in particular the body/landscape relations lived out in the Australian context. But as Cronen (1996, pp. 50–51) points out:

> [T]hese stories are *ours*, not nature's. The natural world does not organize itself into parables. Only people do that, because this is our peculiarly human method for making the world make sense. And because people differ in their beliefs, because their visions of the true, the good, and the beautiful are not always the same, they inevitably differ

as well in their understanding of what nature means and how it should be used—because nature is so often the place where we go searching for the fulfillment of our desires.

And so...

What does *The Second Bridegroom* do, in my reading of it, to change the ways I might think about my embodied being as I live it in the Australian landscape? First, it provides me with metaphors with which to trouble the linguistic patterns through which I see myself as other to the land. The solutions I seek will not be free of that reading of the land as coextensive with my body. Second, it undoes the linguistic boundaries that create separations between people of different "races." The history of brutality of one group against others is made starkly clear. Yet the clear definitions between groups are blurred, transgressed, disrupted. The history of pain and oppression is not glossed over. Rather, a possibility is opened up of erasure of the sharp lines that we constantly draw and redraw in our everyday talk between one set of ancestors and another, between one cultural group and another. The intricately complex and subtle variations in culture can be appreciated quite differently in the finding of linking threads. While the tightly drawn boundaries that the English language creates are still necessary for political argument and for the development of strategies to ameliorate old wrongs, the re-inscriptions made possible through troubling these boundaries promise a rich and quite differently textured future.

It is important to emphasize, in the current political climate in Australia, that I am not referring here to an idea that we are all one and the same and that justice can be achieved through a fiction of sameness or oneness. However much we might all profit from deconstructing the us/them binaries, we cannot ignore the work that needs to be done to ensure justice for all people. Quite often, justice can only be done if the group who has been treated unjustly is named as that group and so the category kept tightly drawn while we find just solutions. At the same time, the conceptual possibilities opened up by moving beyond simplistic assumptions about difference can help undo old patriarchal and colonialist hierarchies. In the space between old hierarchies and the simplistic assumption of sameness lies a possibility of mutual understanding and mutual responsibility based on threads of sameness, and threads of difference. The convict's story enables us to live the pain of the deeply conflicting ways of knowing through which we are folded into Australian body/landscape relations. The living of an imaginary text is not a passive act, nor is it simply a pleasurable, repetitive act in which we view that which is already known. It is a text that holds the possibility of bliss—and bliss sometimes imposes a painful sense of loss. Hall's fiction holds the possibility of shifting perceptions in such a way that we can reenter our cultural landscape differently, seeing it against the grain of old perceptions, finding it differently inscribed. That reentry may make possible new lived possibilities—possibilities that arise because we have allowed his text to shift the palings that guard our hearts.

Body/place:
Living on the ground
and learning a language of place

Breathing in the air of trees,
walking with 'exquisite notice and care,'
listening with the ruffled surface of the body

Margaret Somerville
(1999, p. 226)

~10~ (Be)longing in the writing of Janette Turner Hospital: Eclipsing the constitutive force of discourse

I MET WITH JANETTE TURNER HOSPITAL while she was visiting Australia to launch her book *Oyster*. Although much of her writing is located in Australia, she spends most of her life in other countries, and so I felt myself very lucky that she was here, and that she agreed to meet me. Over lunch in a hotel in Brisbane she expressed a sense of vulnerability about the interview, telling me she was not very articulate when it came to spoken words, and that what she had to say was already in her books. But when the tape was turned on, her words were like perfectly formed jewels. She spoke with insight and emotion about the embodied nature of her writing. I was, during our hour over lunch, panic-stricken that we did not have enough time for all my questions, in a state of rapture at the careful and profound answers she made to my questions, and delighted to find so many moments of her life echoed in my own memories. We were both born in the 1940s in Australia and so had grown up through the same historical and discursive shifts through which we had become "girls," "people," and "Australians." For her part, Janette Turner Hospital expressed surprise and pleasure at the careful, detailed reading I had made of her texts, and at the fact that I treated her with such respect. Through our talk about her life and her writing, in working through the transcripts later, and in our subsequent communication about aspects of the interview and my interpretations of it, I developed a deep sense of affinity with and respect for her.

Janette Turner Hospital's life was, as a child, and is, as an adult, one in which she often feels deeply precarious. Her subjection within the various discourses through which family and Australian colleagues are constituted is not something she takes for granted for herself. The difference between family and school and family and work makes the terms of subjection in each highly visible to her. She described to me the effect of this while on her lecture tour and, at the same time, visiting her family:

I felt exhausted—psychically exhausted at the immensity of the difference and the fact that I've learnt to pass as a native in both worlds and in fact I feel profoundly alien and deeply precarious in both because I just—there are days when I simply feel fraudulent, there are days when I just feel I can't manage it . . . (Turner Hospital, 1996a)

Janette Turner Hospital describes herself as a child who did not accept the terms of her subjection without question. She wanted to interrogate the discourses that her family insisted must be taken on trust. Her childhood home, she says, was a place where you didn't ask questions, particularly about the apparent irrationality of stories in the Bible. School, too, was a place where you didn't ask questions. In her novel *Charades* she created a character, Kay, who attempts to pass as one who is acceptably subjected in school terms, but who finds that her fraudulence is visible to teachers and the other students who "know" without question the terms of their subjection. In the following excerpt from *Charades*, Kay's lack of knowledge about a famous horse race held each year in Australia leads to her being positioned by teacher and students as outsider, as one who has no right to know as they know, to be as they are:

Kay felt she would run out of storage room for all the puzzling things she knew. Most of her knowledge was of the wrong kind. She could, for example, rattle through the names of the books of the Bible, from Genesis to Revelation, but could not produce the name of a single horse in the Melbourne Cup. She had never even heard of Phar Lap— "the *legendary* Phar Lap," Miss Kennedy said, incredulous.

On the other hand she knew that the blue bodypaint of Boadicea's warriors was called *woad*, and that King Harold had been felled by an arrow in the eye at the Battle of Hastings.

Miss Kennedy, surprised but grudgingly pleased, asked: "Now just *where* do you pick up these things?"

"In the library," Kay said guiltily. In the library, while the rest of the class engaged in Maypole dancing and sundry other forbidden licentious acts. "In the picture-book encyclopedia."

Not acceptable, she knew it instantly. She could feel the disapproval like a sudden tropical fog. They would *do* things again, the boys would, if Patrick wasn't with them and they caught her alone after school. Don't tell, don't tell, they would taunt. If you tell we will get you tonight . . .

. . . she had gone and *memorised* the page on Phar Lap in the picture-book encyclopedia. She waited and waited and when at last he was mentioned again by Miss Kennedy, her hand shot up. "His greatest win was the 1930 Cup," she said, breathless. "He had thirty-seven wins, the last one in America. And then," she rattled on, "he was murdered by the Americans, but his heart was one and a half times the normal size for a thoroughbred."

There was an eerie silence.

They all looked at her very strangely, she could feel the stares like pins and needles on her skin.

"What would *youuuuu* know?" someone taunted.

Wowser, wowser, wowser! voices said.

"*Youuu've* never been to the races in yer life."
What would you know you know you know? voices chanted later in
the playground. And the circle formed a kind of dance, a skip, a game.
(Turner Hospital, 1988, p. 132)

Such experiences of not belonging, which make Turner Hospital
(and Kay) feel so vulnerable, lead to a capacity to see beyond the
taken-for-granted everyday world. She does not write with the clichés,
the obviousnesses that form the *settled* certainties of existence. She
writes out of her own embodied existence—the flow of her writing
comes from the *in(terre)conscious* zones. *In(terre)conscious: between
earth and consciousness.* She draws on all the subterranean possibilities
earthed in the human body as a result of experiencing life where she
does not belong—possibilities that take her beyond the kind of knowledges and practices of the taunting children in Kay's classroom. Cixous
uses the term *in(terre)conscious* zone when she talks of the writing of
Derrida. She says, "I see in him this brilliant explorational cast, which
brings him to discover structures or logics that have never before been
thought, to sketch the course of rivers that flow in the '*in(terre)con-
scious*' zones" (Cixous, in Cixous and Calle-Gruber, 1997, p. 88).
Turner Hospital troubles the separation of consciousness from the
earth (*terre*): she writes from the space between (*inter*) earth and consciousness. She invites us into an imaginary space in which we
encounter (and in part become) embodied beings not separated from
the earth, but of it. She writes into the space between landscapes and
bodies and finds them, on occasion, inseparable:

In the green pool the two heads floated with their dark hair fanned
about them: waterlilies on lily pads. (Turner Hospital, 1995a, p. 200)

Uncle Seaborn's hair is soft as water, crinkly (one thinks of wavelets
rippling back over sand), the colour of seaweed.... A gleaming creature, barebacked and slick with sweat.... Behind him ... the Great
Divide falls away to the coastal plain, and the wet tendrils of hair drip
down ravines of muscle and bone, of eucalypt scrub, of Fitzroy River
silt, making their way to the Pacific. It sucked at him ceaselessly, the
ocean. (1995b, p. 203)

The cane pushes through the rotting window blinds and grows into the
cracks and corners of the mind. It ripens in the heart at night, and its
crushed sweetness drips into dreams. I have woken brushing from my
eyelids the silky plumes that burst up at harvest time. (1995c, p. 15)

Turner Hospital describes how, in the face of being silenced as a
child, at home and at school, she sought unpeopled spaces in which
to think, to ask the questions she wanted to ask. When she climbed

trees or swam in the sea she could explore the concepts that seemed weighty to her, and discover a language in which her openness to the flows of the earth and her consciousness opened new possibilities. From as young as six years old, she describes herself as experiencing a "fusion of landscape and body and thought":

And I was told, you know: you don't ask these questions, we don't understand what God's thinking. So I wasn't allowed to ask questions at home, and for quite other reasons at school the questions I would have asked would be deemed stupid or the class would laugh at them. So my first experience of where I could think my own criminal and puzzling and unanswerable thoughts was a fusion of landscape and body and thought. I would climb and hide up our mango tree, you know, or I would go off alone to the beach or I would actually be in the surf . . . so actually for me freedom, intellectual freedom and critical thinking and language and bodily pleasure and the eroticised highly speaking landscape all seemed to fuse extremely early for me you know and I had these thoughts about it, not so highly articulated and verbalised, I'm sure, by the time I was six years old.

She describes her first visit to North Queensland, as a schoolgirl, as one of ecstatic fusion with the landscape. She could not join in the chatter of the other girls—their talk of boys and sex was "totally unknown territory." Instead, she went walking alone: "[I] walked around on Green Island by myself and just was ecstatic. And I found the North Queensland rain forest" (1996a). The "eroticised highly speaking landscape" she experienced then as a schoolgirl and later as a teacher in North Queensland has become a resource she can write out of, not just as a memory of events and places, but as an embodied experience of knowing beyond the already available words that shape her. Her writing opens the possibility for others to enter that space: that which is beyond words is made knowable through sound and imagery, through an invitation to imaginatively enter the bodily and emotional space inhabited by her characters.

In Turner Hospital's short story "The Last of the Hapsburgs," the teacher, Miss Davenport, newly arrived in North Queensland, stands on the Port Douglas beach and hears the landscape speak to her, bidding her to find words to *"Sing me North Queensland":*

The young woman leaves no footprints at all. She stands with her feet and ankles in the erratic line of froth, at the point where ocean and shore eat each other, and reads the Port Douglas beach. Cabrisi's horse [the wild brumby], nostrils flaring with the smell of her, rears: a salute of sorts.

"Caedmon," she says—here, the naming of creatures is all hers—"you beautiful show-off!" Of course he knows it. So bloody beautiful that a cry catches in her throat. Caedmon whinnies again, a high jubilant note, and brushes the air with his delicate forelegs. Another sign. The beach is thick with them, but who has time enough for the decoding, the translating, the recording?

Surf rises from her ankles to her knees. *Sing me North Queensland,* it lisps with its slickering tongues.

I can't, she laments, hoisting up her skirt. *I can't.*

She would need a different kind of alphabet, a chlorophyll one, a solar one. The place will not fit into words.

Surf rushes between her thighs. *Sing me North Queensland,* it commands.

The young woman lifts her arms high above her head and faces the ocean. She begins to dance. She sings. When the sun slides behind Double Point, she climbs the hill at the end of the beach still singing. (1995a, p. 190)

The sea, in which she is partially immersed, "lisps with its slickering tongues," commanding her to "sing me creation." Her silence holds her mute, but the sea commands again, rushing through her thighs, in an erotic salty embrace. This place will not fit the words already available to her, but the sea does not cease in its command. She needs "a different kind of alphabet, a chlorophyll one, a solar one." Existing words fail her, and yet "[s]he begins to dance. She sings." A song without end. And in that singing lies the possibility of a new relation between body, language, and landscape. Though as readers we cannot hear that song, it exists as an imaginary possibility; a voice that responds to the voice of the sea. Turner Hospital says of such writing:

I suppose in a way I know I'm always writing about silent women, mute women who nevertheless are highly in tune with their own bodies and the landscape, and an attempt to speak of a language that is sensually eroticised, quite profoundly communicative, but has to exist outside established language forms because they've just not served the purpose of communicating. So I guess I'm always—that's what my writing is actually looking for. Metaphors that speak of the fusion of body, landscape, and the will to communicate. Will is altogether too analytical, patriarchal a word. The eroticised desire to communicate might be a better way to put it. And seeking to do that in a language that sneaks below the water table perhaps of the existing language forms. I feel as though I will write my way, that I've been writing my way out of silence but that in fact I'll write my way back into it somehow.

The experience of being embodied as silent, unable to speak—an experience fundamental to growing up female (Davies et al., 1997)—is disrupted, and yet it is always there as a possibility to return to. The return to silence she talks of is not necessarily a return in the original terms of exclusion, but a return made possible by the discovery of another way of being beyond words, which is experienced as more

powerful than words. Though in what follows it becomes clear that
these two kinds of silence cannot be so clearly separated out, one
from the other.

Later in the story of the young woman on the beach, Miss Davenport seeks out two of her students who are loners in the school, one
an Aboriginal girl from a poverty-stricken background and one a Jewish
girl with an eccentric family escaped from Europe to a place where
they hope they will be safe. The three young women walk together to
the Mossman Gorge. When they arrive at the Gorge, Hazel, the Aboriginal student, slips off her tunic and dives in. Rebecca, more cautious in
taking off her clothes, hesitates, then follows Hazel. Miss Davenport has
longed all day for the coolness of the pool, but not thought about the
problem of clothes. She has brought the young women with her as a
spontaneous afterthought. She is uncertain of the situation, but she
finds the repeated phrase from the fourteenth-century mystic, Julian of
Norwich, "*all manner of thing shall be well,*" and thus finds the desire
and the freedom to follow the young women into the water:

> Miss Davenport, with a careless rapture, took off all her clothes and
> walked into the water.
>
> The pool, from dark subterranean places, was chilly, a shock to the
> body for whole minutes. Time must have passed, though the three
> women were not conscious of it. They did not speak, but they were
> aware of each other. Birds piped and flashed their colours, the falls
> kept up their subdued chatter.
>
> *This is where we have escaped to,* Miss Davenport thought. One is
> safe in water.
>
> One is helpless in water.
>
> Afterwards, she could never understand how there was no warning,
> no transition. Just peace and then chaos, the jarring laughter and cat-
> calls, the five boys standing on boulders.
>
> *Joanna Goanna's tits?* they whooped. *Cop those black tits! Plain-jane
> hasn't got any tits, she's flat as a bat. Oh struth, cop that! You can see
> old dried up Davenport's pussy!*
>
> The boys, Miss Davenport noted, were in an intense and spiritual
> state, a kind of sacrilegious ecstasy, leaping from boulder to boulder
> around the pool. Like kings of the wild, they stood high on the great
> black rock and pissed into the water. Then one of them, Ross O'Hagan,
> eldest son of the local policeman, an ordinary boy who sat at an ordi-
> nary desk in Miss Davenport's English class, that boy turned his back
> and pulled down his shorts and squatted. A turd emerged slowly and
> hung suspended from his hairy anus. It was long, amazingly long, mak-
> ing its celebrity appearance to a chanted count. One! the boys chanted.
> Two, three, four, five . . .
>
> Miss Davenport, Rebecca, and Hazel watched, mesmerised. The turd
> had attained the count of ten, a plumbline reaching for water. Eleven,

twelve, thirteen . . . It detached itself at last and fell into the pool with a soft splash. Cheers went up, and more whoops of laughter, and then the boys were off like possums, flying from rock to rock. They scooped up the bundle of female clothing, and ran off. . . .

Water lapped at their shoulders. Polluted water. Hazel, inured to indignity perhaps, was the first to move. She clambered onto the boulder below the falls and let the water hammer her. . . .

But what comfort could Miss Davenport give to Rebecca whose face had put on its whitewax look-alike mask? How could she unsay the sentence that had been spoken, become an anti-Circe? In her teacherly mind, she rehearsed possible spells: *This says more about the boys than it does about us.*

But it would not serve, she knew it. It might be true, but it would not serve. That steaming fact, dropping stolidly into the pool, spoke a thick and dirty language. The acts of men, even when they are boys, Miss Davenport thought, are shouts that rip open the signs that try to contain them. We have no access to a language of such noisiness. Our voices are micemutter, silly whispers.

We will have to stay here in the pool forever, she thought. We are dead ends, the last of a line, masters of the genre of silence. We will have to invent a new alphabet of moss and water. (1995a, pp. 201–202)

In such writing and reading from the body, from the vulnerable body, Janette Turner Hospital produces a shock of knowledge of what it is to be embodied as woman—not only woman with all the power of the earth, speaking a new language, but woman vulnerable to the words of boys, boys like possums who constitute them as other, as objects to be desired or rejected, playthings who can be left stranded naked in the forest, their words reduced to *micemutter, silly whispers.* But the inventing of a new alphabet of moss and water momentarily eclipses the dominant patriarchal discourses through which these women and these boys are shaped. Janette Turner Hospital says of that moment:

The kind of language exchanged in the Mossman Gorge, say, in the rock pool at the Mossman Gorge with students, that didn't have words at all and it was sort of shared bodily epiphanies and I don't mean sexual and I don't mean eroticised exactly, although I do think of language and the body as eroticised— instruments, perhaps, is the word.

In creating such a powerful image of the body as instrument for speaking the landscape without words, Turner Hospital does not essentialize such power and so allow us to fall into the naive assumption that such eclipsing of other language forms might be permanent, or capable of rendering powerless those more usually positioned as powerful. The energy that led Miss Davenport to seek something new and different, that enabled her to run against the grain of dominant discourses, is generated afresh in the anger erupting from the fact of the steaming stolid turd speaking the boys' contempt. That anger does not rest with Turner Hospital as author, nor Miss Davenport as character, but is potentially lived again by each reader, in each reading of it. At the same time, Turner Hospital leaves many of her readers with a deep unease, since the new alphabet that makes it possible to go beyond known discourses makes the young women's vulnerability all the more vivid: old discourses that render women and landscape the same, as passive objects to be used and abused, are textually present in their reading of this episode at the Mossman Gorge. The new is always partially generated out of the old and thus partially contained by it. The seeking of ecstatic fusion, the sensual awareness of embodiment in landscape, the discovery of one's body as an instrument that speaks a language beyond words, is partially generated by a desire for escape from oppressive discourses: the oppressive discourse cannot be ignored, therefore, as a generative force.

Cixous describes what writing is for her in comparable ways. She describes how she searches not in the possibilities afforded by rational thought but for what she can find on her own body's deep surfaces, in the *in(terre)conscious* zones. She finds on the deep surfaces of her body jewels and corals, matter of the earth and of the sea, matter earthed in the lived human body. At the same time, that embodied searching is a searching for language, for deeply embodied words that, she finds, spark off the same resonances in her readers as they do in her:

As for this weaving you [Mireille Calle-Gruber] spoke of a minute ago, here to there is nothing voluntary for me; I do not take an element *a* and an element *b* to connect them. This happens in my deepest depths. The signified and the signifier work together without my being able to say which one leads, because the one calls for the other. And vice versa. How? A kind of work takes place in this space that we do not know, that precedes writing, and that must be a sort of enormous region or territory where a memory has been collected, a memory composed of all sorts of signifying elements that have been kept or noted—or of events that time has transformed into signifiers, pearls and corals of the 'language' of the soul. . . . There must be a sort of magnetic 'force' in me that collects, without my knowing it, jewels, materials of the earth, that are propitious for a future book. It is my memory of writing that does this. I say 'my memory of writing' because it is not the memory of life, or the memory of thought. It happens with sound elements, aesthetic elements, etc. Perhaps there is also a recording surface deep in me receiving micro-signs—it must guess that these signs are not solitary and lost, but emitters; in communication with other signs. An example: I had been struck, without realizing it, by the red geranium that lights up in *The Pos-*

sessed of Dostoevsky. It was as if, quite by chance, I had picked from the ground a key that opened a magic world. In the end, the geranium was absolutely not accidental, it was overdetermined. And it was not only my own mania or my own memory, but in effect a clue that functioned in more than one unconscious. Not only my own. Many others. (Cixous, in Cixous and Calle-Gruber, 1997, p. 29)

Turner Hospital's most recent novel, *Oyster,* is a profound exploration of words in relation to embodied being. It tells the story of a teacher who defied the power of men who would control her words, and of how she managed to pass some of those words on to one of her pupils, who used them to escape the extreme domination and control of her oppressive community. It is also a story about young New Age people seduced into their own destruction through the words of a prophet named Oyster.

The novel is set in "Outer Maroo," somewhere in North Queensland. Outer Maroo is in an unmapped zone, free of the surveillance of government bodies, but captive to the surveillance of the local graziers, miners, and religious leaders who have cut their local population off from the outside world in order to take all power to themselves, to make their own fortunes, to wage their own wars. They have removed all traces of Outer Maroo from the map and have closed the lines both out and in. By controlling what can be written and spoken, and what can be read, they hope to take total control of the people and of the wealth of the landscape. One of the characters, Jess, makes her own freedom from control by refusing to speak. Her silence cannot be read, and therefore her thoughts are not subject to control. Miss Rover, the teacher, brings into Outer Maroo books full of dangerous ideas and a will to speak that is so forceful that she chooses the dangerous path of opposing the men—of naming what they are doing and of pointing out to them that their control can never be absolute.

Rover: a nomad, a subject in transition, not overcoded and fixed. *To rove* is to "wander about (a place) with no fixed direction." (*Collins English Dictionary*)

Miss Rover is a subject in process, a subject who exists as verb rather than as noun, a subject who cannot be fixed by the controlling gaze of powerful others (cf. Davies, 1997). Miss Rover sees what is there, she sees the dangerous power of the men in control and she speaks, despite their threats of brutally silencing her. In this she exerts the kind of agency written about in poststructuralist theorizing, in which the subject is aware of being subjected through multiple discourses, and she looks for ways to make that subjection visible and to subvert its power when it works in ways that run counter to other preferred forms of subjection (Davies, 1991).

Unlike Miss Davenport, who could find no words to pass to her students, Miss Rover not only speaks against the will of the men, she passes words in spoken and written form to Mercy, her student, another central character in the novel. Mercy, too, has been raised in a fundamentalist Christian household and community, but her father has lost his faith, and Mercy listens carefully to what Miss Rover has told her. In the following scene, Miss Rover confronts the men in the pub about the fact that no mail comes in or out of Outer Maroo, and she tells them she has found a way to get letters out from their closed community:

> "I think," Bernie said, "that you should apply for a transfer, Miss Rover. I don't think we got that much need for a school after all."
> *Miss Rover, come over,* the children sang.
> "And I think," Miss Rover said, "that you won't shut me up so easily. I think that you don't realise just how many messages are getting out. For example, a letter or two of mine went to Bourke with the Murris, which may be the long way round to Brisbane, but then again, it might be more expeditious than Australia Post."
> "Jesus," one of the men said, seemingly casual. "What big fucking foreign words she keeps in that slutty little mouth."
> "I think maybe she should wash her filthy tongue," someone said.
> "Maybe a few other private places, eh? She admits she's a *Boong-lover*. How many of those black bastards do you reckon she's fucked?" (Turner Hospital, 1996b, pp. 62–63)

The men's strategies for silencing her are primitive. They differ little from the silencing strategies of primary school boys who sexualize the girls who speak in powerful ways (Davies, 1993). Their collective sexual talk nonetheless excites them, excites their sense of power over the woman who will not be silent. The children watch and chant their chorus, the people in the chapel across the road watch, and Miss Rover's one ally, Pete, tries helplessly to take the focus away from her:

> "Listen, mates," and there was a sharper edge of anxiety in Pete Burnett's voice, "just ignore her. Teachers come and go. They come and go and change nothing." . . .
> "Words are like bushfires," Miss Rover warned. She was high on something. She was high on having crossed the line. "You can't stop them. And you can't tell where they'll end up."
>   . . .
> She turned and saw Mercy through the window and waved the remnants of her torn letter, and before Mercy had time to think, she had raised a hand in salute, and Miss Rover put a word there and it burned.
> "Thank you Mercy," Mr Prophet said tightly. "You may sit down. And may the Lord inscribe His Word upon our hearts." The congregation, as

one, was transfixed, its gaze on the scene across the street. "We will bow our heads in prayer," Mr Prophet said, "that the peace which passeth understanding may settle like a dove in every heart."

Something brushed Mercy's heart and her wrist. It was the dove of Miss Rover's word and she closed her fingers round it and kept it in her fist where it fluttered violently and bucked about like a trapped thing. (1996b, pp. 64–65)

The words that pass from Miss Rover to Mercy are words from the *in(terre)conscious* zone. They are words that lodge themselves in the deep surface, in the grain of Mercy's heart and her wrist; they are embodied words that flutter and buck, but which she holds tight. The words of Mr. Prophet provide her with the image of a dove, an image that, like the geranium in Dostoevsky for Cixous, provides a key that opens up a magic world.

Once again Turner Hospital has written about a woman positioned by men as vulnerable, as sexually vulnerable, and as one who can and will be removed from the situation. But this time they do not manage to silence her; she continues to speak despite their overwhelming power. And for the moment her words change nothing, except perhaps for the shifting grain of Mercy's hand and heart. And the effect of words is unpredictable. Text, as Grosz points out, is labile, explosive:

A text is not the repository of knowledges or truths, the site for storage of information (and thus in danger of imminent obsolescence from the "revolution" in storage and retrieval that information technology has provided as its provocation to the late twentieth century) so much as a process of scattering thought, scrambling terms, concepts and practices, forging linkages, becoming a form of action. A text is not simply a tool or an instrument; this makes it too utilitarian, too amenable to intention, too much designed for a subject. Rather, it is explosive, dangerous, labile, with unpredictable consequences. Like concepts, texts are complex products, effects of history, the intermingling of old and new, a complex of internal coherences or consistencies and external referents, of intension and extension, of thresholds and becomings. Texts, like concepts, do things, make things, perform actions, create connections, bring about new alignments. They are events—situated in social, institutional, and conceptual space. (Grosz, 1995, p. 126)

Mr. Prophet knows the power of his words; he utters words to contain the power of his congregation, but one of the words slips out of his control. The familiar words, whose intention is to subject and contain Mercy, do not do so. "The peace which passeth understanding," which Mr. Prophet wishes to "settle like a dove in every heart" and put an end to questioning, instead provides Mercy with an image, alive and fluttering wildly in her hands, opening up new questions, disrupting the promised peace of unquestioning subjection to that which is settled. The conflict for Mercy is agonizing, like warfare in her head between opposing discourses, each vying for dominance:

> Since her departure, Miss Rover has taken up permanent residence as a sniper inside Mercy's head. There are other snipers. There are the irreverent and earthy voices of Ma Beresford and Ma's Bill. And the voices of the elders. And others, and others. Mercy is trapped in the crossfire. Also, there are the clamouring voices of books, Miss Rover's books and her father's library, what used to be her father's library, two different worlds. Is all this listening so exhausting for everyone, or only for Mercy? She feels like the conductor of an orchestra full of musicians who have run amok; they play discordant instruments; they have set up permanent and competitive rehearsal within her mind. (Turner Hospital, 1996b, p. 116)

At the end of this novel Mercy escapes to Brisbane—she gets back on the map, out of the danger zone of a patriarchal attempt at total subjection and the exclusion of all other knowledges. Miss Rover, the teacher who gives her the words that enable her to escape, is lost—the men's will to control and exclude is violent, dangerous. Other young women and men in this novel also lose their lives in a brutal fashion as they are drawn into the discursive web of the prophet Oyster. Only Mercy grasps the possibility handed her by Miss Rover, opens herself to the flow of conflicting words, and, although she almost drowns in the contradictions, finds her way to life. She makes a choice: she has agency—agency that comes from the power of words, agency that arises from subjection. She enables the reader to live what Butler theorizes: she is made a possible subject through conflicting discourses and she eclipses the conditions of her own emergence.

This, for me, is a harrowing text about language and desire, and about resistance to others' will to control and to maintain power. It shows how submitting to domination may seem easier than resistance, but it constitutes such submission as deadly. Turner Hospital makes the power of words visible, and the struggle with them and against them is also made visible. She makes them more than visible: in reading this text, I, and others, find ourselves living and breathing the oppressive force of discourse and the explosive desire for freedom that alternative discourses make possible.[1] Turner Hospital does not set up here a binary in which discourse is oppressive while freedom lies outside discourse, although that is one reading of what she was doing in "The Last of the Hapsburgs." Rather, she invites the reader, as nomad,

---

1. Paula Smith (1998) in her Ph.D., "Syncopations in the Life of a Woman Religious," writes a deeply moving account of her bodily experience of reading this novel.

to move freely in dangerous new places, to live out the enormous differences experienced by her characters, to know life as volatile, labile, capable of movement in multiple directions. She shows the weight and power of language as it is lived by the embodied beings that she (and the reader) bring to life on the page; she shows the force of will and of desire, the potential danger of dominant and dominating discourses, and she shows that the eclipsing of the consitutive power of language is possible.

That eclipsing is brought about through three closely related strategies, lived out through different subjects. The first strategy is to recognize and name oppressive and controlling forces, refusing the power of those who use silencing others as a major strategy for maintaining power. The second strategy is the development of an awareness, beyond words, of embodiment in landscape. This awareness invites the stretching of words to accomplish what is, until that point, unknown, mysterious: it opens the possibility of writing/speaking from the surface/depths of one's own body. Such speaking/writing displaces dead language that exists only as well-practiced clichés or accepted ways of speaking. The third strategy, lived out through Mercy, is the combination of the first two and involves a movement "into different linkages or new alignments" (Grosz, 1995, p. 126). It brings together an awareness of language and its force in/on the surfaces of the body. Mercy lives and breathes words and is able to examine their effects in/on her, and on those around her. She moves beyond the modes of being that are available to the rational humanist self and develops what Turner Hospital calls "the eroticised *desire* to communicate"; she is not limited to and controlled by one discourse, or by the limitations of rational forms of thought, or by the will of others; she is able to read her own embodiment, and its inscription through language, to recognize the multiplicity of it, and to act in ways that enable her to move beyond the existing patterns of power and powerlessness.

And so...

Several readers of this chapter have found themselves deeply shaken by it without being quite sure why. I suspect this is because although Janette Turner Hospital's writing opens up the possibility of eclipsing patriarchal discourses, it also takes us, bodily, into landscapes where we are deeply vulnerable. Turner Hospital says of this aspect of her writing:

[In Australia, though nowhere else] I've frequently been charged with writing too eloquently, too "beautifully," too "disturbingly" about violence. I was completely mystified and shell-shocked when these charges first began cropping up. To me it's like accusing a war vet of having nightmares that are too vivid, too colorful, too dramatic. As though he has any control over that! For god's sake, what else is violence and trauma if not disturbing?

. . . The process of writing is, to use Clément's terms, a long syncope for me. I climb down into the bat cave of sensory, moral and philosophical and interrogative data, and I grope around down there, and things happen, things both euphoric and terrifying, and I set them down during this long syncope when I lose track of everything else (of time, of my body, of my normal functions in the world; I am seriously dysfunctional when I am writing), and when I climb out again with written pages, they are as mysterious and alarming and beautiful to me as an opal pulled out of the dark. (Turner Hospital, 1996a)

The process of writing that Turner Hospital engages in is the writing Cixous describes in her book *Three steps on the ladder of writing*, and the embodied writing I have been searching for in this book. Cixous (1993, p. 118) says of such writing:

Writing is not put there, it does not come from outside. On the contrary it comes from deep inside. It comes from what Genet calls the "nether realms." . . . It is deep in my body, further down, behind thought.

. . . Since we are shaped by years and years of all kinds of experiences and education, we must travel through all sorts of places that are not necessarily pleasant to get there: our own marshes, our own mud. And yet it pays to do so. The trouble is we are not taught that it pays, that it is beneficial. We are not taught the pain nor that in pain is hidden joy. We don't know that we can fight against ourselves, against the accumulation of mental, emotional, and biographical clichés. . . . There is a whole list of institutions, media and machines that make for the banishment of birds, women and writing.

Cixous takes the idea of those birds that the Bible forbids us to eat, calling them unclean, and connects the forbidden joy of the birds' flight to the forbidden joy of writing as a woman, from the body. She uses the term *imund*, forbidden, to refer to books that dare to break away from "the accumulation of mental, emotional, and biographical clichés."

[I]f we are in joy and in love with writing, we should try to write the *imund book*. The imund book deals with things, birds, and words that are forbidden. . . .

The imund book is the book without an author. It is the book written with us aboard, though not with us at the steering wheel. It is the book that makes us experience a kind of dying, that drops the self, the speculating self, the speculating clever "I."

It's the book of the Act of Writing. The book that takes life and language by the roots. . . . It's the book that's stronger than the author: the apocalyptic text, whose brilliance upsets the scribe. How can it be written? With the hand running. Following the writing hand like the painter draws: in flashes. The hand leads to the flowers. From the heart where passions rise to the finger tips that hear the body thinking: this is where the Book *(Alive)-to Live (le livre Vivre)* springs from. . . . (Cixous, 1993, p. 156)

The critics who berate Turner Hospital for writing of women who suffer are apparently not looking at her writing from within a fold in the body/landscape that enables them to see her climbing down into herself/the earth to bring back the startling, mysterious, and disturbing things she finds there. The radical feminist fold they stand in needs powerful women, incapable of being subjected by oppressive discourses, and they wail their displeasure at not finding the images they desire in her writing. Such critics know what the author should find: and if it is not to be found on the depth/surfaces of her body, well, then, she should presumably invent it. Powerful women, in control of their own fate, are what is desired in the fold of the landscape in which they stand. Those powerful women may well exist (at least in the radical feminist imagination), but in literary criticism applied to Turner Hospital's writing those impervious critics are like Cixous's spare wheel that is mistaken for the bird (Cixous, in Cixous and Calle-Gruber, 1997, p. 4). Spare wheels might be useful if the machine one is driving is broken down, but the bird, Turner Hospital's bird, is capable of eclipsing the machinery and taking us somewhere else—into another fold in the landscape altogether, albeit a fold in which she does not become impervious or blind to the horror of the patriarchal machine. To read her fiction requires the willingness to go with her, to examine what she finds as she makes that interior journey "reintegrating the earthly, the earth, and the earth's composition in one's body, imagination, thought" (Cixous, 1993, p. 150).

Our hands are led to the dance
By the wing and the song of birds

Paul Éluard
(1996, p. 85)

~ Conclusion: The ways and the song of the book

THE BODY IS (IN)SCRIBED, THEN, but not in any final way. What I have shown in this book are bodies in landscape, bodies as landscape, and landscapes as extensions of bodies, all being worked and reworked, scribed and reinscribed. I have shown how the physical, discursive, emotional, political, and social landscapes with/in which we are subjected and with/in which we become speaking subjects are both solid and coercive, *and* fluid and shifting. In particular I have shown how we work at our subjection, how we take enormous pleasure in our subjection, and how we suffer extreme pain through our subjection—and through being subjected, we become appropriate(d) beings in the landscape, and in that same process, beings who can (re)appropriate its meanings and patterns, (re)constitute bodies in relation to landscapes, (re)signify what we find we have become.

This is a book made up out of embodied readings and embodied writings—both of my own and of others. In that writing, we have sought for, and partially found, ways of knowing the materiality of the body, the thinking body, the body that materializes with/in landscapes, the body that comes to know itself through the rich possibilities (and also the restrictions) of the languages lodged on its depth/surfaces. Like Clarice Lispector, whom Cixous writes about, this book seeks to integrate the earth and the body with imagination and thought. It explores the lived matter of bodies through a series of interior journeys—into the *in(terre)conscious zones*—between the spaces of one act of consciousness and another—relying on intuition, on feeling the way, and also on a variety of writing and analytic strategies derived from poststructuralist theory. Of Clarice's explorations to find the way to write of matter, Cixous (1993, p. 150) writes:

> Matter [for Clarice] is not abstract but intelligent, alive, and powerful. One has to follow a path to arrive at matter. . . . Clarice effects an interior return journey, since we began as matter before moving away from whence we came. . . . [S]ometimes she gets very close to matter, to earth—she's almost there—then she takes a step too many and breaks through the earth, passes to the other side, and comes back on the side of abstraction and the idealizing thought she constantly criticizes. . . .

The bodies in these explorations (of mine, of the other writers here, of Clarice) do not have a final, fixed essence. These are bodies that shift, stretch, coextend with/in multiple landscapes and with/in language in all its multiplicity. These are bodies that, like prisms, remain multidimensional and emergent, startling in their capacity to occlude (to eclipse)—and even make seemingly impossible—previous perspectives while (un)folding new ones. But unlike prisms, these bodies are capable not only of pleasurably repeating themselves, in each of their facets, but also of using their own matter to erupt in a moment of bliss, unfolding a new perspective not already found in the depth/surfaces of their existing matter. These bodies (un)fold themselves in time and space and in relations of power and powerlessness, and, occasionally they stretch and break the linguistic possibilities they find (in)scribed on their bodies. These are bodies responsive to forces apart from discourse: like the force of gravity that holds them on to the earth and in relation to which they build their musculature and bones; like the force of water after heavy rains or during a tsunami; like the force of trees and earth when they take back even those parts of the earth that human bodies have controlled for millennia.

I did not set out at the beginning of this book with a theory of body/landscape relations and data I could use to elaborate and somehow "prove" my theory. I was intrigued by the realization that in coming to understand the constitutive force of discourse we had somehow lost sight of (and touch with) the material body. I set out to explore, with the aid of writers like Cixous and with the analytic possibilities opened up in poststructuralist writing, what that materiality might be, and how we might write about it. *How we might write about it* was indeed the first puzzle. The line into the missing material body seemed to require a more poetic writing, a writing issuing from the body, a writing that could allow and even comprehend that the constitutive force of language does not always and necessarily render us passive. Poetic writing takes itself to be powerful, to be active, to take the material of the body and of lived experience and to make meanings not bound by logocentric abstractions that seek a complete and timeless Truth. Poetic writing seeks to find the details of the lived moment that are most likely occluded by Truth. The understanding sought in such writing is what Deleuze calls "sense" (*sens*) "carrying with it the dual meaning of both intelligibility and direction" (Thomas, 1999, p. 45).

Cixous describes herself, in the process of writing such emergent, "always becoming" books, as being a scribe, a linguistic receptor for words that arise out of the womb/world—out of the "flux of living events." She secretes the thing called a book, which is, in the process, taking on life—from the landscape of her body:

> But beforehand, where is it, that which will come into the world, how does it prepare itself? I do not feel it. *The womb is all the world.* The child is made from all sides. Throughout months, years. It is not me, *it is at the crossing of my thinking body and the flux of living events* that

the thing is secreted. *I will only be the door and the spokesperson supplying words. The linguistic receptor. The scribe.*

There comes the time of imminence. A desire to write rises in my body and comes to occupy my heart. Everything beats faster. The entire body readies itself. I say to my daughter: 'I feel like writing.' Thirst cannot be refused or rejected. I do not say: 'I have an idea.' I have no idea what this book will be. But very quickly scenes, sentences press forth and scarcely have I noted down twenty pages or so when I discover not the content but the direction, the ways and the song of the book. (Cixous, 1998, pp. 144–45, *my italics*)

Such writing from the *thinking body* emergent with/in *the flux of living events* is quite different from ideologically driven writing—one doesn't quite know where it will lead, or what will emerge—what the ways and the song of the book will be. Janette Turner Hospital used the term "syncope" to tell of the "miraculous suspension" (Clément, 1994, p. 5), the apparent death to the ordinary world, the space from which she returns with written pages that "are as mysterious and alarming and beautiful . . . as an opal pulled out of the dark."

"Secreted" as it is from my body, and from the bodies of others, as we each move through and take up our being, with/in different landscapes, this book has multiple and overlapping ways and songs. The "mysterious and alarming and beautiful" jewels emerging from those bodies trouble the certainties of so many boundaries laid down in our familiar, pleasurable, repetitive (what Morrison calls "dead") patterns of language. Old established boundaries may temporarily dissolve in the specificity and materiality of the texts of embodied being. My beginning point was the exploration of body/landscape relations and the practices of reading and writing through which bodies and landscapes and body/landscape relations are (in)scribed. In that process I have stumbled, miraculously, it seems to me, on moments in which words are blissfully, disruptively freed from some of their "sinister, frequently lazy, almost always predictable" patterns (Morrison, 1992, p. xiii).

This writing invites a tuning into and a listening to the landscape as a potent and relevant force, coextensive with the force of the body. Such an awareness of landscape makes thinkable the body/landscape connections the participants in the collective biography on Magnetic Island longed for, Robert Dessaix glimpsed when he traveled into the Gibson desert, the Australian environmentalists sought in their own bodies in "natural" spaces, Sam Watson sees as the basis of ancient earth-based cultures, Janette Turner Hospital's characters live in their bodies, and the Japanese studies reveal as the element that binds Japanese people to the four seasons and their unfolding.

In troubling the separation of bodies from landscape, I have thus sought to return some recognition to the body as powerful. In doing so I am not drawing on totalizing and essentializing physiological discourses in which the matter of the body is understood as causing everything that the body experiences. My interest in the materiality of the body lies more at the intersections between bodies and landscapes, bodies and language, bodies and imagination, bodies and relations of power. The explorations here trouble some of the physiologists' shibboleths, such as the idea of mind lodged in or generated by the brain. Mind is explored here, rather, as a brilliant idea, a possibility, of the embodied being in landscape. The creativity and inventiveness of bodies-in-landscape is celebrated in this writing. And it is understood as following from, or inhering in, subjection rather than in escape from subjection.

This book troubles our taken-for-granted/"naturalized" understanding of embodiment as separate from landscapes and shows how (in)scriptions come to be read as naturalized through providing the terms with which we interpret ourselves and the world. At the same time, it explores a different relationship with language—a relationship in which the speaking body seeks the precise words that will express what it finds when it turns its reflective gaze upon its own embodied self. Such a shift does not turn its gaze upon the body to find an answer to the question *how has language constituted me* (as male, as female, as Australian, as Japanese, as indigenous, as nonindigenous). It asks, *how can I get past clichéd and explanatory language to know this speaking/writing/embodied being?* Language is reclaimed in this shift, as a tool—not an invisible tool as it was (and is) in most social theory, but a tool like the song of the young woman on Port Douglas beach, who listens to the sea and its slickering tongues, who reads the signs of the beach, and who finds the capacity to sing the landscape of North Queensland.

What has previously been placed at the center of social theorizing, the all-seeing human eye or, in some cases, the eye or hand of "god," has placed everything else as that which is around that eye/I. *Environs, encirclement.* And certainly we may be encircled in the landscape, as we are as babies prior to birth. But what encircles us is *both* human *and* landscape, and at the same time we ourselves are also landscapes. By removing the human from the center as the all-seeing eye/I, I have generated a set of images and metaphors for understanding humans as integral to multiple folded and unfolding landscapes. And in writing from the body/landscape, in finding ways for others to do the same, and by working with fiction writers who write from "the bat-cave of sensory perception," I have found myself troubling boundaries other than those between bodies and landscapes. The song of the book is about bodies, bodies that we are not very well practiced at knowing. What we find when we tune in, with all our senses, to our bodies, is body as process, as (un)folding or (un)furling in different contexts, as becoming now one thing and now another through relations of power, located and positioned in discursively and ongoingly created contexts and histories. And what we find in such (un)furlings of bodies with/in landscapes is that the division into "natural" categories of male and female has been disrupted, as have categories based on race and on patterns of division laid down in discourse and in history.

Each of the stories in this book can be understood as revealing an irreducible difference about the person whose story it is, being specific to the space and time in which it happens and the particular lived history that led up to that moment. At the same time, they reveal the embeddedness of each in recognizable discourses, in recognizable patterns of desire, and in recognizable patterns of power and powerlessness. There were startling moments of sudden insight, for me, in finding the ways and songs of this book where I stumbled across completely unexpected boundary crossing. One such moment was when I attended the Buddhist funeral ceremony for Masako's grandfather. The assumed separation and difference between Japan with its ancient Buddhist and Shinto traditions and indigenous Australian culture suddenly dissolved. As I reflect back now, over the multitude of ways and songs, I can see many boundaries being crossed and dissolving.

If I think, for example, of the vivid image of Joseph, diving down into the murky depths of the sea, losing his boundaries and communing with big fish, I cannot help also thinking of Tommy, the Kadaitcha man, diving into the Brisbane River and talking to the ancient grouper. (Colonizer/colonized dissolves, like tears, releasing the sedimentation of bodies divided.) I am also aware of Cath as a small girl child, diving again and again into the waves of the sea, lost in the magic of the colors of light in water and intent on establishing her own power and competence alone in the water. (Girl/boy dissolves like hot tears.) And, of course, Miss Davenport in the Mossman Gorge, her immersion in the water and her silence enabling an ecstatic "fusion of landscape and body and thought." And then Takeshi, when I went with him out to the Reef, found the same amazement and wonder in water. (East/West dissolves in the jeweled light of the sea.)

Or, to take another example, the vivid image of Charade, at one with the trees in the Australian rain forest. This image reminds me first of Rodney Hall's convict overwhelmed by the beauty of the light in the trees. Then of Rosie, lying on her back in the creek bed looking up at the light on the leaves. Of me walking in the Fushimi-Inari forest. Of Shingo, intensely aware of the gingko tree budding out of season, like himself, or of Takeshi writing to me about his springtime experience of being at one with the cherry tree. (Australia/Japan, male/female, child/adult, now/then—each dissolves in the lived moment of specificity, washing away sedimented boundary lines.)

To make such a shift beyond all those binaries that have come to seem natural requires a greater use of the imagination combined with quite rigorous intellectual work, work aimed at freeing oneself from the apparent inevitability of the coils of those ways of speaking that loop themselves around us and define our limitations. Probyn (1993, p. 6) says:

> Finally I am brought back to the importance of imagination. . . . In order to . . . work at the very edges and ends of ourselves in order to envision change, we must engage our imaginations more fully. Without blurring the material conditions of our difference, we can nonetheless stretch ourselves to the point where we break into other realms of possibility. In other words, the question of "who is she and who am I?" necessitates a fundamental reworking of the theoretical and social terrain in which we are positioned. This also entails a radical rethinking of how we use and position ourselves. It is only at the extreme limits of who we think we are that we can articulate, respect and use our differences.

Cixous (1998, p. 137) also writes of using imagination to explore the possibility of each of us becoming multiple, of moving across the boundaries, to know the possibilities of a self not caught in the boring constriction of being a "single self and a single sex." Like Probyn, she acknowledges both the difficulty and the importance of this work of the imagination and of the intellect:

> [H]ere, in this kingdom that stretches beyond oppositions or exclusions, it is well known, from having had the experience so often, that it's the soul, that is, the heart—and its moods—that makes the face, the voice, the inexplicable and complicated truth of a human creature. *May I* thus be another woman, another man, who am not myself? In this human crucible of ours, who would call into doubt 'the equality of the sexes [of the races]?' Who even thinks of it? The creature is. All creatures contain infinite possibilities of being another. One possibility is just as good as another. If our internal world were reduced to a single self and a single sex, what a boring scene it would be, what sterility. It's up to us to be peoples and be placed under the spell. But to accomplish this one must have the utmost courage to let go of the ballast of the self, to leave oneself unweighted on the celestial platform. Let go of the weight of the self, but not the memory, or the trace. For heshe becomes not simply quite-other. The most delicate and most precious aspect of the transfiguration, without which there would be neither joy nor learning, is that I-can-be-another (creature)-whom-I-am-not-myself: it is perhaps the most wonderful of experiences to be able to pluck the chance and pleasure of being another person all the while knowing that I am not the other, only the place with the scent of the other, and that me-my-other is taking place. For a little while at least.

In writing and reading from the body, in using language to write precisely the body's knowledge, rather than in the usual lazy ways of seeing through the simplistic binaries and descriptors of everyday language usage, we find in the texts of this book no evidence that the binaries are embodied in any essential or final way. The binaries can still nevertheless be used as useful political tools as Spinoza suggested: "to create a politico-ethical organization where all, in their own manner, seek to maximize the possibilities of their activity" (quoted in Gatens, 1996, p. 56). At the same time, it is useful to be vigilant in finding the ways those same categories distort political action and mislead it with false and unnecessary division. This is most likely, I would suggest, precisely where the binaries used as political tools are simultaneously understood to describe real people, real bodies, real and essential boundaries.

Reading and writing from the body generates an understanding of language as an expressive force of embodied beings. This is different from the idea of language as shaper of all possibilities, and from language as separate from and controlling the body. Language in this embodied reading/writing is not separate from and controlling the body, but is a force of the body, a possibility of individual and collective bodies. How language is used, and how it relates to the bodies of the individuals who speak it, hear it, write it, or read it, depends on patterns of power and powerlessness, but it also depends on how "language" and its relation to the body is understood. In Chapter 9 I wrote about Barthes's concepts of texts of pleasure and texts of bliss. A text of pleasure is that predictable, familiar pattern of language use that "comes from culture and does not break with it . . ." (Barthes, 1989, p. 14). Texts of bliss unsettle "the reader's historical, cultural, psychological assumptions, the consistency of his [her] tastes, values, memories, brings to crisis his [her] relation with language." I have added, here in this book, a third kind of text, a text that begins with the material, thinking body. Such texts are produced through writing/reading the embodied self in landscape. This third kind of text may be like the text of bliss in its capacity to go beyond what is already understood—but it comes less from a play with language and more from an embodied reading/writing of bodies in landscapes, bodies as landscapes, and landscapes as extensions of bodies, and from the use of that embodied reading/writing to go beyond the limits of those discourses that we thought held us captive.

~ References

Ashcroft, B. and J. Salter (1994). "Australia": A rhizomic text. In L. Dobrez (Ed.), *Identifying Australia in postmodern times.* Canberra: Anutech.

Attenborough, D. (1998). *The life of birds.* BBC Worldwide Ltd.

Attridge, D. (Ed.) (1992). *Jacques Derrida: Acts of literature.* New York: Routledge.

Barthes, R. (1989). *The pleasure of the text.* Oxford: Basil Blackwell.

Benterrak, K., S. Muecke, and P. Roe (1984). *Reading the country.* Fremantle, Australia: Fremantle Arts Centre Press.

Berque, A. (1992). Identification of the self in relation to the environment. In N. R. Rosenberger (Ed.), *Japanese sense of self.* Cambridge: Cambridge University Press.

Butler, J. (1995a). "Conscience doth make subjects of us all." *Yale French Studies* 88, 6–26.

———— (1995b). Contingent foundations: Feminism and the question of "postmoderism." In S. Benhabib, J. Butler, D. Cornell, and N. Fraser (Eds.), *Feminist contentions: A philosophical exchange.* New York: Routledge.

———— (1995c). For a careful reading. In S. Benhabib, J. Butler, D. Cornell, and N. Fraser (Eds.), *Feminist contentions: A philosophical exchange.* New York: Routledge.

———— (1997). *The psychic life of power.* Stanford, CA: Stanford University Press.

Carter, P. (1996). *The lie of the land.* London: Faber and Faber.

Chaloupka, W. and M. Cawley (1993). The great wild hope: Nature, environmentalism, and the open secret. In J. Bennet and W. Chaloupka (Eds.), *In the nature of things: Language, politics, and the environment.* Minneapolis: The University of Minnesota Press.

Cixous, H. (1993). *Three steps on the ladder of writing.* New York: Columbia University Press.

———— (1998). *Stigmata: Escaping texts.* London: Routledge.

Cixous, H. and M. Calle-Gruber (1997). *Hélène Cixous rootprints: Memory and life writing* (E. Prenowitz, Trans.). London: Routledge.

Clément, C. (1994). *Syncope: The philosophy of rapture*. Minneapolis: University of Minnesota Press.

Collins English Dictionary. (1979). P. Hanks (Ed.). Sydney: Collins.

Conley, V. A. (1991). *Hélène Cixous: Writing the feminine*. Lincoln: University of Nebraska Press.

Cornell, S. (1990). Hélène Cixous and les etudes féminine. In H. Wilcox, K. McWatters, A. Thompson, and L. R. Williams (Eds.), *The body and the text: Hélène Cixous, reading and teaching*. New York: Harvester Wheatsheaf.

Cronen, W. (Ed.) (1996). *Uncommon ground: Rethinking the human place in nature*. New York: W. W. Norton and Co.

Davies, B. (1982). *Life in the classroom and playground: The accounts of primary school children*. London: Routledge and Kegan Paul.

———— (1989). *Frogs and snails and feminist tales: Preschool children and gender*. Sydney: Allen and Unwin.

———— (1991). *The concept of agency: A feminist poststructuralist analysis*. Social Analysis 30 (Dec.), 42–53.

———— (1993). *Shards of glass: Children reading and writing beyond gendered identities*. Creskill, NJ: Hampton Press, Inc.

———— (1997). The subject of poststructuralism: A reply to Alison Jones. *Gender and Education* 9(3), 271–83.

Davies, B., S. Dormer, E. Honan, N. McAllister, R. O'Reilly, S. Rocco, and A. Walker (1997). Ruptures in the skin of silence: A collective biography. *Hecate: A Women's Studies Interdisciplinary Journal* 23(1), 62–79.

Davies, B. and H. Whitehouse (1997). Men on the boundaries: Landscapes and seascapes. *Journal of Gender Studies* 6(3), 237–54.

Davis, K. (1997). Embody-ing theory: Beyond modernist and postmodernist readings of the body. In K. Davis (Ed.), *Embodied practices. Feminist pespectives on the body*. London: Sage Publications.

Dessaix, R. (1998). *(and so forth)*. Sydney: Macmillan.

Dixon, R. M. (1972). *The Dyirbal language of North Queensland*. Cambridge: Cambridge University Press.

Drewe, R. (1996). *The Drowner*. Sydney: Macmillan.

Einosuké, I. (1962). Nightingale. In I. Morris (Ed.), *Modern Japanese stories: An anthology*. Tokyo: Charles E. Tuttle Co.

Éluard, P. (1996). *Unbroken poetry 11*. Newcastle upon Tyne: Bloodaxe Books.

Falconer, D. (1998). "Wild Imaginings": People, places and objects that induce longing and sustain fantasies. Paper presented to the Brisbane Writers' Festival: Qld Cultural Centre.

Falk, P. (1995). Written in one flesh. *Body and Society* 1(1), 95–105.

Foucault, M. (1977).What is an author? In D. Bouchard (Ed.), *Language counter-memory practice*. Ithaca, NY: Cornell University Press.

—— (1980). In C. Gordon (Ed.), *Power/knowledge: Selected Interviews and other writings 1972–1977*. New York: Pantheon.

Gardner, W. H. (1953). *Gerard Manley Hopkins: A selection of his poems and prose*. Harmondsworth: Penguin.

Gatens, M. (1996). *Imaginary bodies: Ethics, power and corporeality*. London: Routledge.

Grosz, E. (1989). *Sexual subversions: Three French feminists*. Sydney: Allen and Unwin.

—— (1994). *Volatile bodies: Towards a corporeal feminism*. Sydney: Allen and Unwin.

—— (1995). *Space, time and perversion*. Sydney: Allen and Unwin.

Hall, R. (1994). The second bridegroom. In R. Hall (Ed.), *A dream more luminous than love: The Yandilli trilogy*. Sydney: Picador.

—— (1996a). *The island in the mind*. Sydney: Macmillan.

—— (1996b). The lonely traveller by night. In R. Hall (Ed.), *The island in the mind*. Sydney: Macmillan.

—— (1997). Interview with Bronwyn Davies, Bermagui.

Haug, F. et al. (1987). *Female sexualization*. London: Verso.

Kasama, H. (1992). A study of certain aspects of "Informal Education" in the English early childhood education system: Towards a re-examination of Japanese pre-school education practices. *Kushiro Ronshu* 24, 117–55.

Kawabata, Y. (1957). *Snow country* (E. G. Seidensticker, Trans.). Tokyo: Charles E. Tuttle Co.

—— (1969). *Japan, the beautiful, and myself: The 1968 Nobel Prize acceptance speech* (E. G. Seidensticker, Trans.). Tokyo: Kodansha International Ltd.

—— (1970). *The sound of the mountain* (E. G. Seidensticker, Trans.). Tokyo: Charles E. Tuttle Co.

Kerr, A. (1996). *Lost Japan*. Melbourne: Lonely Planet Publications.

Kodansya International Ltd. (1998). *The Kodansya bilingual encyclopedia of Japan*. Tokyo: Bunkyo-ku.

Koren, L. (1994). *Wabi-Sabi for artists, designers, poets and philosophers*. Berkeley: Stone Bridge Press.

Kurosawa, A (1982). *Something like an autobiography*. New York: Vintage Books.

Lacan, J. (1985). *Ecrits: A selection* (A. Sheridan, Trans.). Tavistock: London.

Lovelock, J. E. (1991). *Gaia: The practical science of planetary medicine*. Sydney: Allen and Unwin.

―――― (1995). *The ages of Gaia: A biography of our living earth* (2nd ed.). Oxford: Oxford University Press.

Lowitz, L., M. Aoyama, and A. Tomioka (Eds. and Trans.) (1994). *A long rainy season: Contemporary Japanese women's poetry (Vol. 1)*. Berkeley: Stone Bridge Press.

McQueen, H. (1991). *Tokyo world: An Australian diary*. Port Melbourne: William Heinemann Aus.

McVeigh, B. (1996). Standing stomachs, clamoring chests and cooling livers: Metaphors in the psychological lexicon of Japanese. *Journal of Pragmatics* 26, 25–50.

Margulis, L. and L. Olendzenski (1992). *Environmental evolution: Effects of the origin and evolution of life on Earth*. Cambridge, MA: M.I.T. Press.

Modjeska, D. (1990). *Poppy*. Ringwood: McPhee Gribble Publishers.

―――― (1994). *The orchard*. Sydney: Macmillan.

―――― (1999). *Stravinsky's lunch*. Pan Macmillan.

Morrison, T. (1992). *Playing in the dark: Whiteness and the literary imagination*. Cambridge, MA: Harvard University Press.

―――― (1994). *The Nobel lecture in literature, 1993*. London: Chatto and Windus.

Nast, H. (1998). The body as "place": Reflexivity and fieldwork in Kano, Nigeria. In H. J. Nast and S. Pile (Eds.), *Places through the body*. London: Routledge.

Neilsen. L. (1998a). *Bodies of knowledge: Literacies and landscapes for ways of learning* (unpublished course notes GEDU 6156[10]). Nova Scotia: Mount Saint Vincent University.

———— (1998b). *Knowing her place: Research literacies and feminist occasions*. San Francisco: Caddo Gap Press and Great Tancook Island, Nova Scotia: Backalong Books.

Nitobe, I. (1969). *Bushido. The soul of Japan: An exposition of Japanese thought*. Rutland, VT: Charles E. Tuttle Co.

O'Brien, G. (1997). *Hotere. Out the black window: Ralph Hotere's work with New Zealand poets*. Auckland: Godwit Publishing.

Oe, K. (1969). *A personal matter* (J. Nathan, Trans.). London: Picador.

———— (1996). *Japan, the ambiguous and myself: The Nobel Speech Prize and other lectures*. Tokyo: Kodansha International.

Oppenheimer, J. and B. Mitchell (1989). *An Australian clan: The Nivisons of New England*. Kenthurst, Australia: Kangaroo Press.

Ortner, S. B. (1971). Is female to male as nature is to culture? In M. Rosaldo and L. Lamphere (Eds.), *Women, culture and society*. Stanford, CA: Stanford University Press.

O'Shane, P. (1998). Sin of omission. *The Weekend Australian* (November 7–8), p. 29.

Pateman, C. (1988). *The sexual contract*. Cambridge: Polity.

Pizzey, G. and F. Knight (1997). *Field guide to the birds of Australia*. Sydney: Angus and Robertson.

Probyn, E. (1993). *Sexing the self: Gendered positions in cultural studies*. London: Routledge

Rosenberger, N. R. (1992). Tree in summer, tree in winter: Movement of self in Japan. In N. R. Rosenberger (Ed.), *Japanese sense of self*. Cambridge: Cambridge University Press.

Smith, P. (1998). *Syncopations in the life of a woman religious*. Unpublished doctoral dissertation, James Cook University, Townsville.

Somerville, M. (1999). *Body/landscape journals*. Melbourne: Spinifex Press.

Suzuki, D. (1995). *Declaration of interdependence*. Vancouver: The David Suzuki Foundation.

Suzuki, D. and K. Oiwa (1996). *The Japan we never knew: A journey of discovery. Sydney: Allen and Unwin*.

Sykes, R. (1997). *Snake cradle*. Sydney: Allen and Unwin.

Thomas, D. (1999). *Reading Nietzsche rhetorically*. New York: The Gilford Press.

Tobin, J. (1992). Japanese preschools and the pedagogy of selfhood. In N. R. Rosenberger (Ed.), *Japanese sense of self.* Cambridge: Cambridge University Press.

Trinh, Min-ha (1991). *When the moon waxes red: Representation, gender and cultural politics.* New York: Routledge.

Turner Hospital, J. (1988). *Charades.* St. Lucia: University of Queensland Press.

———— (1995a). The last of the Hapsburgs. In J. Turner Hospital (Ed.), *Collected stories.* St. Lucia: University of Queensland Press.

———— (1995b). Uncle Seaborn. In J. Turner Hospital (Ed.), *Collected stories.* St. Lucia: University of Queensland Press.

———— (1995c). You gave me hyacinths. In J. Turner Hospital (Ed.), *Collected stories.* St. Lucia: University of Queensland Press.

———— (1996a). Conversation with Bronwyn Davies, Brisbane.

———— (1996b). *Oyster.* Sydney: Knopf.

Watson, S. (1990). *The Kadaitcha Sung.* Ringwood: Penguin.

———— (1996). *Black Man Down.* The Australian Film Institute. (Writer/co-producer: Sam Watson; director: Bill McCrow; producer: Bruce Redman.)

Wilson, E. O. (1984). *Biophilia.* Cambridge, MA: Harvard University Press.

Winterson J. (1995). *Art objects: Essays on ecstasy and effrontery.* London: Jonathan Cape.

Yoshimoto, B. (1991). Kitchen. In H. Mitsios (Ed.), *New Japanese voices: The best contemporary fiction from Japan.* New York: The Atlantic Monthly Press.

Yovel, Y. (1989). *Spinoza and other heretics: The adventures of immanence.* Princeton, NJ: Princeton University Press.

~ Index

A

abacus school, 96–98
abandonment, stories of, 56–57
Abe, Dean, 136–137, 147
agency, 62, 167, 244
Ainu people, 102, 110, 133, 146
Ainu village, 134, 135
Albania, 214
animal/human binary, 23
animals, in Japan
    endangered, 157–160
    extinct, 157
ants, 26
appropriate(d) embodiment,
    stories of, 58–61
appropriation
    of bodies, 164
    of landscape, 164
    with/in landscape, 11
Aranda religion, 202, 206
art, and life, 218
Arthur (environmentalist), 69,
    75–76, 78
Asayama, Professor, 148, 155,
    156
Ashcroft, B., 216
Attridge, D., 218
Australian landscape, as a
    contested terrain, 229
author, what is an, 7
autobiographical writing, 40–41
autobiography, 38–39
    author's, 21–22
    as rewriting of culture, 41
    See also Sykes, Roberta
autonomy, as illusion, 59, 60

B

bare attention, 20
Basho, Matsuo, 92–93, 112,
    132, 178
before-the-naming, 50
being out of place, stories of,
    54–57
belly, as locus for thinking,
    19–20
belong, definition of, 37
belonging, definition of, 37
(be)longing/belonging
    in the environment, 78
    in Japanese landscapes, 109
    to landscapes, 37, 45, 59,
        60, 81
    as a political experience,
        39–40
    stories of, 37–39, 51–54
Benterrak, K., 16–17, 32
Berque, A., 149, 159
binaries
    black/white, 199, 201, 203
    body/landscape, 23, 37
    built environment/natural
        environment, 26–28
    colonizer/colonized, 28–29,
        32, 228
    culture/nature, 65, 66–67,
        68–69, 77, 79, 83
    dissolving, 253–254
    East/West, 101, 214
    emotion/control, 130
    good/evil, 199, 201
    human/animal, 23
    individual/group, 103

binaries *(continued)*
   inside/outside, 36, 214
   insider/outsider, 89
   macho masculinity/environ-
      mentalist, 71–72
   sameness/otherness, 37
   student/teacher, 47–48
   us/them, 230
binary thought, Western, 103
biography. *See* collective biography
birth, 27–28
Black Man Down (film), 198
black/white binary, 199, 201,
   203
bliss, 217, 218, 223, 226,
   230–231
Blofeld, John, 126
Blomfield, Bruce, 222n2
bodies
   awareness of, 14–15
   as changing, 13
   deep/surfaces of, 33, 76, 85
   of environmentalists, 68
   as expressive, 28
   as fiction, 16
   as inscribed, 16, 40
   as inseparable from land-
      scape, 11, 19
   as inseparable from lan-
      guage, 33–34
   as landscape, 11, 23, 38, 39
   materiality of, 11, 16n1,
      252
   "natural" state of, 67
   poetic, 168
   as powerful, 251–252
   as shaped, 15–16
   shaped and disciplined, 18
   theoretical writings about,
      13
   as thinking, 19–20, 49
bodily competence, stories of,
   58–61
body/landscape binary, 23, 37

body/landscape relations, 21–28
   changed by environmental-
      ism, 149
   changed by industrializa-
      tion, 149
   current Japanese, 153–155
   embedded in ancient
      Japanese poetry,
      137–139
   indigenous, 65, 83
   indigenous history of, 40
   and Japanese language, 19,
      24
   made visible by fiction
      writers, 20
   original, 24–25
   traditional Japanese, 149
   traditional Western, 65, 149
Booka (character in *The
      Kadaitcha Sung*), 192,
      200, 208, 209
Bower, Olivia Spencer, 25
bowls, Chinese/Japanese,
      136–137
Brisbane, 197, 204–206,
      213–214
Bruce (environmentalist), 68–69,
      74, 76, 77, 78
Buddhism, 112, 155, 157
built landscape, in Australia, 65
built enviornment/natural envi-
      ronment binary, 26–28
Bushido: The Soul of Japan, 89
Butler, J., 34, 58, 59
butterflies, 26, 214
Byodo-in Temple, 125, 127

C

Calle-Gruber, Mireille, 33
calligraphy school story, 98–100
Carter, P., 202, 207
Charade (character in
      Charades), 37–40,
      52–53

Charades, 234. *See also*
    Charade; Kay
cherry blossoms, 134, 143,
    187–188
children, Japanese
    and conservation, 162
    and industrialization, 145
    and tradition/change, 150
    See also day-care centers;
        preschool children, in
        Japan
children, Mexican, 150–151
children's play, 150–151
Chinese characters. *See* kanji
chopsticks, 136, 142–143
Cixous, H., 33, 43, 45, 50,
    167–168, 170, 235,
    240–241, 246, 249,
    250–251, 254
Clément, Catherine, 194
collective biography/memory
        work, 13–14, 43–51, 46
    Australian stories, 38–40,
        51–61
    Australian/Japanese experi-
        ence, 165, 183
    Japanese stories, 94–102,
        103–108
    nature of, 14
    stories, 31–32
    "truth" in, 43
    workshop, 43, 48–51
    writing in, 50
collective school experiences,
    44–45
collective unconscious, 33
colonial history, 41
colonizer/colonized, 28–34
colonizer/colonized binary,
    28–29, 32, 228
conservation
    and Japanese children, 162
    of wetlands, 158
convict (character in *The Sec-
        ond Bridegroom*), 215
    abandons control, 224–225

comes to Australia, 219–221
    desires recognition, 227–228
    escapes, 221–222
    as invisible, 225–226
crane, Japanese, 158–159
Cronen, W., 229–230
crows, 27
cultural commentators, 43
cultural spectators, 43
culture
    as active, 67
    earth-based, 195
    and Western philosophical
        thought, 66
    See also nature
culture/nature binary, 65, 66–67,
        68–69, 77, 79, 83
    in *The Second Bridegroom*,
        222
    and Western philosophical
        thought, 66

D
dams, 71
dashi, 117
Davenport, Miss (character in
        "The Last of the Haps-
        burgs"), 236–237,
        238–240
Davies, Bronwyn, 17, 62, 63n1,
    214
day-care centers, 55–56,
    151–152
death, fear of, 197–198
Declaration of Interdependence,
    68, 76, 156
deconstruction, 14
deep, meaning of in
        English/Japanese, 182
Deleuze, Gilles, 169, 250
Derrida, Jacques, 43–44, 217,
    235
desire, and landscapes, 40
Dessaix, Robert, 63–65, 66, 82,
    213, 214

discourse, 24
  constitutive power of, 14,
    16n1
  of environmentalism, 63–65,
    75, 161–164
  indigenous, 67
  patriarchal, 245
  postcolonial, 28–29, 65
  as powerful, 11
Dixon, R. M., 30
Drewe, Robert, 66–67, 69
Drowner, The, 66–67, 69, 71
dry tropics, 70

E

East/West binary, 101, 214
eclipse, 169
education system, Japanese,
  109
embeddedness, in family and
  community, 103–105
embodied appropriate(ly),
  stories of, 58–61
embodied reading, 168,
  191–192
embodied writing/writing from
  the body, 34, 45,
  168–170
  strategies for developing,
    19
embodiment
  appropriate(d), 58–61
  in Australian landscapes,
    184–186, 217
  bringing to consciousness,
    13
  as environmentalists, 11
  as Japanese, 89–90,
    147–148
  in relation to landscape, 13,
    26
  in relation to the seasons,
    93–95, 106–108
  in the tropics, 9
emotion/control binary, 130

emperor system, 110, 145, 146
environment
  as coextensive with self, 65
  dictionary definition of, 66
environmental destruction, in
    Japan, 134–135, 136,
    142, 155
environmental discourse, 76
environmental ecology, 68
environmentalism
  Australian, 164
  and government, 160–161
  Japanese, 152, 164
  Western, 149
environmentalists
  Australian, 163–164, 165
  embodied experiences of,
    77–84
  Japanese, 163–164, 165
environmentalists, male
  as different from "other"
    men, 66, 67, 73–74
  female aspect of, 71, 73–74
  See also macho; male
    bonding
Éluard, Paul, 247

F

Falconer, Delia, 40
Falk, P., 67
festivals, 148–149
  kite, 111, 113, 115–116,
    117–118, 148
  Matsuri, 101–102
fisherman's house, in Otaru,
  137
fishermen, in Japan, 137
fishing stories
  Australian, 73–74, 79–80, 82
  Japanese, 103–106, 104–106,
    107
folds/folding/unfolding
  in bodies, 14, 61
  of body/landscape, 20, 23,
    86

folds/folding/unfolding (*continued*)
    deep and knotty, 16, 41
    of Japanese landscapes, 87
    in the landscape, 14, 61,
        163, 167, 202
    of meaning, 204–205,
        212–213
    reconceptualized by fiction
        writers, 20
    in song, 202
    in the writing, 34–35, 87
forbidden, 246–247
forests, 125–127, 158
    clear-felled, replanted, 142,
        158, 162–163
    connection with, 84
    power of, 126
    as sacred, 131, 146
Foucault, M., 7, 18–19
frogs
    breeding habits, 23
    colonizing human spaces,
        25–26, 27, 36
funeral ceremony, Buddhist,
        116–117
furyu, 138
Fushimi-Inari, 125–127

G
Gannon, Sue, 46–49, 52, 58–59
gay men, 72–73
geckos, 27
Gibson desert, 63–65
good/evil binary, 199, 201
Graham (environmentalist), 68,
        77, 83
gravity, 15
Grosz, Elizabeth, 15–16, 67, 243
grouper, 79, 209, 213
guilt, postcolonial, 29, 31–32

H
haiku poem, 138
Hall, Rodney, 32, 48–49, 185,
        215, 217, 225n4
Hamamatsu, 113–118
Hamish (environmentalist), 68
Hannyaji Temple, 119–121
happi, 115, 116
hara no suwatta hito, 19
Hariu-san, 152–153
Haug, F., 13, 40
head, as locus for thinking,
        19–20
heart (mind), losing its way,
        126–127
Helen (student), 51–52, 59–60
hero-god, 72, 79–80
Hiroko (student), 90, 94,
        96–100, 103–106
hito, 147–148
Hokkaido, 29, 131–142, 146,
        150
Honan, Eileen, 31, 56
Honda, Katsuichi, 102–103, 106
Honshu island, 94, 111–121
Hopkins, Lekkie, 59
human/animal binary, 23
humans, similarities to other animals, 23, 68, 81–82, 107

I
imagination, 168, 254
imperfection of all things, 181
impermanence of all things,
        181
imund, 246–247
Inahata, Teiko, 188
incompleteness of all things,
        182
indigenous body/landscape
        relations, 83
indigenous/nonindigenous
        binary, 214
individual/group binary, 103

industrialization, in Japan, 145,
149
effect on children, 145
effect on the environment,
147
(in)scription, concept of, 11
(in)scription/inscription
constitutive power of, 16
as shaping landscape,
22–23, 231
as shaping the body,
15–16, 22, 66, 67, 68,
77, 78
shifting nature of, 16
inside/outside binary, 36, 214
insider/outsider binary, 89
in-temperate zones, 69
in(terre)conscious zones, 235,
240, 243, 249
Inuit culture, 135
invention, enigma of, 217
Island in the Mind, The, 32

J
Japanese
influence of, by Chinese,
148
self-criticism of, 102–103
Japanese language
and body/landscape rela-
tions, 19, 24
*Japan We Never Knew: A Voy-
age of Discovery, The,*
89
jin, 147–148
Joseph (environmentalist), 68,
71, 73–74, 77, 79–82

K
Kabuki Theater, 125, 128–129
Kakadu National Park, 75–76
Kanda, Professor, 149–150
kanji, 145, 148
Kaori (student), 90, 106–109

Kasama, Professor, 151, 152
Katanuma, Professor, 147–148,
155, 157
Kato, Keiko, 92
Kato, Koko, 110, 165
Kawabata, Yasunari, 91–92, 183
Kay (character in *Charades*),
234–235
Kerr, Alex, 89, 118, 119, 120,
123, 124, 125, 126
Kershaw, Robert, 30
Kikuko (character in *Yama no
Oto*), 173, 174,
175–176, 179–180
"Kitchen," 90
kite festival, 113, 115–116,
117–118
kite-flying ceremony, 116
Knight, F., 26
knowledge, 77
as being, 76
Kodo drummers, 131
Korea, 135
Koren, Leonard, 89, 137, 178
Kurosawa, A., 126–127, 130,
135–136
Kushiro, 142
Kyoto, 121–131, 134
Kyoto princess, 123

L
Lacan, J., 226
land rights, 40
landscapes
appropriation with/in, 11
Australian, 21–22, 31, 32
as bodies, 11, 23
bodies as, 11, 23, 38, 39
built, 65
in childhood, 21–22, 95
city, 63
as colonized, 29
as a contested terrain, 229
control of, 136
definition of, 11, 22–23

landscapes (*continued*)
  desert, 63–65
  and desire, 40
  emotional, 51
  folds/folding/unfolding in,
    14, 61, 163, 167, 202
  immersion in, 52–53
  indigenous dreamings of,
    29
  indigenous stories of, 30
  as inscribed, 17–18
  prior-to-birth, 23–24
  reading, in different ways,
    24–25
  separation from, "being out
    of place," 54–57, 65
  as source of political dis-
    pute, 39, 229
  as speaking, 18
  spiritual connection with, 83
  tropical, 69
  as violent and unpre-
    dictable, 143
language, 40
  Aboriginal, 219, 222
  as collective process, 17,
    33–34
  as dead, 43, 167
  deprivation, 229
  and desire, 28
  and embodiment, 76–84
  failure of, 31
  inventing selves and being
    invented through,
    33–34
  invisible effects of, 18
  in landscape, 18
  longing for, 17–18
  in poststructuralist theory,
    170
  as powerful, 245
  prior to birth, 23–24
  in relation to knowledge,
    17–18, 22, 32, 33
  as shaping memories, 43
  spoken, 17

"Last of the Hapsburgs, The,"
    236–240
Laws, Cath (student), 31, 60–61
linear time, 207
lizards, 17, 21, 26
Lonely Traveler by Night, The,
    32–33
longing, definition of, 37

M
macho masculinity, stereotype
    of, 71–72
macho masculinity/environmen-
    talist binary, 73
Magnetic Island, 41–42
male bonding, 74, 75–76
male superiority, assumed, 66–67
Maori culture, 135
maps, of Japan, 118, 122, 124
masculinity, 71–72, 73, 85. *See
    also* male bonding
Matsudaira, Meiko, 143
Matsuri festival, 101–102, 113
McCann, Helen, 51–52, 55–56,
    59–60
McLaren, Rosemary (student),
    53–55
McQueen, H., 131
McVeigh, B., 19–20
medaka, 102n2, 109
Meiji Restoration, 146, 147
memories, 40, 43
memory
    as embodied language, 33,
      43, 45
    as having weight, 40
    retrieval of, 43–45, 46
    of sexual abuse, 46
memory work, as research
    strategy, 46
men
    gay, 72–73
    inland (Australia), 70–71
    macho, 66–67, 71–72, 73
    of northern Queensland, 70

Mercy (character in *Oyster*), 242–244
Mexico, 150–151
Migloo, 192, 196, 202, 206
mind
  as idea of the body, 19, 252
  as rational and dominant, 78
Modjeska, D., 20, 25, 27–28
morality
  disruption of certainties about, 34
  as resting in conscience of group, 103
  resting in group practices, 105–106
Morgan, Sally, 39
Morrison, Toni, 43, 49, 167, 189, 191
Mossman Gorge, 240
mountains
  destruction of, 134, 135, 142
  as sacred, 131, 142
  sound of, 179, 183–184
Mt. Fuji, 139, 141
Muecke, S., 16–17, 32
Murri people, 190–192, 199
  as powerful, 193
  survival of, 201

N
Nara, 118–121
Nast, H., 40
"natural" state, of the body, 67
nature
  as an illusion, 11
  as coextensive with environmentalists, 11
  as coextensive with humans, 13
  as devalued, 66
  in Japanese culture, 155
  as passive, 67

rhythm of, 123
  as saturated with desire, 13
Neilsen, Lorri, 46
Nick (environmentalist), 69, 72–73
Nietzsche, Friedrich Wilhelm, 45
Nikko, 143
nin, 147–148
Nitobe, Inazo, 89
nomad, 32
nomadological texts, 169
North Queensland, 30, 69, 70, 72, 236
northern Queensland. *See* North Queensland
nostalgia, in Japan, 146

O
objectivism, 41
Oe, Kenzaburo, 89, 101, 122, 146, 147, 150
Oiwa, Keibo, 89, 102–103
Okinawa, 134
omote, 129–130
Onoda, Masako (student), 90, 92, 94, 100–101
open-schooling movement, Australian, 152
Orchard, The, 25
Ortner, S. B., 66
Osanai, Professor, 111
O'Shane, Pat, 39, 41
Otaru, 134, 137
ownership, in *The Second Bridegroom*, 229
Oyster, 241–244
oyster farming, 158
ozizo-san, 132

P
pagoda, golden five-story, 120–121
patriarchal discourse, 245

Paula (student), 57
Personal Matter, A, 122
philosophical writing, 45
Pizzey, G., 26
plural "I," 41, 51
poetic writing, 45, 167, 168, 170
poetry, 109
   ancient Japanese, 137–140
   contemporary Japanese, 90
   haiku, 138
   implicit knowledge of, 140–141
   nature described in, 185, 186, 187
   sabi, relation to, 113
   tanka, 140, 187
   traditional Japanese, 91
   translation of, 138–141
   and *wabi sabi,* 112
postcolonial discourse, 28–29, 65
poststructuralist theory, 170, 241
poststructuralist writing, 201
post–World War II Japan, 146, 147
power/powerlessness, patterns of, 18
preschool children
   in Australia, 51–52, 55–56
   in Japan, 129, 151–152
primitive, notion of, 28

R
rain forest
   immersion in, 37–38
   on Magnetic Island, 41
Rain (poem), 86
Ramsar Convention, 161
reading
   poetic/embodied, 168
   Western linear, 204
Reef, 184–185, 188
reforestation, in Japan, 158

reverie, 20
rhizomatic texts, 169
rivers, 67
   in Brisbane, 206
   in *The Kadaitcha Sung,* 207–209
Rocco, Sharn, 46
Rock, The. *See* Magnetic Island
rocks, sacred, 120, 122
Roe, P., 16–17, 32
Rover, Miss (character in *Oyster*), 241–243

S
sabi, 119, 138
   relation to poetry, 113
   relation to tea ceremony, 113
Sakakibara-san, 161
Salter, J., 216
Sapporo, 136, 137
scarification, 15
schools, Australian, 44–45, 152
schools, Japanese, 95–96, 129
   abacus, 96–98
   calligraphy, 98–100
   walking to and from, 95–96
science, 77, 90
scription, 16
sea, 78, 83
   (be)longing to, 80–81
   bringing to life, through metaphor, 220
   as having voice, 239–240
   as life-saving, 78–79
   love of, 71
seasons, embodied sense of, 93
   chart, 108
Seiji (student), 90, 94–96, 102, 111
settlement/invasion, 216
shark-feeding, 73–74
sheltered space, 20
Shibecha, 158
Shimamura (character in *Snow Country*), 183–184

shimenawa, 131, 132, 133
Shindo, Professor, 148–149,
    159–160
Shingo (character in *Yama no
    Oto*), 173
    attitude toward aging/death,
        175, 178, 181
    experiences *wabi sabi*,
        175–176
    as father of the family, 176
    loses control over life,
        176–177
    and love, 176, 180, 182
    mental condition of, 179
    as representative of older
        generation, 174
Shintoism, 102, 145, 146–147, 157
shrines, 117, 120, 133
    with bamboo pipes in
        pond, 123, 132
    Fushimi-Inari, 125–127
    Nikko, 143
    Shinto, Hokkaido, 146, 149.
        See also Shintoism
    Tenmangu, 124
Shunida, Tada, 152, 156
silence, as method of control,
    241
silencing, of females, 237–238,
    241, 242–243
singing
    in Kabuki Theater, 128–129
    of monks/priests, 117, 128
Smith, Paula, 57–58, 244n1
snake
    as one's self/landscape, 39,
        225–226
    on the verandah, 25
Snake Cradle, 39
Snow Country, 183
Somerville, Margaret, 8, 223n3,
    231
Space, time and perversion, 16
Spinoza, 13, 19, 37
spritual embodiment, 82–83

student/teacher binary, 47–48
subjection, 11, 61, 168–170,
    233–234, 241, 249, 252
    as condition of possibility,
        58, 169
    to language, 33–34,
        235–236
    questioning the terms of,
        236
    as submission and mastery,
        58
subjectivism, 41
suicide, 78, 150, 173, 176–177
sunbirds, 25–26, 27, 28, 29
Suzuki, David, 68, 76, 89,
    102–103, 156–157
Sykes, Roberta, 38–40, 41
symmetry, 137
syncope, 194–195, 196, 199,
    251

T
Tanaka, Professor, 133–134,
    137–138, 185
tanka poem, 140, 187
Taoism, 155
tea ceremony, 111–112, 113,
    123, 137
temples, Japanese, 119–121
Tenmangu, 124
terra nullius, 28
Terry (environmentalist), 69,
    70–71, 83, 84
Tetsuro, Watsuji, 149
texts
    of bliss/pleasure, 217
    as explosive, 243
    multivocal, 7
    as nomadological, 169
    rhizomatic, 169
    strong, 220
    as volatile, 16
therapy workshops, and mem-
    ory, 45–46

thinking, with the body, 19–20
Thomas, Andy, 15
Three Sisters Inn, 121–122, 124
Three steps on the ladder of writing, 246
time
   linear, 207
   in living memory, 206–207
Tobin, J., 129
Tom (environmentalist), 69,
   83–84
Tommy (character in *The Kadaitcha Sung*), 192
   and alcohol, 210–212
   as Kadaitcha man, 207–209
   and love, 212–213
   mixed heritage of, 192,
      200, 203, 204
   as powerful, 193–194
   as violent, 199–200
   as water dweller, 208–209
torii gates, 122, 124, 125, 126,
   127, 146
tours, in Japan, 119, 159
tradition/change
   and children, 150
   tension between, 100–101
trees
   gingko, 180, 183
   as sacred, 100, 120, 131
Trinh, Min-ha, 41, 51
tropical landscapes, 69
tropics, life in, 9, 27
trouble/troubling, 14, 35
   compared with deconstruction, 14
Turner Hospital, Janette, 17–18,
   37, 48–49
Tuwhare, Hone, 86

U
Uluru, 213
ura, 129–130, 151
us/them binary, 230

V
verandah
   author's, 21, 24–25, 26
   compared to kangaroo
      pouches, 25
   as a place for doing collective biography, 49
   as a place for dreaming, 25
   Robert Dessaix's, 63
   Rodney Hall's, 215
   sunbirds', 26, 29
violence, 15
   in *The Kadaitcha Sung*,
      197–198
   toward women, 197,
      238–239

W
wabi, 111–112, 119, 138
wabi sabi, 111, 159, 178
   as active and passive, 160
   colors of, 127–128
   as imperfection, 137
   nature in the context of,
      175
   and Western conception of
      beauty, 182
   wisdom of, 181–182
war, Japanese memory of,
   100–101
water
   and control, 70–71
   and emotions, 71
Watson, Sam, 48–49
Western body/landscape relations, 65
wetlands, in Japan, 136, 154
   conserving, 158
   cultivation of, 162
Whitehouse, Hilary, 8, 63*n*1
Winterson, J., 218
women
   powerful, 247
   silencing, 237–238, 241,
      242–243

women (*continued*)
supposed inferiority to
man, 66–67
violence toward, 197,
238–239
Woolf, Virginia, 191, 217, 218
workshops, collective biogra-
phy/memory work, 43,
48–51
World War II, 110. *See also*
post–World War II
Japan
writing
against the grain of dominant discourses, 34, 167
autobiographical, 40–41
in collective biography, 50
in collective
biography/memory
work, 50
fiction, 191, 217–218
poetic/embodied, 45, 167,
168, 170
poststructuralist, 201
See also embodied writing;
scription
Wulgurukaba people, 42

Y
Yamato spirit, 146
Yasuko (character in *Yama no
Oto*), 173, 174
Yoshinaka-san, 147, 157
Yukiguni, 183
Yuramiru, 225*n*4

Z
Zen, 111, 114

~ Permissions

Hélène Cixous and Mireille Calle-Gruber, extracts from *Hélène Cixous Rootprints: Memory and Life Writing* by Hélène Cixous and Mireille Calle-Gruber © 1997. Reprinted by permission of Routledge Press, London.

Janette Turner Hospital, extracts from *Oyster* © 1996. Reprinted by permission of Janette Turner Hospital.

Sue Gannon, untitled poem. Reprinted by permission of Sue Gannon.

Chapter 3, "Australian Men Talk about Becoming Environmentalists." Printed with the permission of Hilary Whitehouse.

Robert Dessaix, extracts from *(and so forth)* by Robert Dessaix © 1998. Reprinted by permission of Australian Literary Management.

Hone Tuwhare, "Rain" from *Hotere: Out the Black Window. Ralph Hotere's Work with New Zealand Poets,* by G. O'Brien © 1997. Reprinted with the permission of Random House New Zealand.

L. Lowitz, M. Aoyama, and A. Tomioka, untitled tanka or haiku from *A Long Rainy Season: Contemporary Japanese Women's Poetry* by L. Lowitz, M. Aoyama, and A. Tomioka (eds. and trans.) © 1994. Reprinted by permission of Stone Bridge Press.

Chapter 7, "An Exploration of Body/Landscape Relations in Kawabata's *Yama no Oto.*" Reprinted by permission of *Interpretations* and Takeshi Osanai.

Chapter 8, "Reading and Writing *The Kadaitcha Sung*: A Novel by Sam Watson." © 1999. Reprinted by permission of *Interpretations* and Sam Watson.

Sam Watson, extracts from *The Kadaitcha Sung* © 1990. Reprinted by permission of Penguin Press and Sam Watson.

Chapter 9, "*The Second Bridegroom*: A Narrative of the Australian Landscape and Captivity." Reprinted by permission of *Interpretations.*

~ About the Author

BRONWYN **D**AVIES is a professor of education at James Cook University in the far north of Australia. Over the last decade she has played a major role in translating the philosophical principles of poststructuralist theory into research practice. Most notable was her bestselling book *Frogs and snails and feminist tales: Preschool children and gender*, which has been translated into several languages and received considerable acclaim. Other books include *Life in the classroom and playground: The accounts of primary school children; Shards of glass: Children reading and writing beyond gendered identities; Power knowledge desire: Changing school organisation and management practice;* and *Poststructuralist theory and classroom practice.* Her current work explores the ways in which poststructuralist theory can inform not only the way we ask research questions, but also the way we collect and analyze data. As well, she is particularly fascinated by the processes of writing—how it is we can write differently about what emerges through the research process and also how the act of writing itself is fundamental to that process. Her work seeks to make the principles of poststructuralist theory understandable and usable, and in that process she has made valuable contributions to the body of writing about and within the field of poststructuralist theory.